A Consipracy of Crowns

The True Story of the Duke of Windsor
and the Murder of Sir Harry Oakes

A Consipracy of Crowns

The True Story of the Duke of Windsor and the Murder of Sir Harry Oakes

Alfred de Marigny
with Mickey Herskowitz

GARRETT COUNTY PRESS

©2005

Photograph credits appear with the captions. Those not credited are from the personal collection of Alfred de Marigny.

ISBN: 9781939430267

Cover design : Kevin Stone

All rights reserved. No part of this publication may be reproduced, stored in a retrieval system, or transmitted in any form or by any means, electronic, mechanical, photocopying, recording, or otherwise, without the prior permission of the publishers.

Garrett County Press
931 N Tonti Street
New Orleans, LA 70119

For more information, please address www.gcpress.com

To Curtis Thompson,
known as George,

and to Montreal's Jewish community of the mid-forties,
led by Moses Miller, Philip Joseph, and Harry Rajinsky.
In the darkest hours of my life, they defined for me
the word *friend*.

CONTENTS

Acknowledgements I

PART ONE

Fool's Gold: The Cast, the Scene, the Crime
Wind, Rain, and Fire - 1
To Cross a King - 24

PART TWO

The Case Against Alfred de Marigny
The Arrest - 45
The Frame - 65
The Jail - 85

PART THREE

In Search of Nassau
Mauritius - 103
This Was London - 113
Out of Europe - 121
Coming to America - 136

PART FOUR

Islands in the Sun
Pirates' Island - 148
Guilty of Marrying Nancy - 163
The Trial - 187
The Verdict - 210

PART FIVE

The Odyssey
Cuba Libre - 257
Canadian Sunset - 274
Journey's End - 290

EPILOGUE - 309

Selected Bibliography - 321

ACKNOWLEDGMENTS

I made a promise to certain loved ones not to refer to them, or thank them, by name. But they know who they are and what they have meant to my life and this book.

In expressing my gratitude elsewhere, there are no such restrictions. Scott Williams, a young and brilliant friend, was always supportive and helpful in interpreting legal details. It also helps to have an attorney in the family; my daughter-in-law, Sidney de Marigny, was helpful in obtaining documents that had been previously classified.

In organizing literally thousands of pages of transcript and early drafts, my coauthor was assisted by Patrick Bishop, whose insights were welcome.

In the tedious process that involves keeping the computer running and the printer printing and the pages in the right order, thanks are due to Sid Clinton and Ida Levinson.

I was challenged by, and enjoyed comparing notes with, the writer Charles Higham, whose book *The Duchess of Windsor* included a provocative chapter on the Oakes case. Another author who fell under the thrall of this story was Geoffrey Bocca, who encouraged me, up to the time of his death from cancer, to tell my side of it.

As a patient and understanding editor, the best kind, Betty Prashker guided us with gentle hands. Her associate, Lisa Healy, gave us the friendly and essential closing push.

I approached the task of writing this book with the most tangled of feelings. Now it is done. I am more convinced than ever that no one will resolve the contradictions of the case, either the murder of Sir Harry Oakes or the attempt to frame me for it. The description of my trial is based on the transcript of the testimony as kept by the Chief Justice, who wrote it by hand, with a quill pen. Although not all of his notes are legible, the accounts of the testimony vary little in the newspapers of the day and the books that appeared later.

What I can add to the dryness of the daily record is truly my own—my thoughts, my knowledge of the characters, how I appraised the evidence and the people who gave it. On the subject of how Oakes died, and why, I differ emphatically with most of what has been written. But to all who have kept alive an interest in this case, and the injustice that grew out of it, I give my thanks.

Predestination brought everyone in this book to play a part in my life. Each one had a definite place at a definite time, similar to the units of a jigsaw puzzle. Every piece was part of a whole.

PART ONE

FOOL'S GOLD: THE CAST,
THE SCENE, THE CRIME

WIND, RAIN, AND FIRE

THERE is a cycle in life in which friends become enemies, and winners become losers, and the cycle goes the other way as well. This is true among men as it is among countries, and it is part of a story that began on a summer's night in Nassau, the Bahamas, and continues nearly half a century later. The islands were not yet the tourist attraction they would in time become, but even as the globe was engulfed in war, Nassau fulfilled its role as a sanctuary for the rich, the spoiled, and the shadowy.

Between midnight and dawn on the morning of July 8, 1943, one of the richest men in the British Empire was murdered in his bed, in a sprawling home at the water's edge. He was Sir Harry Oakes, sixty-eight, an eccentric and complicated man who roamed the earth before discovering a legendary gold mine.

Doctors would find four wounds to the head, each the size of a fingertip, behind the curve of the left ear. The bed had been set afire, scorching the body in no discernible pattern, and reducing to rags the front of his pajamas. Only tatters of mosquito netting still dangled from the ceiling.

Blisters were visible on Sir Harry's neck, chest, and groin, and on the left knee and foot. His face was blackened by smoke and soot, and feathers from a torn pillow were pasted to the raw skin, stirring slightly, like moths, in the air of an electric fan facing the bed a few feet away.

He had been found lying on his back in bed, but, oddly, a line of blood seemed to flow in the wrong direction, upward, from the left ear, over his cheek, and across the bridge of the nose. Either the law of gravity had been defied, or his killer had left him facedown, his head hanging toward the floor.

A trail of charred carpet led across the bedroom, into the hallway, and down the staircase, and yet no flames had reached the ceiling, and the bedroom walls were almost undamaged. When the first doctor reached the scene, the mattress still smoldered in one small spot beneath the body. The doctor doused it with water from a drinking glass.

Muddy tracks ran through the house. A typical Nassau storm had blown up during the evening, squalls with winds fierce enough to bend the tall palms as if they were made of rubber.

A million tourists have come and gone in the years since the morning of that gruesome discovery. Reporters, authors, amateur detectives, even a few pros have poked around the islands, searching for the missing clue that would solve the crime. Still the same questions are heard:

Who killed Harry Oakes? Why? And how?

For reasons that are still a matter of conjecture, no specific instrument of death was ever established. Theories about the murder weapon would spread like crabgrass. From that moment on, half a dozen lives would be rearranged, and a mystery would surface that endures to this day.

That week, the Allied forces had invaded Sicily, and Mussolini's Fascist government was on the verge of collapse. Tens of thousands were dying across Europe, Asia, and Africa. But the murder of Harry Oakes landed on page one of newspapers around the globe. Who would have dared to invent such a melodramatic crime: a stormy night, an exotic island, a grizzled old gold prospector, all at the doorstep of a former King of England?

The Bahamas had just begun to emerge as a playground of the idle rich. But this act seemed a throwback to other eras, to a long history of what might be called institutional violence: piracy, shipwrecking, bootlegging.

No stranger to the rougher edges of life, Oakes boasted of

the enemies he made. He might have been killed out of fear or greed or hate.

Oakes was crude and ill-tempered, his nature made tough by early hardship and suspicious by late wealth. He was, from all accounts, a man of modest sexual experience when he married at forty-eight. His wife, Eunice, was half his age. He had traveled around the world in search of the riches he never doubted he would find, and had worked his claims in places that are now a part of folklore: Yukon Territory, the Klondike, the Belgian Congo, Death Valley.

In his reading of many geological maps, and from the experience of his own eye, Oakes had devised a theory that veins of gold all led to the richest concentration at dead center, like the spokes of a wheel. This was the mother lode. He found his in Canada, in 1912, at a place called Kirkland Lakes in northern Ontario. He had searched and sacrificed for thirteen years, and now he was sitting on a virtual river of gold. He would need eight more years to win his legal battles and raise the cash to work the claim. But Lake Shore Mines would turn out to be the second richest in the world.

To keep going, to survive, Oakes borrowed whatever he could, from his family, friends, and strangers. He traded shares in the mine for supplies, and the Chinese grocer who stocked him became a millionaire. An early Oakes partner, Bill Wright, invested his money in publishing and went on to found the *Toronto Globe*.

No one could say Oakes had not earned his fortune. He went days without food or sleep; survived bone-chilling Alaskan winters and suffocating Death Valley summers. No physical deprivation could deter him. He shared the meanest of mining camps with drunks, whores, perverts, and psychos, the human refuse that a gold rush always drew. But he kept no company except his own.

He was a pit bull of a man, five-foot-six, strong enough to carry an eighty-pound pack on his back. Whatever polish he had acquired from two years of medical school, or growing up in a family of lawyers, had disappeared. When he returned to polite society, wealthy beyond his dreams, he found it unnecessary to eat his meals with any utensil other than a knife. At dinner parties, he would spit grape seeds and fruit pits across the table.

Marriage gradually changed him, made him civilized, but he would never be a sophisticated person. Oakes would never look like anyone's idea of a multimillionaire. He looked like a union boss or a butcher. But he tried.

He settled in Canada with Eunice, built a chalet near Kirkland Lakes and a mansion in Toronto, and fathered two daughters and three sons. But Harry Oakes was a man besieged all his years by demons, real or imagined. When the Canadian government raised his taxes, he sought duty-free relief in the Bahamas.

His presence there was instantly felt. He moved his family into a mansion, bought the British Colonial Hotel, added a wing to the hospital, laid out a polo field and a golf course, and built an air base that bore his name, Oakes Field. He did not find peace. He bought a title from the British Crown, but he did not find nobility.

Now, in Nassau, in 1943, he had acquired new anxieties. The production of his Lake Shore mines had begun to dwindle. The war was coming closer—there had been submarine activity in the shipping lanes off Nassau—and he feared that the colonial office would decide to levy taxes, making new demands on his fortune. He had taken to sleeping with a loaded gun on a table at his bedside—a reaction, perhaps, to rumors that Sir Harry kept in his home a hoard of gold coins and sovereigns. Two night watchmen patrolled the grounds of Westbourne, his estate on the edge of town.

He had grown disenchanted. His recent business ventures had taken wrong turns, and he believed he had been cheated by a friend, Harold Christie, the island's foremost real-estate promoter. Oakes had, in fact, made a final decision to leave the islands and move his family and investments to Mexico.

Harry could scarcely wait for Friday to arrive. And yet, in the final hours of his life, in spite of his suspicions and the gun within his reach, he slept with the windows and screens open to the weather and not a door in the house was locked. The watchmen had been given the night off by Christie, acting, he said, on Sir Harry's instructions.

When people with money or potential reached Nassau, somehow the first person to befriend them was Harold Christie. He was responsible for persuading Sir Harry to settle in the Bahamas, and Oakes quickly became his most important client. Harold lived high, dreamed large, and was always strapped for cash. He resented, at times bitterly, having to accept scraps from the rich man's table.

Harold kept an office on Bay Street, Nassau's main artery. He had been elected to the House of Assembly, and emerged as the leader of that select circle of power brokers known to some as the Bay Street Boys, and to others as the Bay Street Bandits.

Christie was from an old Nassau family, Scottish, the son of a restless father who wrote poetry, did not work long at any job, including advertising, disappeared on impulsive trips that lasted months, and finally came home to preach the gospel of a sect called the Plymouth Brethren.

Harold Christie was a world-class salesman, who sold not just real estate but dreams. He had more or less appointed himself as Nassau's ambassador to the rich and restless. The job was less colorful than an earlier one, running rum to Florida in the 1920s, but the long-term prospects were more stable.

Rumpled and homely, Christie had the gift of persuasion. But he also had Nassau's considerable resources going for him. He was in his finest form raving about the emerald waters and the pristine beaches, but he really captured a prospect's interest when he talked taxes. In the Bahamas, the income tax was unknown and unwelcome. The state took only two percent of a man's personal estate on his death, and didn't touch his real estate. With that kind of bait, Christie went trolling for millionaires in Canada and the United States, to the playing fields of Palm Beach, Long Island, and Bar Harbor.

There was another attraction for Canadians. In the colony's only bank, money could be changed from one currency to another in a matter of hours, beyond the reach of tax collectors. The art of money-laundering was raised to new levels during the war, when American dollars came pouring in. New and more creative schemes were hatched.

Harold Christie had a talent for making money, but not for keeping it. He was an erratic manager, leaving most of the details and paperwork to his brother, Frank.

By the spring of 1943, Christie was heavily in debt to Oakes, who had learned only recently that his partner had double-crossed him on the contract to build a new military airfield on the island.

Among the men whose ambitions would become entangled in Nassau, fact and fantasy seemed to compete. Oakes and Christie, one wealthy and the other hungry, were each at various times praised as "the uncrowned king" of the Bahamas, a title flattering to both. And then, as if to mock their pretensions, and his, along came the genuine article, the uncrowned King of England, the former Edward VIII, now David, the Duke of Windsor, the Royal Governor.

That mix might have been volatile enough. New Providence was civilized enough; Harry Oakes had bought a home in the center of it, called Westbourne, where the American actress Maxine Elliott once lived. He was reported to have paid $250,000 for it, a vast fortune in 1934. But Hog Island was not yet renamed Paradise, and Lyford Cay, on which Christie gambled his hopes for a fortune, was still a barren waste.

For all the potential of the tropics, it was fair to wonder if there was room enough for the egos of Oakes, Christie, and Windsor. And then, in their midst, arrived a provocative figure, every inch a maverick, named Alfred de Marigny.

He stepped off a cruise ship in 1938, flush with monies he had made in the commodities market in Europe, searching for his future. Her name was Nancy Oakes, Sir Harry's oldest daughter.

Born on the island of Mauritius, in the Indian Ocean, de Marigny had the year-round suntan of men who are at ease on water. In later years, as he aged gracefully, and his hair and beard turned white, he would look like the model for a character created by Ernest Hemingway, who, in fact, had been his friend. He was six-foot-three, a meticulous dresser, who broke freely into a smile or a laugh. In appearance, attitude, and taste, he and his father-in-law were exact opposites.

The war had slowed to a crawl the tourist traffic in Nassau, and stopped the talk of new hotels and gambling casinos. Nightlife meant home life.

There were four for dinner at Westbourne, on the last night of Harry Oakes's life, and eleven at de Marigny's home on Victoria Avenue. His guests included Fred Ceretta, an American engineer whose company had obtained the contract—over Oakes—to build the new airfield. He had bumped into Ceretta the night before in the bar of the Prince George Hotel, in the company of two RAF wives, Jean Ainslie and Dorothy Clark. Their husbands were on a mission, and he invited Ceretta to bring them along. It was casual, rather impromptu. Were these the actions of a man constructing an alibi?

He had space for another guest at his table. He called Harold Christie, who begged off, explaining he was to spend the night at the home of Sir Harry.

At Government House, the Windsors played bridge with friends and retired after ten, the Duchess nagging the Duke to finish his cigar and brandy and whatever story he was telling.

And so they were accounted for, these men of wildly contrasting histories, whose paths had crossed on a chain of islands that were mere flyspecks in the Caribbean.

What curious forces had been joined to bring them together? Each would spend the prime of his years adrift, roaming from country to country, living in a kind of limbo.

Harry Oakes was born in America, became a citizen of Canada, found his wife in Australia, died in a British colony. The absence of taxes, not the beauty of the beaches, lured Oakes to the Bahamas.

De Marigny, tall, elegant, well born, but irreverent about class and wealth, thought he had found serenity.

The Windsors were in an early stage of what would become a vagabond life, a self-imposed exile from the country the Duke had ruled, briefly, as king. Now the government had posted him to the Bahamas, far from the war in Europe, out of harm's way—and theirs.

Of course, some ships came in the night, in silence, like common thieves. Shortly before midnight on the eighth of July 1943 a cabin cruiser killed its engine and was seen gliding the last few feet to the dock at Lyford Cay, at Nassau's far west end. The boat would have been at least fifty feet long, of enough size to make the crossing through rough waters from Miami. Two men, shadows in the dark, walked across the creaky wooden pier and climbed into a waiting black sedan.

There were no crowds or pageantry that night when the passengers from the unidentified boat went ashore.

Some yards away, a caretaker and his assistant watched the car swing around and head east toward town, into a swirling rain. He would see the car, carrying the two men, return less than three hours later, would watch the boat cast off. He noted that the men were not dressed for fishing ... or for sailing.

For most, arriving in Nassau was the best part of the trip. The tourists came on the grand cruise ships and docked before noon, with the native boys diving for coins and the tour guides waiting on the shore, chattering like auctioneers. At the end of the gangplank they melted into the milling crowds. The shops beckoned. Black men in loud shirts and pretty, slender black women in colorful smocks caught the eye.

It had been that way in 1934 when Oakes, the discoverer of the Lake Shore Mines in Canada, landed with his wife and five children. So it was four years later, when de Marigny stepped ashore. And the crowds were never larger, the colors never brighter, the reception never more festive than in mid-August of 1940, when the Duke of Windsor and his Duchess sailed into port as the new governor and first lady of the islands.

Under a white-gold sun, a police band played and welcoming banners whipped in the wind. But there was no relief from the choking midday heat. As the ceremonies dragged on, stains of sweat appeared on the back and under the arms of the Duke's uniform, spreading until his heavy khaki coat was all a darker color. Sweat trickled down his sleeves, blurring his signature on the oath of allegiance, the ink running off the page.

The moment was symbolic. The Windsors had walked into a cauldron. Here, flesh-and-blood reality would collide with the romantic legend of the storybook couple, the king and the woman who was more desirable than a kingdom.

Nothing in her adult life, in society's circles and on the fringe of royalty, had prepared the Duchess of Windsor for the intolerable heat or poverty of the Bahamas.

For the latter she did what she could, visiting neighborhoods and such schools as there were, and instructing the natives on hygiene. The squalor was not of a kind she had known before. A Benedictine monk had written: "They had tumbledown shacks for homes, but most managed to have a Sunday dress or Sunday suit. They were not filthy . . . you could eat off the floor. One day a man came to Father Arnold to ask him if he could have a box. Asked why, he said: 'To sit on. I have no chair in the house.'"

The islands depressed the Duchess, and the heat drained her spirit and wit. Fair-skinned, she suffered under the tropical sun. Driven indoors, she found small comfort in the plainness of the Governor's House, whose furnishings and meager art offended her every taste.

One story worth repeating tells how, in a single gesture, she described her feelings. In the first letters she wrote to friends, she took her pen, scratched the address from the official stationery, and wrote instead one word: *Elba.*

Nothing about his duty, that steamy July morning in 1943, could have pleased Major Cray Phillips, one of the Duke of Windsor's aides-de-camp. He knew that at 7:00 A.M. he would be disturbing the sleep of the royal couple. The news he brought them was not going to improve their mood; it was grim, shocking, ghastly. Sir Harry Oakes had been found dead, the cause unknown. A fire had started in his bedroom. The body was partly burned.

The third time he pounded on the door, Phillips heard the muffled sounds that indicated the Windsors were stirring. The Duke came to the door, knotting the belt of his white silk bathrobe on which the royal coat of arms was embroidered in red and gold over the pocket.

The conversation lasted just long enough for the major to repeat the essential details. He had taken two calls, the second of which was from the superintendent of the local police, the first from a flustered Harold Christie, who had discovered the body.

Phillips left and the governor closed the door behind him, leaving the Duke alone with his Duchess to collect his thoughts. And in that room, with all of the various options and actions available to him, what happened next was the most remarkable of all.

Nothing happened.

For three hours and fifty minutes the Duke of Windsor, Royal Governor of the Bahamas, did nothing. One can only guess at the spiral of dread and confusion and indecision that gripped him. The Duchess urged him to act; there were orders to be given, official and private sources to be informed.

Any other thoughts that might have engaged him had to compete with the knowledge that the death of Harry Oakes had the potential to create enormous problems for him. They were partners, along with a shadowy figure named Axel Wenner-Gren, in a scheme to smuggle millions of dollars out of the Bahamas. The money was to be banked in Mexico, and kept available for judicious postwar investment. Christie had helped broker the deal.

Wenner-Gren was a Swedish industrialist, one of the richest men in the world, whose American holdings included the Electrolux Company. He had represented the Krupp family in its international munitions sales. In the files of certain intelligence agencies, he was under suspicion as a Nazi agent.

Mexico was a neutral country, but could be of immense strategic value if Germany elected to launch direct attacks on the United States. On its face, the plan violated the British currency laws. Any deeper reading might well find that the former King of England had betrayed his country and the Allied cause.

At some point it may have occurred to Windsor that one other person on the island would be aware of these dealings and in a position to do him harm. The man was Alfred de Marigny, the son-in-law of the murder victim.

One year earlier, in May 1942, two days after she turned eighteen, Nancy Oakes had eloped with de Marigny without the consent or knowledge of her parents. The groom was then thirty-two. It was a marriage that delighted the local gossips. Typically, de Marigny volunteered to answer any questions Sir Harry might have about his past. And, just as typically, Oakes replied, "I have nothing to ask. I don't give a damn about your past. No man with any guts bothers about his or anybody else's past life. The only thing that matters to me is that you make Nancy happy."

De Marigny had never feared hard work. He built the first modern apartment complex in the Bahamas, invested in land, bought a grocery, and opened a beauty parlor (partly to accommodate the Duchess of Windsor). He astounded Nassau society by starting a chicken farm and running it himself. When large orders came in, he often worked side by side with his black employees.

Oakes admired his business judgment, but his son-in-law's independence was a frustration to the crabby old miner.

To the white establishment, de Marigny was a puzzle. He violated one of the unwritten rules of the colony by inviting Jews to Nassau, renting them apartments, socializing with them. Nor did they understand his sympathy for the island's impoverished blacks. They were confused by the ease with which he moved from one role to another: delivering his chickens to his neighbors' door in the morning; returning to dine at their table that same night.

The gossips kept a close eye on de Marigny. He arrived in Nassau near the end of a failed marriage. For a few months after the divorce, he and his ex-wife, Ruth Fahnestock, continued to live together. Descriptions of him invariably relied on the word *playboy*, but the label was slightly off center. He did not smoke or drink, and his language was refined, his accent very French. His real weakness was sailing. There were few things Bahamians, old or new, white or black, appreciated more than good seamanship, and de Marigny was a champion yachtsman.

Meanwhile, Oakes had been eager to cultivate a friendship with the Duke of Windsor. They were occasional golfing partners, and the Duke had solicited donations from Oakes for charities he or the Duchess favored. When the Windsors had found Government House to be unlivable by their standards, and in need of immediate and sweeping repairs, one of the homes they borrowed was Westbourne. They had slept in the room where Harry Oakes now lay dead.

Through Windsor, Oakes had met Axel Wenner-Gren, whose yacht, the *Southern Cross*, previously owned by Howard Hughes, was anchored in Nassau harbor. With world currency markets fluctuating wildly, Wenner-Gren had dangled in front of his friends the prospect of huge postwar profits, through banks and silver trusts he controlled in Mexico.

De Marigny was not invited to participate, and would not, at any rate, have chosen that company. He had little use for the Duke of Windsor and made no effort to conceal his feelings. They had met years ago in London, when Alfred was a young stockbroker and the royal heir was still David, the Prince of Wales. He had observed even then the pro-German sentiments of the young prince, marked him as weak, and foreseen long before others did what he would become: an unnecessary person.

Curiously, each had found his way to Nassau on the wings of war and love. De Marigny had come to escape a bad marriage, Windsor to maintain one that had become a piece of history.

The arrival of the Windsors had been a reluctant one. The Duke believed that Winston Churchill had deliberately arranged to isolate him, to keep him outside the orbit of the war. The Duke, commissioned as a major general by his brother, had been given a trivial job on the military staff in Paris, but had resigned within weeks, leaving just ahead of the arrival of the German army. With what remained of their entourage, they had traveled to Lisbon and Madrid, while around them assorted Nazi plots swirled and each wild rumor was replaced by the next.

For six weeks after his posting to the Bahamas was announced on July 9, 1940, the Windsors were involved in a sort of tennis game with London, lobbing cables back and forth. They delayed, hoping to bargain for an assignment closer to the action, or at least closer to Washington and the American society the Duchess so enjoyed.

The Duke was going through another of life's cycles. As the young Prince of Wales, he attracted huge crowds wherever he traveled, arousing in the masses an excitement seldom inspired by royalty, of a kind associated today with rock stars. Then came the Abdication, a publicized trip to Germany as the guest of Hermann Goering, and statements seen as naïve or, worse, as pro-Nazi. His government feared any move that might make it more convenient for the enemy to use him as a pawn in the propaganda war. This nervousness eliminated any hope he had of receiving a military command, or even a meaningful diplomatic post. Given these conditions, the Duke's public friendship and secret dealings with Wenner-Gren become even more perplexing.

He had accepted his appointment to the Bahamas as a probationary period, a chance to rehabilitate himself. That he might spend the entire war there did not seem to occur to him. To obtain a more suitable position, he believed, would only require a clean record and an avoidance of scandal. All the Windsors really wanted of the Bahamas was a way out.

Blacks outnumbered whites on Nassau by nine to one. At the instant Harold Christie said he was walking toward the room of Harry Oakes, few of the whites on the island were rising. They did not usually wake up with Alfred de Marigny's chickens.

Windsor and Oakes had a date to play golf on the morning of July 8, 1943. Sir Harry was to leave by plane the next day, Friday, to rejoin Lady Oakes at their summer home in Bar Harbor, Maine. He already had his ticket and his travel permit.

The ticket would go unused, the golf game unplayed. Oakes died sometime after midnight and before 3:30 A.M. During those hours an intruder, or more likely two, murdered Oakes as he slept.

Harold Christie, who said he spent the night in the next bedroom, no more than twenty feet from where Oakes slept, heard none of it. Not the sounds of a struggle, of footsteps on the stairs, of a weapon smashing against a human skull, not even the knob turning and his own door opening, if one may judge by the bloody handprints that were found there.

Nor was he aware of the smoke that curled through the second floor, or the sicky sweet odor of burning flesh.

He was awakened twice by mosquitoes, he said, and once by a thunderclap. He killed the mosquitoes and went back to bed. Otherwise, he slept routinely through a tropical storm, a fire, and a killing.

A policeman noted that Christie's bed was only lightly

disturbed, rather than disheveled, as if someone had lain on top of the sheets. The account he gave them was a strange and rambling tale, filled with inconsistencies, each point stretched to reinforce his claim that he had not left Westbourne the night Sir Harry died.

Why he would feel so urgent a need to establish his presence at the scene of a murder isn't clear. But Harold Christie clung to his story as to a life preserver.

This is the story Christie told:

He had decided on the spur of the moment to stay the night at Westbourne, his third of four nights as a guest there. They had been joined for drinks and dinner by one of Sir Harry's neighbors, Charles Hubbard, a retired Woolworth executive, and Mrs. Dulcibel "Effie" Henneage, the wife of an army officer stationed in England. It was widely rumored on Nassau that Mrs. Henneage had been the mistress of Harold Christie.

Hubbard and Mrs. Henneage left at eleven, after a game of checkers. Half an hour later, Christie borrowed a pair of Sir Harry's brown silk pajamas, picked up that week's copy of *Time* magazine—Russia's Marshal Vasilevski was on the cover—and said good night.

Before Oakes drew his mosquito netting around him, he pulled out the first drawer of his dresser and carefully placed the blue gun on top of a pile of letters and a roll of bills.

Etienne Dupuch, the editor of the *Nassau Tribune,* and a reporter from the *Guardian* were due to drop by around nine to interview Oakes about his recent shipment of 1,500 sheep from Cuba. He had intended to breed them to help offset the wartime shortage of meat. Oakes had confided in de Marigny, when they were still talking, that the sheep didn't exist. Christie had used the money instead to cover his mounting expenses at Lyford Cay. Sir Harry was planning to confront Christie with this deceit, and to confirm the rumors that he intended to leave the Bahamas. Sir Harry enjoyed his cat-and-mouse games, and having Christie as a houseguest was a convenient way to enjoy Harold's discomfort.

The next morning, around seven o'clock, Christie stepped onto the veranda and walked barefoot, still in his pajamas, to the bedroom of Harry Oakes.

He called out to his friend, heard no response, opened the door, and entered the room. Then and only then was he aware of the foulness of the scene, bloody handprints on the wall, a wisp of smoke—and the body of Harry Oakes, battered and unmoving.

He found the body still warm, from life or from the heat of the fire he couldn't know. He lifted Sir Harry's head, he said, and put a pillow under it. Then he took a flask of water and put it to the dead man's lips. He wet a towel and wiped his friend's face. He opened the door to the balcony and called for help, hoping to be heard by Madeline Kelly, who lived next door. Her husband managed the country club.

When no one responded, he ran downstairs to the phone. He reached Mrs. Kelly and asked her to come quickly. Next he dialed his brother, Frank, and told him that Oakes was hurt, maybe dead, and to bring a doctor. In his haste, he neglected to say where he was. Oakes might have stayed at any of four addresses. Frank, however, headed immediately for Westbourne.

Only a few minutes had passed. The police commissioner, Colonel R. A. Erskine-Lindop, wasn't home, and Harold left a message with his wife. He telephoned the Duke of Windsor, and gave the first sketchy details to Major Phillips. Then he walked back up the stairs to look again on the lifeless form of the richest man in the colony.

One glance would have convinced even a casual viewer that Oakes had been slain in the most savage way. An inflammable fluid, possibly kerosene, had been splashed on the bed and the carpet, and around the room and along the staircase. The fan on the floor was still humming. It might have been placed there, at the foot of the bed, to whip the flames.

A smoke-smudged Chinese screen near the bed was splattered with drops of blood. There was more blood on Christie's door, in his bathroom sink, on towels.

The police had not yet arrived when the phone rang at Westbourne. Christie, startled, picked it up. Etienne Dupuch was calling to confirm his interview with Oakes. Harold shouted into the phone, "He's dead! He's dead!"

"Who?" asked the newsman.

"Sir Harry," said Christie. Then he added an extraordinary remark, one that was not repeated or quoted at the trial: "He has been shot!"

"Shot? Are you serious?"

"Of course I'm serious. I've just discovered him. He's dead."

Dupuch made an effort of will to remain calm and professional. "This is a very big news story, Mr. Christie, and I'm a journalist. I propose to cable it around the world. You *are* certain?"

"Yes, yes," Christie said wearily. "I'm certain."

At nearly nine o'clock the Duke of Windsor decided to use his war powers to impose press censorship on the story of Sir Harry's death. He instructed Major Gray Phillips, his aide, to inform the newspapers and the local radio station that a blackout was in effect. His dramatic action was spoiled only by the fact that it came too late. Etienne Dupuch had wired his story, though meager in its details, to the news services, and at that instant the word was buzzing around the globe.

All calls on the Duke's private line were logged in by British intelligence. There was a long conversation with Harold Christie, and there were several short ones with Erskine-Lindop, the police commissioner.

At ten minutes of eleven, the Duke had made up his mind. In a move that would later seem mystifying, a towering display of poor judgment, he placed a call to the Miami police department. This decision would baffle and frustrate all those who would study the case in years to come.

The Duke asked for Captain Edward Melchen, chief of

the homicide bureau, who had been his bodyguard on his occasional trips to the States. A prominent citizen had died, Windsor told him, "under extraordinary circumstances." He asked Melchen to come at once, and to bring a colleague with him to assist in the investigation.

What else was said can't be certain. One question that would linger was whether the Duke led Melchen to believe that the death was a suicide. Or was a story concocted later to cover the bungling of the Miami detectives?

The possibility of suicide had been raised in a wistful way by the Duke of Windsor, expressed as not much more than a hope that the island would be spared the bad press he saw coming. A doctor who had not yet finished his examination, and had found only the first wound, attempted to humor him. Yes, the doctor mused, if a bullet had caused the hole, it could have been suicide.

Pan American Airways held its noon flight to Nassau for Melchen and Captain James Otto Barker, described as a fingerprint expert. Barker, a former ambulance driver and motorcycle cop, had been twice demoted for departmental infractions.

The Duke could have called in Scotland Yard or the FBI, or assigned the case to his own Criminal Investigation Division, headed by veteran British officers. His failure to contact the Bureau irritated J. Edgar Hoover, and gave Hoover one more reason to keep open a file on Windsor's activities. With these options at hand, the Duke chose two obscure officers from a police department then considered one of the most corrupt in the country. To complicate matters, he announced that he would take personal charge of the investigation. He wanted, needed, indeed expected a quick solution.

At least the notion of suicide was dismissed as soon as the detectives saw the death scene. The deceased could not have inflicted four wounds to his head and then burned his own body.

Whether they believed it or not, the police soon circulated the theory that the killer, or killers, had intended to burn down the house and conceal the nature of the crime. The weather had intervened to foil their plan: winds from the storm had blown through Sir Harry's open windows and extinguished the flames.

Leaping from house to house, phone to phone, rumors sped across the island. No fact was too gross to lend itself to one or more of the prevailing theories. Photographs of the corpse made it appear that the eyelids and testicles of Harry Oakes had been burned as if by design, by a flame applied to those areas at close range, after death. Any of several conclusions could be drawn, and were:

This was the work of a sadistic killer-for-hire.

The killer knew Oakes and hated him with such passion that the mutilation was a gesture of vengeance.

The burning of the eyes and testicles was a symbolic act, an act of voodoo, and suggested that a woman was involved.

The killer wanted it to appear that the murder was a voodoo ritual.

Such was the setting when the Miami lawmen arrived in Nassau, to be met at the airport by Eric Hallinan, the Attorney General of the Bahamas, who would prosecute the case. He had been handed the prize assignment of his life.

Hallinan was slender, austere in manner and appearance. Born in County Cork, he had attended Catholic schools in England, and had the starchy loyalty often found in Irishmen who embrace the service of the British Empire.

Hallinan announced to the press that the Miami detectives had brought with them the most technologically advanced equipment used for fingerprinting.

In fact, he knew the exact opposite to be true. They had brought no equipment at all, advanced or otherwise. The only reason for Barker to make the trip was his status as a fingerprint expert. Yet he had forgotten to bring a camera.

They were unshaken, announcing that the search for

prints would be postponed to the next morning. The atmosphere, they complained, was too humid for dusting powder to do its work. Neither officer had any clue, any idea, as to what murder weapon had been used, nor did they order any search to be made. Muddy footprints had been left on the stairway, but they were obliterated by the police and neighbors, who tramped freely through the house.

No area was sealed off, no objects were shielded. The visitors left their prints on lamps, chairs, doors, and windows.

Meanwhile, the Duke of Windsor was calling at hourly intervals, impatient, eager to know what progress had been made. Roughly fifteen hours had passed since someone arranged four precise holes in the skull of Harry Oakes.

Erskine-Lindop was visibly embarrassed as his constables waited for orders from the Miami imports. He was every inch a professional, who kept his silence about the case for decades. Off the record, he dropped broad hints that his department would have conducted "a proper investigation," that the identity of the killer was known to him, and that justice could have been done.

The Duke bypassed the local force on at least two counts: he believed that they lacked the training needed for a case that might tread on delicate ground; and, reflecting his own sensibilities, he regarded their ranks as too black.

The Nassau police were given no assignment until days later, when they were told to scrub the hallway outside Sir Harry's bedroom, as well as the bedroom walls. They were to remove all handprints and fingerprints because, as one constable would testify in court, such prints "did not match those of the accused" and, according to Captain Melchen, would only "confuse the evidence."

No one yet had been charged, but by late Thursday, the ninth of July, one name was already making the rounds. No one would be really surprised by his arrest except the accused himself.

Alfred de Marigny.

De Marigny had grown a beard, a Vandyke, and enjoyed the idea of surprising his wife when Nancy returned from spending her summer in the States. She had always liked ballet and had enrolled in Martha Graham's school in Vermont. She indulged herself even as she slowly regained her strength from the illness and dental surgery that had marred her honeymoon.

In Nancy's absence, Alfred filled his days tending his farm and shops and apartments. Nights he spent with friends. He did not exactly lead a monastic life.

That night, around eleven, as Oakes was saying good-bye to two of his guests, the lights failed at de Marigny's house. His butler, Harris, brought in two candles and hurricane shades. As de Marigny reached in to light them, the flame ran up the back of his hand and he jumped.

His dinner partners laughed as de Marigny gave his hand a shaking. The incident hardly seemed significant at the time.

It was after midnight when the guests began to leave. Jean Ainslie and Dorothy Clark were growing anxious about the storm, and needed to be driven to their homes at Cable Beach, just beyond the estate of Harry Oakes. De Marigny asked Ceretta and then Basil McKinney to join him, but both declined.

George Thompson, who had been hired off a fishing boat and now helped around the house and farm, held an umbrella over each lady's head as they darted through the rain to de Marigny's Lincoln Continental.

Lightning zigzagged across the sky as they turned onto the highway. Powerful gusts of wind caused the car to sway, and de Marigny slowed down. As they passed the sign of Lightbourne's pharmacy, Jean Ainslie wondered how late it was. She checked her watch and said, "One-twenty."

De Marigny glanced at his own, which had a dial that glowed in the dark. "One-oh-five," he corrected her. She held her watch to her ear and shook it. "Mine must be running fast," she said. "Are you sure?"

"I am certain," he said.

Those brief, idle words about the watch had established the time of de Marigny's movements. Unwittingly, the RAF wives, strangers to him, meaning him no harm, had placed the son-in-law of Harry Oakes near the scene of the crime.

Driving home, he passed Westbourne. The upstairs lights were still burning.

When he reentered his house that night, Alfred de Marigny found that his guests had gone, save one. His cousin and boyhood friend from Mauritius, Georges de Visdelou, had been ailing with a cold, and his date, Betty Roberts, was still sitting by his bed.

The rain had developed a rhythm, falling with force, then lightly, as the squalls passed. Alfred went to de Visdelou's apartment and asked if he should take Betty home. Georges said he would take her later, and de Marigny accepted that as his cue to go to bed.

At roughly the same time, a brief and curious scene was taking place on the otherwise deserted streets of Nassau. Captain Edward Sears, the superintendent of the Bahamas Police Force, was driving along Bay Street. Sears was a veteran of many years as a lawman; he was a cautious man, respected by all. The rain was still falling hard. As he passed the old Island Bookshop, a station wagon met him going the other way, traveling at about fifteen miles an hour. He could not make out the driver sitting on the right side of the car—British rules—but he had a perfectly clear view of the man sitting in the front passenger seat, no more than five feet away.

It was Harold Christie.

Around three in the morning, a noise interrupted the sleep of de Marigny and he sat bolt upright in bed. Then he realized the noisemaker was Grisou, the Maltese cat owned by de Visdelou. The cat seemed to be playing in the Venetian blinds.

De Marigny swore softly and tried to go back to sleep. Then he heard the voice of his cousin, outside his window, talking to Betty Roberts. They drove off, and a few minutes later the car returned. He heard the door slam.

"Georges!" he called out.

"Yes?"

"Come and take your damned cat out of here."

At the door, de Visdelou said, "Sorry," and called Grisou. Alfred de Marigny rolled over and went back to sleep. The storm was subsiding. Once the Caribbean sun rose over Nassau, his life was never going to be quite the same again.

TO CROSS A KING

WITHOUT realizing it—he would not have been greatly troubled by the thought, if he had—Alfred de Marigny had made an adversary of the former King of England. Most men—and women—would have been elated to find themselves in proximity to David Windsor and the former Wallis Warfield Spencer Simpson, perhaps eventually to claim a friendship. But de Marigny was not most men.

To begin with, he had an enduring contempt for royalty, one of the products of a childhood that was cold and lonely and scarred by a family secret. He was born Marie Alfred de Fonquereaux, the son of a sugar planter. He had rejected a family title, avoided using it, and was embarrassed when society hostesses—and his ex-wives—enjoyed doing so.

He had believed his mother was dead until he met her by chance when he was eighteen. He adopted her name, de Marigny, as a deliberate affront to his father, who he believed had neglected and deceived him.

These circumstances would be soon used against him, by a prosecution bent on painting his past as shady, his character as questionable, his way in society as having been eased by a dubious title.

In light of his own difficulties and the Duke's contribution to them, de Marigny was never inclined to view with charity the misadventures of Windsor, neither then nor in retrospect.

History may judge the former King less narrowly than does de Marigny. Certainly, to the generations that came along before and after the war, he was not a venal man but a lovesick one: weak, too easily used, trained to rule a kingdom but not to hold a job. If at one time his ideas and his words coincided with what the Nazis wanted to hear, his defenders would argue that the Duke thought he was on the side of peace. In his heart, the choice was never between England and Germany. He was for England and a negotiated peace, against war and Communism.

Even as late as his duties in the Bahamas, the Duke had not caught on to the diplomatic nuance: "negotiated peace" was a euphemism for capitulation to Hitler and the Third Reich.

But it would be misleading to suggest that the differences between the Duke and de Marigny were political.

In his determination to show that he was not in awe of the Royal Governor, de Marigny ignored the royal protocol, and his attitude ranged from rudeness to open disrespect. At the least, his behavior was unwise, and reinforced among Nassau's white establishment a sense that de Marigny was arrogant, stubborn, and altogether too foreign.

The feud that simmered between the ex-King and the ex-count was in part fueled by pettiness, but one or two cases turned on basic issues of fairness and compassion.

They had met twice before, the first time briefly, socially, when de Marigny was twenty-two, studying economics in London and beginning to play the stock market. Windsor was then the Prince of Wales, and ten years his elder. De Marigny was introduced to the Prince at Ascot by a Lord Ronald Graham, who had befriended him. His first impression was quite favorable. The Prince was polite, attentive enough to chat a minute about Mauritius, de Marigny's birthplace.

He was surprised by His Royal Highness's stature—five-foot-seven, of average build, neither slight nor sturdy. It was easy to see why women were so easily smitten. They found him boyish, almost "pretty," with a face unwrinkled and untroubled by thought.

It was not until later, when he accepted an invitation to

the château of a man named Charles Bedeaux, that de Marigny understood the attention he had been paid. Lord Ronald was a Nazi sympathizer, or more, and hoped to recruit Alfred and others like him. The dinner was attended by people of similar persuasion, and their star exhibit that night was the Prince of Wales.

Their host, Bedeaux, would later commit suicide in prison after being arrested by the Allies as a collaborator. To the end, the Windsors defended him.

Initially, in the Bahamas, the Windsors' contacts were pleasant, and they welcomed de Marigny as an interesting presence at their official and social activities. His stock soared with the island's discriminating hostesses.

He met the Duchess for the first time at a formal, white-tie reception given in honor of the royal couple aboard Wenner-Gren's yacht, the *Southern Cross*. He recorded his impression: "She was a remarkable-looking woman, not a hair out of place, the makeup perfect, the dress exquisite, from one of the great couturiers. She wore little jewelry, and then simple but elegant pieces. . . .

"I was surprised at how tall she looked next to the Duke, who seemed overshadowed by his wife. She looked the part of the aristocrat, and he the attendant. When she spoke, only her lips moved. Her face was wrinkle-free. Everything about her had been studied meticulously. I watched her in admiration. She had tumbled a king from his throne and she played her role with poise and dignity."

To his surprise, the Duchess thanked de Marigny for opening the island's first beauty parlor, now located in the rooms above his grocery. She informed him that she had flown in a hairdresser from New York to instruct his manager, Mrs. Bethel, on how to do her hair.

Unsure that the Duke would remember him, or acknowledge it if he did, de Marigny kept his silence as the Duchess introduced him as "the gentleman who had the beauty salon installed for my benefit." The Duke studied him for a moment and said, "We met in England, did we not?"

"Once at Ascot" he replied, "through Lord Ronald Graham, and again at a château in Scotland."

The Duchess moved away to greet her guests. A waiter passed by, carrying a silver tray of champagne glasses. The two men lifted their glasses, and the Duke recited in perfect French, in a low voice: "Man is a strange animal... *il brule ce qu'ila adore et adore ce qu'il a brule.*" ("He burns what he adored and adores what he burned.")

The meaning of those words escaped him, but de Marigny passed off the toast as a sample of the Duke's taste for the theatrical gesture.

Shortly after the evening on the *Southern Cross,* he was invited to a reception at Government House, the first since the Duke and Duchess had returned to the official residence. The Duchess greeted him as an old friend. Her pride was evident as she pointed out the improvements in the old pink stucco mansion, which stood high on a hill, amid a grove of tall palms. De Marigny thought he was seeing a glimpse of her real self, the usually unrevealed Duchess. "I could understand," he wrote in a diary he kept at the time, "how a frail and effeminate little man like the Duke could have lost his heart and his throne over her. She had the charm of a femme fatale, and a serene control that made her irresistible. I had a glimpse through her eyes of the warmth and passion that she disguised so well under her cool appearance."

De Marigny considered himself a serious observer of the female species. He was prepared to add the Duchess to his list of women who by their beauty or cunning rearranged the future, along with Helen of Troy, Cleopatra, and Madame du Barry—women who have always attracted man's imagination and sexual desire. He admired the Duchess and what she represented: an elite sorority of women, not necessarily beautiful, whose well-disguised talents gave them power.

From then on, de Marigny became part of the accepted

group to invite whenever His Highness and the Duchess were in attendance. He dined with them at the home of Frederick Sigrist, who, with Tommy Sopwith, designed the Hurricane fighter plane; again at the Wenner-Grens', on Hog Island; and twice as the guest of the William Taylors. He thought it odd that he never met Sir Harry and Lady Oakes at these more intimate functions. They had lent their estate to the royal couple, and yet had once again failed to step across society's threshold.

The excitement that greeted the surprise arrival of the Windsors soon paled. Beyond the stately pink house on the hill, the island's blacks lived in squalor in a ghetto called Grant's Town. Many of the houses had dirt floors, and water was scarce. Some Nassau businessmen had begun to regard the Duke as an expensive luxury to a colony where eighty percent of the people lived in poverty. It had been the custom for previous governors to return their yearly salary of six thousand pounds to the island's treasury. His Royal Highness kept his. Breaking tradition was to be his way of life. To add to the colony's debt, the Executive Council had to pay ten thousand pounds to repair and redecorate Government House to the satisfaction of the new occupants.

Finally, there were four or five episodes that caused the bad blood between the Duke of Windsor and Alfred de Marigny, one consequence of which may have been the trial of an innocent man for murder.

The first, most personal, and most damaging of these bouts involved the water rights to property de Marigny had acquired on Eleuthera, one of the cays (pronounced "keys") sprinkled around Nassau like pebbles in an aquarium.

He was building a home there, and had taken on as another project a system that would supply fresh water from his well to the black villagers, who had none. They boiled sea water or captured rain in buckets, when it rained, and in the thin, barren soil nothing flourished except disease and hardship.

So de Marigny provided the pipes, the windmill, and a reservoir, and the House of Assembly approved the project. All he needed was the signature of the governor to begin.

One day de Marigny was visited by a new neighbor, a well-known British writer who had built a lavish home east of his. Her name was Rosita Forbes, and she was an old friend of the Duke of Windsor.

She arrived on horseback, looking very sporty and very British. During tea she lamented the fact that she had no source of fresh water on her property. Missing the hint, de Marigny suggested that she install gutters and a water tank.

He was still waiting for a permit to be signed, when he heard from a source in the colonial office that the delay had to do with Rosita Forbes. She had asked the Duke to intervene, and divert the water lines intended for the natives to her exclusive use instead.

A confrontation with the Royal Governor was inevitable. De Marigny drove to Government House, where an aide-de-camp, Captain George Wood, led him into the library used by the Duke as an office.

He explained the reason for his visit. Windsor tapped tobacco into his pipe and seemed pensive. "As a matter of fact," he said, "I was about to write you on that matter. I'd hope you would be reasonable. Mrs. Forbes has spent a tremendous amount of money to build that house of hers. Not only did she provide work for dozens of needy people, she will spend more money and employ more people to develop the gardens. This is a factor one should not overlook."

He took a pull on his pipe and added, "Between us, my friend, the Negroes on the Cay have been living without running water from the time they arrived here. They have managed."

De Marigny was startled by the shallowness of the argument. "I am afraid that the governor does not see the picture as I see it," he replied. "Here is an Englishwoman who spent a fortune on a place before first determining whether fresh water was available. I humbly remind the governor that the water in question is mine. I would have never thought that the governor would place the whim of Mrs. Forbes against the vital necessity of native Bahamians, who need water for their survival."

The Duke left his desk, walked to a bookcase at the other end of the office, and began flipping the pages of a book. He watched de Marigny out of the corner of his eye. The captain tried to explain that one rose when His Royal Highness rose, and that the interview was now closed.

"Captain Wood," said de Marigny, stretching his long legs, "we are not in Buckingham Palace. We are here on a glorified reef. The welfare of the majority should be his one and foremost objective."

"His Royal Highness, sir. You are talking about His Royal Highness."

"Captain," said de Marigny, "if the British government felt that the Duke was someone of importance, he would not have been sent to rot on this miserable reef. Like them, I sometimes feel that our Prince is nothing more than a pimple on the ass of the British Empire."

The Duke of Windsor slammed shut his book and left the room, ending, with the same finality, any chance of a civil relationship between de Marigny and himself. De Marigny rose deliberately and made his way out of the building. In the weeks and years ahead, de Marigny's closing line would be widely repeated and quoted, and it would not endear him to those who would soon hold his fate in their hands.

Three days later, the permit was signed by the governor, and the blacks of Eleuthera were at last to receive free, fresh water.

If those words were meant to wound the Duke—"a pimple on the ass of the British Empire"—de Marigny surely succeeded, for he had said openly what Windsor knew to be true. Decades of British neglect had made the Bahamas almost impossible to govern. He had no real power; the House of Assembly passed the laws, and the Bay Street Merchants controlled the rest.

The white power structure in the Bahamas opposed many things, change foremost among them. There was a mentality very close to what existed in the American South in the 1940s. In his approach to relations with the black race, the Duke regarded the segregation of the South as a fine model. He pictured a kind of paternalism that kept blacks in their place: no voting rights; separate housing and schools and health care, as good as could be afforded on the wages their bosses believed in keeping low to make the economy work.

The Duke of Windsor made nice speeches about improving their wages and eliminating their hunger. But during his tenure, no black entered Government House through the front door.

Nor did the Bahamas want or seek financial support from London, or the influence that might go with it. That was an echo of the South's long opposition to federal aid as a threat to states' rights and a way of life that has now vanished from the American scene, along with the American scene itself.

In another episode, de Marigny challenged the Duke's prejudice against Jews. On a visit to New York, he learned from a friend, Walter Seligman, an oilman, and Charles Revson, the founder of the Revlon cosmetics company, that the policy in Nassau barred Jews from the hotels and golf club. To meet the Duke, and possibly play a round of golf with him, was like a fantasy to them.

On the spot, de Marigny offered to rent them apartments in his new Cable Beach Manor, which automatically included guest privileges at the golf course. He quoted them a price, and left with a check for the full amount. The Duke and Duchess were a valuable tourist attraction.

As his first order of business the next day, de Marigny converted his dollars into pounds. He was aware that the step he had taken so lightly would be seen as a challenge to powerful forces—not only the Duke, but the merchants and politicians.

The policy of exclusion had been rigidly enforced. The Bay Street Boys feared that once they opened the doors to Jews, Nassau would quickly turn into another Miami Beach. De Marigny counted on Harold Christie to smooth out any problems.

Christie's first reaction was shock, then anger. Calmly, de Marigny handed him a check for six thousand pounds. "This is your commission," he said, watching his eyes, "for the rentals."

Harold offered a deal. He would join the chorus of curses that would greet de Marigny's news, then plead his case on the grounds that he was ignorant of the island's "traditions." And Harold must promise the Bay Street Boys that, after the season, de Marigny would sell his Cable Beach development. With some reluctance, de Marigny accepted the quid pro quo.

It may not have been a clean blow for religious tolerance, but one way or another the barriers were coming down in Nassau.

Yet another episode, another link in the chain, occurred the week that France fell to the Nazis. This one would put de Marigny at odds with Windsor, and on a collision course with the Attorney General, Eric Hallinan.

Among those who followed the war, some wept and sank into a depression. Of French stock, de Marigny suddenly felt useless. He looked around and saw an island that catered to society's parasites, while Paris lay trampled under German boots.

He inquired about enlisting with the Free French army of Charles de Gaulle, and a physical examination was arranged with Dr. Ulrich "Ricky" Oberwarth, an old friend. Tests confirmed a history of hypoglycemia and chronic stomach pain. Dr. Oberwarth told him bluntly that there was no chance of his being accepted into the armed forces.

De Marigny had allowed himself to feel temporarily noble,

with the prospect of doing something patriotic. Now, for one of the few times in his life, he felt defeated.

That was his mood when extraordinary news reached him from Governor's Harbour. A small sailing boat with seven half-dead men on board had washed up on de Marigny's beach. Four of the men were French, three were Vietnamese.

They had come from Devil's Island.

With the fall of the French government, the penal colony had been closed, and the inmates given their freedom. All had documents to prove they had served long prison terms and were now classified as free men. Their leader, Henri de Boynes, a middle-aged man of excellent family, had brawled with his captain during a period of military service, and had served twenty years on Devil's Island.

Two of the group were homosexual and had been convicted of robbery. The last one introduced himself as a banker, a wry way of saying that he robbed for a living.

The three Vietnamese had come from Saigon. They were in wretched condition and nearly starved. De Marigny fed them and, after they had rested, had them delivered to Nassau. As a sailor, he was stunned by the pluck they had shown in sailing from Guiana to Venezuela, where they wrecked their first boat, which they then replaced with a smaller one and, with no knowledge of sailing or navigation, crossed the rough windward and leeward passages to Nassau.

News that de Marigny was bringing into town seven convicts from Devil's Island preceded him, as if someone had driven through the town in a sound truck. He was met by the captain of the Salvation Army and the bishop of the Baptist church, who between them provided clothes, food, and shelter for the miserable group.

With support from the two local newspapers, Christie led an immediate campaign to dispose of the ex-convicts. He considered their presence on Bay Street an embarrassment to the island, a danger to the residents, and a threat to what was left of the tourist trade. The Attorney General offered a fast solution: he had them slapped into jail.

Seeing people abused had often awakened in de Marigny a response that was almost paternal. He had risked his life to salvage two friends from Germany. He was to do the same in a different way, in another era, after the rise of Fidel Castro in Havana. And now the citizens of Nassau, led by the Attorney General, were prepared to treat seven miserable, destitute souls like meat for the sharks. They were unable even to express themselves in the tongue of the country whose shore they had reached.

No one cared, or understood, that they had spent years in the most infamous prison since the Dark Ages, and had faced death for over sixty days in fleeing that hellish place to freedom—only to be thrown in jail without due process of law.

No lawyer, including his own, Godfrey Higgs, would assist de Marigny in what must have struck them as a quixotic cause. The captain of the Salvation Army knew just enough law to guide him. They petitioned the local magistrate to free the men on a writ of habeas corpus, only to have Hallinan refuse to release them.

They must have made an unforgettable pair, the missionary and the yachtsman, when the two men burst into Hallinan's office and demanded an explanation.

The Attorney General looked at de Marigny with loathing painted on his face. He replied that the unwanted visitors were vagabonds, criminals, escapees from justice. "Why," he asked, addressing de Marigny, "are you so concerned with this scum?"

"Because they are human beings," he said emotionally.

"Under the War Act, I can keep them in jail indefinitely."

"That is not so. Under the War Act, you must set them free without delay. Those men have sworn that they are pro-de Gaulle and anti-Vichy. They are therefore our allies and should be treated as such. Too, they are shipwrecked sailors. Under international law, they are entitled to humane care, food, and a place to stay. Not a jail cell. Then they must be provided with a seaworthy boat, with sails and provisions, and permitted to leave, all expenses to be borne by the local government.

"You have no reason to keep them in jail one minute longer. I am willing to respond for them, and they shall not become a public charge. If bail has to be posted, I am prepared to do so now."

His intensity startled Hallinan. That same day, the men were transferred to the hospital to be checked for contagious diseases.

Jobs were found for them, and the refugees from Devil's Island settled quietly into the community. The one who called himself a banker became the foreman for an American lady who raced speedboats and owned an island north of Nassau. The three Vietnamese found work at the Chinese laundry.

The favorite of de Marigny turned out to be Henri de Boynes, the refugees' leader. Alfred provided the dowry when de Boynes decided to take a wife. He opened a small shop where he carved and sold coconut husks. As far as is known, all the former prisoners worked hard and made honest livings.

An earlier boatload had been less fortunate. They had been dumped in a mental hospital until the governor decided what should be done. He had ruled that if the prisoners were not Free French, they would be provided with a boat and provisions and put to sea. Eventually, they cast off for America, with blankets and clothing and food, but no visas or charts. They were never heard from again.

Not long after his defense of the men from Devil's Island, Alfred de Marigny found himself in jail, on trial for his life. On Sundays he was certain to have visits from six friends who never forgot or abandoned him. It was more than he could have said about a large number of people who had eaten his food, drunk his wine, borrowed his money, and, soon after his arrest, drifted away and seemed not to know him.

Even in such remote ports as Nassau, profiteering in wartime was not considered good form. He was not proud of those rare occasions when he did so, but de Marigny took satisfaction at least once in outbidding the Duke of Windsor.

He made a splendid buy on an insurance auction of wines saved from a warehouse fire. The insurers were obligated to advertise the sale in the newspaper, but a friend arranged to have the ad buried on a back page, in the smallest possible type, giving only the time and date. In those days a box of cigars was a worthy bribe. On the day of the auction, only a handful of people came to bid.

The booty included five cases of Hennessy Five-Star cognac, a find worth a small fortune, especially at a time when cognac country was occupied by the Germans.

Several days after the auction, de Marigny received a visit from Captain Wood, on behalf of His Royal Highness. The captain was a typical officer of the period, infused with the attitude that colonials are lesser breeds whose only function is to serve the desires of the English overlord.

His Royal Highness had been distressed to learn that the auction of the warehouse inventory had already taken place. His Royal Highness had had his eye on the Hennessy's. Now he was in the awkward position of asking a favor of a man he disliked. Would he be kind enough to spare a couple of cases?

De Marigny replied that the bottles were not for sale.

Wood was amused. "You did not expect that His Royal Highness would *buy* them, did you, old chap?"

De Marigny ignored him. "I will make an exception for the governor. I could let him have two cases for five hundred pounds, and a bargain at that."

Captain Wood brushed his mustache. "That is absurd. I have never heard such rubbish." He took his leave.

A week later, two of the bottles of cognac were delivered to Government House with de Marigny's card. The Duke sent back a personal note of thanks.

It was not true that Alfred never missed an opportunity to

taunt or annoy the Royal Governor, but most of the episodes clearly ended in his favor.

In spite of the war, and the local politics, the parade of distinctive visitors to Nassau continued uninterrupted. The actress Madeleine Carroll arrived with her leading man, Sterling Hayden, to make a film called *Bahamas Passage*. Most of it had already been filmed in a studio in Hollywood; exterior shots of Nassau would give the picture an air of authenticity.

At a party given by Christie, Miss Carroll met de Marigny, with whom she chatted in fluent French. She paid discreet visits to the house on Victoria Avenue, where de Visdelou joined them for long, relaxed talks and quiet meals. She disliked the cocktail parties and the crowds that pestered her with silly remarks and requests for autographs.

They formed a fast friendship. The film stars liked de Marigny's idea of entertainment: a flying visit to Eleuthera and a day on the pink sandy beach; a bicycle ride around Nassau; picnics with fresh lobsters caught and prepared before their eyes.

Months later the cast returned to Nassau for the film's premiere. Madeleine asked de Marigny to host a small party at his home after the showing, saying with some coyness that she had a surprise. As it happened, the Duke and Duchess had planned a larger, formal affair at Government House in the actress's honor. Someone—Harold Christie or Captain Wood—had remembered to invite everyone but Miss Carroll. She was unaware that a reception had been scheduled.

The theater was packed, and when the film ended, the crowd rushed out to watch as the lovely actress departed. The Windsors dawdled long enough to see her emerge to cheers—she curtsied to the Duke and bowed to the Duchess—then grab the arm of de Marigny and hurry to his car.

The Duke looked on, astonished. He canceled his party on the spot.

With glee, some newspapers reported that Miss Carroll had been whisked away in an act of mischief by the local

Casanovas, de Marigny and his cousin, de Visdelou.

Madeleine Carroll's surprise was the announcement of her engagement to Sterling Hayden.

If life in the tropics seemed anecdotal, at times trivial, much would change in July 1943.

On the morning of Thursday, July 8, de Marigny rose at dawn, popped an Alka-Seltzer for his complaining stomach, and fixed his own breakfast: Ovaltine, two poached eggs, and toast. It was the same breakfast, without variation, he ate every day.

He stopped by the farm, leaving at 8:45 A.M. and making two trips, an hour apart, to the Central Police Station, to register his truck. On his first attempt, around nine, the officer he needed to see wasn't in. Basil McKinney and Oswald Moseley, another of his sailing companions, could verify the time. He bumped into them near the post office and spent a few minutes chatting about the yacht races.

He returned to the farm and then, just before noon, he drove into town on another errand. Outside the Pan American Airways offices, John Anderson hailed him. Anderson ran the Bahamas General Trust and, some said, was a bagman for Axel Wenner-Gren. He seemed excited.

"Have you heard?" he asked, eager to see de Marigny's reaction. "Harry Oakes is dead."

Alfred wasn't sure he should believe him. He peered into his eyes and said, "You're kidding me, Andy."

"No, I have confirmed it with Dr. Fitzmaurice."

Any white man's death was news in Nassau. But Harry Oakes. Nancy's father. Good God. De Marigny wondered how he had died—a stroke, a heart attack? He thought of Sir Harry's rages; neither would have surprised him. Anderson didn't know.

They were not even sure which house he had used, but Alfred suggested they take Anderson's car and start with Westbourne. From the number of police cars parked outside, they knew they had picked the right place. It was a little after 1:00 P.M.

Two hours later, the stretcher-bearers finally carried out the body of Sir Harry Oakes.

The next twenty-four hours would be a dizzying time. When he learned from Mrs. Kelly how Oakes had died, he thought he might be sick. Inside the house, he saw Harold Christie using the phone in the downstairs hallway. When he realized Harold was talking to Lady Oakes, in Bar Harbor, he insisted on speaking briefly to her. As the only family member in town, he offered to do anything he could. He wanted to be helpful. He felt ignored, and was beginning to feel rising annoyance.

He went through the rest of the day, in his words, "like a zombie." Lunch. Another trip to the farm. Endless, circular conversations. That night, at around 10:00 P.M., Colonel Erskine-Lindop called at his home and asked if he would return to Westbourne. The house was still crawling with people. The police were interviewing witnesses, anyone who had contact with the deceased: Christie, his brother Frank, Mrs. Kelly, the doctors, house servants. De Marigny wondered why total strangers were wandering in and out of the house.

This time he finally met the Miami detectives, Melchen and Barker, who had encountered some unexpected handicaps. For one, they had no murder weapon. They could not explain the source of the fire, and they surmised that the muddy footprints, over which dozens had now walked, led *down* the stairs. They had yet to lift a single fingerprint.

But they knew who de Marigny was, and had heard the stories of the elopement with the deceased man's young daughter, the quarrels with the father, his antics, his gadfly reputation. They wanted to examine his arms and hands for signs of burnt hair.

They returned with him to the house on Victoria Avenue, and there was a comic charade while Melchen and Barker went through his clothes. De Marigny could not single out, from the many identical shirts in the dirty clothes hamper, or the three dozen neckties, the shirt and tie he had worn the night before.

He still felt no alarm, sensed no threat, when Colonel Erskine-Lindop asked if he would mind having a guest for the night, Lieutenant John Campbell Douglas. Alfred did not mind, and served him coffee in the morning.

On the morning of Friday, July 9, Douglas drove him back to Westbourne, and their casual chitchat would later haunt de Marigny. He was questioned again by Melchen, and sent upstairs for a strange interlude with Barker, involving a drinking glass and a pack of cigarettes.

At around four o'clock on Friday afternoon, the Duke of Windsor made a personal appearance at Westbourne. He asked to see Barker, and found him alone upstairs, in Sir Harry's bedroom. There is no record of what was said in the twenty minutes of earnest conversation that took place between the Duke and the Miami detective. The Royal Governor left, and within two hours, Alfred de Marigny was charged with the murder of Harry Oakes.

The reactions to de Marigny's arrest were swift and mixed. The Duke of Windsor found himself in a quandary, as revealed by a plaintive letter he sent to London. "The whole circumstances of the case are sordid beyond description," he wrote, "and I will be glad when the trial is over and done with." He had drawn a puzzling conclusion, in view of how little time had passed and his own record: "The older and more conservative elements and the whole Negro population suspect de Marigny's guilt."

Since when did the Duke of Windsor speak for "the whole Negro population"?

He continued: "On the other hand de Marigny, who is a despicable character and has the worst possible record, morally and financially, since his adolescence, has insidiously bought his way with his ex-wife's money into the leadership of the younger generation, born of bootlegging days, and for whom they have an admiration bordering on hero worship."

The Duke of Windsor, the man who married Mr. Simpson's wife, had claimed the moral high ground in what would be billed by the tabloid press as "the crime of the century."

The trials of Alfred de Marigny, out of the courtroom as well as within, had begun.

PART TWO

THE CASE AGAINST
ALFRED DE MARIGNY

L'homme est un aprenti. La douleur est son maitre,
et nul ne connait, tant qu'il n'a pas souffert.

("Man is an apprentice. Pain is the master, and no one
has lived who has not suffered.")

LE MOTTE HOUDAR

THE ARREST

EVERY day of your life you retrace your steps. You roll out of bed in the morning, drive to work, eat, laugh, lose your temper, make love. And then one day someone you know, someone in your own small circle, is murdered. And you are accused of the crime.

One tries to imagine such a thing happening. It is like trying to imagine a piece of a meteor falling out of the sky and crashing through the roof of your home.

Nothing about the eighth of July 1943 was out of the ordinary. It began as just another languid day in the tropics—except that it was to be the last pure day of freedom I would know, the last for many years that I would call my own.

I was awake at sunup, as usual. The storm of the night before had cleared the air, and the sun was out, the sea calm. At the farm, George Thompson worked hard to fill a backlog of orders created the last two days by **the** unfavorable weather.

I took a place on the line next to George, and helped pass the chickens over a flame. A machine removed most of the feathers, but the down had to be burned off. There is no way to make the business of raising chickens, killing and dressing them, sound glamorous, even if one were tempted. The work was hard and slow and mostly by hand.

It was George who reminded me that I needed to stop by the police station to register our new truck. I went to the station, but the officer I needed to see had not yet arrived. I waited an hour or so and returned, signed the proper forms, and headed back to the farm.

I was soon to discover how incriminating the most mundane errand can seem when you are pulled into the web of a violent crime. The most normal and innocent of actions, what one said or didn't say, can be made to appear sinister. I had not given a second thought to the events of the night before. I had not left my house except briefly, when I drove two of my dinner guests back to their cottage, a few blocks from Westbourne. The next morning, in the hour when the first police had arrived, and a doctor was examining the body, I had appeared twice at the Nassau police station.

Now time seemed to accelerate. There was the chance meeting with John Anderson, where I learned of Sir Harry's death; the spur-of-the-moment ride to Westbourne to seek more information; my hearing from Madeline Kelly that he had died of a head wound. Mrs. Kelly did not use, did not have to use, the only word that described the case: Oakes had been murdered.

My first thoughts were of Nancy, who needed to be told of her father's death. There was no way to guess how long it would take for an operator to put a call through to Vermont, where Nancy had spent the summer attending Martha Graham's ballet school. I would need to cable her.

To add to my confusion, Mrs. Kelly told us that the governor had used his war powers to impose a strict censorship on the island, banning all calls or wires about the death. (How she knew this, I had not thought to ask.)

I had been bothered during the night by stomach pains; now I felt queasy and fought against it. Not an easy man to mourn, Sir Harry Oakes. All those bitter years of prospecting for gold, of scratching for a stake, of nights with only the unforgiving earth for a bed, had wrung from him whatever humor or compassion he might once have had. He had struggled so hard to make it, had lived so long as a tramp, that he could never truly enjoy his great wealth. Yet I could not imagine him dead.

I was still concerned about getting word to Nancy when

Anderson and I entered the house. The first person I encountered was Christie. He hurried past us, with no word of recognition, only a quick glance and a muttered "Long distance." He took the call in the living room. I stood close enough to realize he was talking to Lady Oakes. "Yes, yes, there is no doubt," I heard him say. He paused, listening, then said, "We are doing everything we can. I have already spoken to the Duke. He is bringing in investigators from Miami to take charge here."

I tapped his shoulder. He looked at me, his green eyes reduced to slits, and I said, "I wish to speak to Lady Oakes when you are through." He nodded. Moments later he said, "Eunice, I shall keep in touch if there is anything to report."

I placed my hand on the telephone before he could hang it up. I repeated that I wished to speak to my mother-in-law. I took the receiver from him and heard her crying. "Alfred, this is horrible," she said. "He was such a kind man. I cannot imagine such a monstrous thing."

I told her how sorry I was, still not knowing the details of what had happened. I reminded Lady Oakes that Nancy needed to be notified. I asked her to have Nancy call me later in the day.

Harold hadn't moved. As soon as I had hung up the phone, I grabbed his arm and demanded to know what Lady Oakes meant, the reference to "a monstrous thing." Exactly what had happened to Sir Harry? Christie was evasive, and his attitude puzzled me. "We are friends," I said. "And yet you cannot find one minute to call and tell me that my father-in-law is dead?"

Only yesterday I had invited Christie to join my other guests for dinner at my home.

"Try to understand," he stammered. "I meant no offense. I have been out of my mind ... I am sorry." He looked past me, saw Eric Hallinan, and pulled away. "I must speak to the Attorney General," he said. The two of them started up the stairs. I tried to follow, but Colonel Erskine-Lindop, the police commissioner, stopped me. "Sorry," he said, "but no one can go upstairs. There is a police investigation."

I was, for the moment, speechless. Even as we talked, neighbors, friends of the police, and strangers were milling around, drifting in and out of rooms. Erskine-Lindop lowered his voice and said, in a less official tone: "Between us, Alfred, there has been foul play. The governor has called in two detectives from Miami to head the investigation. My hands are tied."

The full meaning of what he had said was lost on me. I only knew that the Duke, for whatever reasons, had taken charge of what normally would have been a routine police proceeding.

At about 11:30 A.M., we watched the body of Harry Oakes, wrapped in a bedsheet, being carried down the stairs to the ambulance. I was really aghast. Now I understood the reaction of Lady Oakes. She had been talking with someone who was able to give her the ugliest details of the tragedy: Christie had spent the night in the next room. He had discovered the body, he said, around seven in the morning. And it had to have been on information from Harold that the Duke of Windsor acted when he summoned outside help from Miami.

The time of death was fixed at between 1:00 and 3:00 A.M. It was still unclear to me how Sir Harry had died, and, amid the activity all around us, no one seemed willing to take the time to enlighten me. Already forces had been put in motion from which no one could turn back. But I analyzed none of it. I was at that point still feeling slighted, disturbed by what I saw as Christie's discourtesy. Whatever was going on, he had helped take charge of it, a role I knew he enjoyed. He aspired, long before I had met him, to be the kingpin of the establishment.

Harold and his brother, Frank, left the house. I watched their car pull away from the curb and follow the ambulance carrying the body of Harry Oakes.

That afternoon I called Dr. Ricky Oberwarth, who was on the staff of the General Hospital, and who also served as the Nassau prison doctor. When I tried to bring up the death of Sir

Harry, he cut me off, and said he would drop by later for tea.

In the meantime, Nancy called. Her distress was evident on the telephone. She told me that she was flying to Bar Harbor to be with her mother for the funeral. Then, in a voice choked with emotion, she added, "Dearest, I am terribly worried." I sensed that she had started to say something else, then stopped. Instead she said, "Freddy ... please be careful."

Ricky Oberwarth dropped by soon after my conversation with Nancy. He was troubled by the manner in which the investigation had been undertaken. He was under instructions not to discuss the murder. The Attorney General had stressed that all information should be referred to him and kept confidential. Any medical reports were not to be put in writing. Ricky had told me perhaps more than he should have. He seemed pensive.

It was almost dinnertime on Thursday when Lieutenant John Campbell Douglas, of the Bahamas police force, appeared at my door. He said that Colonel Erskine-Lindop had asked to see me. We drove to Westbourne and found the house now teeming with people. There were no evident security precautions being taken.

While I waited for Erskine-Lindop, the Duke of Windsor arrived with one of his aides, Major George Wood. He passed within a few feet of me and stared without speaking. He walked upstairs with Erskine-Lindop and returned ten minutes later, again looking me directly in the eye. He hesitated for just a moment, then continued to his car.

Time dragged while I waited for Erskine-Lindop. I wondered why the Duke had not spoken, even to express a word of sympathy about the death of the man who was, after all, my father-in-law. Nearly an hour later I was ushered into the living room. It soon became clear that I would be questioned by the two American detectives.

This was my first chance to observe them. The one who introduced himself as Edward Mclchen was a burly man with a large pot belly and a prominent nose that supported a pair of eyeglasses. He asked me point-blank to describe my whereabouts throughout the evening of July 7 and the early morning of July 8. No suggestion was made that I should have an attorney, nor did it occur to me that I had any reason to need one. I described my actions in detail.

Major James Barker sat opposite me at a specially lighted tabic. He was tall, slim, ruggedly handsome in a way that today would be characteristic of a television cop. In front of the detective were a magnifying glass, a pair of scissors, and several gadgets related to his work. All other lights had been turned out except for a floor lamp at the other end of the room. The atmosphere, I thought, was contrived to appear dramatic.

Either the pace of events had dulled my mind, or my self-confidence had made me unable to see the danger. It had still not sunk in that I was suspected of having murdered Sir Harry Oakes.

Since Nancy's departure I had cultivated a Vandyke beard. I wanted to see her reaction before I shaved it. Now Barker inspected my hands as a fortune-teller would: he studied the palms, then the backs of my hands. He then looked at them through his magnifying glass, and gave special attention to my beard. He sat up, his eyes riveted on mine.

"The hair is singed on your hands and beard," he said, in a low, measured voice. "Moreover, you have ash residue in the pores of both your hands. Do you have an explanation for that?"

The thrust of this questioning was impossible to miss, but I saw it as no threat to me. Offhand, I could give him three or four reasons. I explained the process of scorching the chickens at the farm. I mentioned that I smoked a half-dozen cigars a day and that, in the dampness of Nassau, they required frequent relighting. And I mentioned the hurricane lamps during dinner the previous night, and burning my hand. Still, the reference to the ash residue puzzled me. I had showered twice since the morning, and had given my hands a hard scrubbing after working at the farm.

They made a point, a little show, of clipping hairs from my head, beard, and arms. Lindop asked if I would permit the detectives to accompany me to my home. I found the request unusual, but made no objection. In my eagerness to show them I had nothing to hide, I played right into their hands.

It was getting late, and when we reached Victoria Avenue, I told the servants they could leave. All did, except for George Thompson.

Melchen asked to see the clothes I had worn that night. I could not pick out the particular necktie from among the thirty or so that were hanging on a rack in my cabinet. Nor could I tell him which of the shirts that we emptied from a laundry basket was the correct one. Melchen stared at the articles he had spilled on the floor, handkerchiefs and socks and five or six nearly identical shirts. Of the fifteen or so shirts I owned, all were white or cream-colored, either linen or silk.

"Do you refuse to show me the shirt you wore last night?" he insisted in a sharp voice.

"You must be joking," I said. "Perhaps the maid can answer your question in the morning. If you like, you may take my laundry with you and inspect it at your leisure."

There were no bloodstains on any of my clothing, or burn marks, or even the scent of smoke, which tends to linger—of this I was certain, and no claims to the contrary were made. Still, if my intent had been to deceive them, it would have been a simple matter to indicate any white shirt or dark tie.

Melchen turned away from me with a grunt and walked into the living room. In the meantime, Barker, who had been looking through the closets, brandished one of my suits and said, in a loud and triumphant voice, "Is this the suit you wore last night?"

"Yes," I replied. It was actually a light brown sportcoat and slacks of a darker brown.

"This suit is freshly pressed. How do you account for that?"

I was trying to bottle up my temper when Erskine-Lindop joined us. "Is anything wrong?" he asked.

Barker held out the suit. "I found this in his closet. It is freshly pressed."

Wearily, I said, "Mr. Barker, I see nothing unusual in having a suit pressed. The laundress does it every day." I turned to Erskine-Lindop. "Am I right, Colonel?"

Erskine-Lindop confirmed to Barker that it was the custom in Nassau to have a suit pressed after it had been worn. "It gives one a good presence," he said, "and is a very British tradition."

It belabors the obvious to point out that labor was cheap, the weather difficult, and wrinkle-resistant fabrics not yet available. But on such slender threads, I would literally discover, evidence in a murder trial can be concocted.

As Barker, taking my suit with him, and Mclchen were leaving, Erskine-Lindop asked if I would mind having Douglas spend the night in my living room. I was exhausted and didn't care where he stayed. Douglas was a tall, pleasant Scotsman with a soft burr in his voice.

Within minutes I was in bed and asleep. I don't know how long I had slept when I realized Douglas was shaking me. He asked if I was all right. I said yes and went back to sleep. This performance was repeated every hour, and each time Douglas called out to someone to say that I was all right.

No matter how irritable I grew, I knew Douglas was at least as miserable. He told me this was to have been his night off, and he had to break a date and keep me company instead. "All this," he complained, "*is* because Sir Harry had plenty of money. If it was some poor colored fellow in Grant's Town, I would be asked to fill out a report and that would be the end of it."

At five in the morning I was wide awake, and after a light breakfast I left the table and went to the bathroom to take my shower. Suddenly, Douglas was in my doorway. "Please, Fred.

Please!" he begged. "Do not shave your beard."

His agitation baffled me. "You must be crazy," I exploded. "Why in the name of heaven should I shave a beard that took so long to grow?"

Douglas looked embarrassed. "I am sorry," he said. "Those are Hallinan's orders."

I washed my face and frowned at Douglas in my mirror: "If I really wanted to shave my beard, who would stop me?" I asked. "And why? You are all playing games instead of using your energy to find the man who killed Oakes."

Douglas shrugged his shoulders. "You know that I am your friend. I can only repeat that this is not my doing. The Irishman orders and I obey."

In time, much would become clear to me that then seemed only idiotic. I have recalled these encounters, these conversations, as my memory, together with whatever notes I kept, tell me they happened. I cannot say whether I have made them more or less dramatic than they seemed at the moment. For an impatient person, it is difficult to be cool and understated when the subject of murder hangs in the air.

For all my annoyance, I understood that the actions of Erskine-Lindop were within the line of duty. As a native of Mauritius he was a countryman, and I knew him as a man of integrity. Nor did I see anything irregular in the work of the detectives from Miami. So hectic had been the twenty-four hours since the discovery of Oakes's body, the rumor of one moment displaced by the allegation of another, that I had found no time to attach the least importance to their posturing. My conscience was clear. I was anxious to cooperate to the limit of my abilities; I had all but insisted on it. Ironic as it may seem, I considered myself the representative of the family.

Now, after a night of interrupted sleep, the intrusion of the police into my home, the charade of the laundered clothes and the burned whiskers, I could not set aside my forebodings.

To the American reader, conditioned all his life to call for his lawyer at the first provocation, my reactions must be those of one living in a fool's world. In truth, it was just implausible to me that from the outset of the investigation I was to be their prime suspect. Their only suspect. I had been judged guilty within hours of the crime, and no consideration would be allowed to interfere with that conclusion.

To put this thought more bluntly: If you were white and important and discreet in Nassau, you had no problems with the law, except possibly an occasional conflict with the banking system. I was not always discreet. But I considered myself a serious person, known more for a tart tongue than a bad temper. The idea that anyone could think I had murdered my father-in-law was preposterous. It was to be treated as an insult, and taken not much more seriously.

The next day, Friday, the ninth of July, I confronted my own doubts. Unfortunately, my lawyer and friend, Godfrey Higgs, had been in Miami for a long weekend and was not due back until the next day. I did not think it necessary to call on Fred Adderley, the only criminal attorney in Nassau.

(In 1939, after Harry Oakes had been knighted, he desired a seat in the House of Assembly. To create an opening for him, a young black lawyer resigned and was appointed to the Executive Council. The man Oakes replaced was Adderley.)

I had a business to run. I could not spend the day examining my own uneasiness. We drove to the farm, where I worked until 9:30 A.M. Douglas had told me that we were to return to Westbourne by ten. Our idle chitchat along the way would come back to haunt me.

The ride to the Oakes estate was like a trip to a morgue. Again people were coming and going; even sightseers had been allowed to move timidly through the first floor. At 10:30 A.M. exactly, Melchen appeared and asked me to follow him upstairs. I thought he wanted to show me Oakes's bedroom. I had not seen it, and had no impression of how much damage the fire had done.

Instead, we stopped on the first landing and entered a small area furnished as a sitting room. Melchen sat down and gestured to a chair across from him. Almost casually, he asked about Christie and Oakes. He asked if I knew whether Christie had been in debt to Sir Harry, or held a grudge against him.

Whether he was actually pursuing this line or was trying to mislead me, I could not tell. But his tone offended me. I replied that Harold was a friend of mine and that I had no intention of answering such a question.

Melchen took no notes and referred to no records. He moved on, and asked about my dinner party. Abruptly, he stopped talking and walked to a small table by the door, on which were a pitcher of water and two glasses. He invited me to pour a glass of water for both of us. He drank his slowly; I emptied mine in one swallow. He tossed me a pack of Lucky Strike cigarettes. I removed one and handed it back to him.

In the middle of this scene, Barker opened the door and asked if everything was okay. Melchen replied that it was, and Barker closed the door behind him. Moments later, he told me the interview was over. We walked downstairs, where Douglas was still waiting in the same chair.

"I will drive you home," he said.

Douglas looked at his watch, a reflex, and I did the same. The time was exactly 11:45 A.M.

The time of our arrival at Westbourne, the time of my interview with Melchen, and the time it ended and we departed all were duly registered by Douglas and presented in court as evidence. This seemingly minor attention to detail would become a pivotal point in breaking down the case against me.

Basil McKinney and John Anderson were waiting for me at my home. Douglas stayed, and we decided to have lunch together. It was one of the marvels of British society then, and possibly today, that a crisis was no reason to postpone lunch. My cousin, de Visdelou, came down from his apartment to join us and began to needle Douglas about the failings of the local constabulary, who needed the help of the sleuths from Miami to solve a murder. Even Doug laughed. The Duke of Windsor's decision to recruit help from the States would embarrass him later, and call into question the integrity of the entire investigation. The Miami police had the reputation of being the most corrupt this side of Chicago, and among the least efficient.

As we lunched on the terrace, two young black marketeers pulled into my driveway with a small truck loaded with two drums of gasoline from the RAF. De Visdelou informed me, as an afterthought, that he had brought them because he planned to go on a fishing trip to the Out Islands, with friends.

My fondness for Georges, our loyalty to each other, had outlasted the occasional lean times. He was at heart a man of unnecessary things, and capable of infuriating me, as he had now, not because I thought he wanted to resell the fuel, or because it occurred to me that anyone would connect it with the attempt to burn Oakes and his home. Only the stupidity of it made me shout at him, "You must be insane! This is high-octane gasoline, and it will blow the engine, the boat, you, and your friends to high heaven." I ordered the two bandits to get the hell off my property.

Once I was alone, I could not help thinking back with dismay to the day before, and Harold Christie's strange behavior, the obvious effort he had made to avoid me. For months he had confided in me his business problems with Harry Oakes. He had sought my advice on the showdown he feared was coming. Now Oakes had been murdered, and not a word had been said to me by Harold on that subject.

At around four o'clock that afternoon, I would learn later, the Duke of Windsor made a personal appearance at Westbourne. He asked to see Barker, and found him alone upstairs, in Sir Harry's bedroom. There was no record of what was said in the twenty minutes of earnest conversation that took place between the Duke and the Miami detective. The

Royal Governor left, and within two hours, as luck would have it, I would receive another visit from Lieutenant Douglas.

Basil picked me up later for cocktails and dinner with friends of his at the Prince George. The place was packed, and I was greeted with a mixture of stares and merriment. Basil downed his drink and drawled, "Whatever those bastards do or say, one thing is certain. Fred had a watertight alibi. We were eight guests at his house until eleven-thirty."

Douglas appeared from nowhere. He was invited to join us, but declined. "Sorry, I'm on duty," he said, adding that Erskine-Lindop wanted to see me again at Westbourne. I protested that we were having dinner in ten minutes. He insisted, saying we would not be long. It was not yet six o'clock.

Westbourne was dark inside, except for a wedge of light at Barker's table and a small lamp on the piano. Again, I thought, the seance. Barker motioned for me to sit in front of him. As before, he looked at my hands and my beard. He then called over Melchen, who asked, "Are you sure you didn't come to Westbourne that night? Didn't you want to be quits with Sir Harry, and you came here to see him and had an argument and hit him?"

I was too startled to react with anger. I pointed out that I would have called on Sir Harry during daylight hours, if I called on him at all. Anyone who walked in unannounced was likely to find not only Sir Harry, but one or several overnight guests.

Melchen raised his voice and announced that he had witnesses who had seen me enter the grounds in the early morning hours. He was obviously trying to provoke me. "I defy you or anybody in Nassau," I said coldly, "to say any such thing."

Hallinan was glued to one spot, and Erskine-Lindop sat on a stool next to a fireplace, his face a mask.

"Please, step this way," Hallinan said to me. I walked toward him and stopped a few steps short. In a clear, flat voice, he said, "Alfred de Marigny, you are accused of the murder of Sir Harry Oakes. Have you anything to say?"

Confused, I replied, "I do not know what you want me to say."

Melchen broke in again: "I want to warn you about one thing. In this case, nobody is too small or too big to be arrested, and even after we have gone away, we will come back and keep on investigating the case."

I said, "That is all right with me," inasmuch as I was unaware of anyone else, big or small, being threatened with arrest.

The words fell hollow on my ears, as though in an echo chamber. All of my senses were heightened. I could hear every noise, see every crack in the floor. I heard myself say, "This is absurd. You must be out of your minds. Why should I murder Harry Oakes?" What was happening to me, standing in front of Eric Hallinan, seemed to be happening to someone else.

Hallinan called out to Erskine-Lindop to make the arrest.

The colonel, impeccable in his khaki military shorts with Sam Browne belt and red lapels, placed his right hand on my shoulder. "Alfred de Marigny, in the name of the Crown, you are under arrest for the murder of Sir Harry Oakes."

Gone now was any pretense that this had nothing to do with me, that I could afford to be angry or cynical or indifferent. Until that instant I had been as free as the wind that fed the sails of my boat. Now I was in the custody of the Crown. I could not move or act or speak without the permission of a policeman. Hallinan yanked me out of my thoughts.

"Do you wish to call an attorney?"

I said, "Yes. I would like to call Fred Adderley."

"I shall call him for you," said Hallinan. He crossed the room to the telephone in the hall adjoining the living room. In a moment he returned and informed me that Adderley was out, but that a message had been left to have him contact me.

Lieutenant Douglas and two black policemen accompanied me to the Court of Justice. I felt lost, in a fog, unable to collect my thoughts. Victoria Square was empty. The car stopped in front of the Magistrate Court. Flanked by Douglas and one of the officers, I walked into the courtroom. Magistrate F. E. Fields, black-gowned and wearing a powdered wig, was waiting for us. Fields exchanged a few words with Douglas and stepped back to his desk.

He asked if I did not want an attorney present.

I said, "Yes, Mr. Hallinan has left word with Alfred Adderley. He is to represent me."

The magistrate cleared his throat. His next words sent a chill through me. He had been advised, he said, that Adderley had been retained by the Crown to help prosecute the case against me.

The silence in the room was oppressive. I was aware of a ceiling fan turning slowly overhead. Everything seemed to dance around. My head was pounding and my throat so dry I did not think I could speak. I was not allowed to sit. I now had the inescapable feeling that the cards were being stacked against me. I heard the magistrate say, "The Crown will provide a lawyer for you."

Stafford Sands, a corporate lawyer, soon arrived and explained to me that the arraignment was just a formality. Godfrey Higgs was due back on Monday and could begin to prepare my defense.

The fact that I required a defense was staggering to me. For what? For having married Nancy Oakes? I was still dazed. And the nightmare had only begun.

It was indeed a quick formality. The hearing was over in five minutes.

Advised of my rights, I volunteered a statement, hastily written in my own hand, declaring my innocence and labeling the charges as absurd. The statement concluded with these words:

"And I can say, swear, that I have not seen Sir Harry Oakes to talk to since the twenty-ninth of March."

How well I remembered. Oakes and his son, Sydney, had

come to dinner after dropping by a cocktail party given by the Duke and Duchess at Government House, an invitation to which event Nancy and I had declined. Sir Harry was upset with us, and the more he drank of our liquor, the more he voiced his displeasure. We were "asses," he said, lecturing us on the importance of mingling with the right people.

When I laughed and replied, "To hell with the Duke," the old man's temper burst from its moorings.

"That's the trouble with you young fools," he shouted. "You'll never learn, will you, that in a small place like this you can't go around saying to hell with everybody. You've been doing that sort of thing too long around here."

We carried the argument out to the sidewalk, where Oakes threatened to horsewhip me, and I countered by offering to apply my big foot to his behind.

As he reached for his car door, Sir Harry threw out a final complaint: "As far as that girl in the house is concerned"—Nancy, the adored oldest daughter, had now become "that girl"—"she has caused enough trouble to her mother, and I don't want to have anything to do with you." He ordered the boy Sydney into the car and drove off, his tires spitting gravel as he pulled away from the curb.

The next day Nancy celebrated my birthday with a party, and invited Sydney. When the hour grew late, he decided to stay the night in a spare room. We were awakened by a fearful racket at four in the morning; Sir Harry was pounding on the door and yelling threats. When I opened the door, Sir Harry brushed past me in a rage. He found Sydney in the guest room, grabbed his foot with one hand, and slid him off the bed. He ordered him to get dressed and out of the house.

As before, insults were exchanged all the way to the car. Then, as quickly as it blew up, the tantrum passed. Days later, his son, then sixteen, would tell us what had happened next. Sir Harry had leaned back in his seat and said calmly, "Not a bad sort, de Marigny. You have got to get to know those Frenchies."

Sydney had looked at his father in amazement.

News of my arrest raced across the island. A crowd had already gathered in the square, including a hundred or more Negroes who had followed on foot the police car that had taken me to the courthouse. Hallinan claimed later that he feared an attempt would be made to lynch me. I heard the crowd chanting, "God help Mr. Fred."

Nassau Jail had been built a hundred and fifty years earlier. It sat on top of a hill in the Negro district, and appeared to have been a fortress of a bygone era. It was surrounded by a high stone wall, and a huge iron door in that wall swung open to let our car in. The superintendent of the prison was a former officer in the Royal Mounted Police, Captain R. M. Miller. He was known for his fairness, and from the first I sensed in him a sympathy for the prejudice he saw building against me.

Miller accepted the remanding order from Douglas, and said to me, "The turnkey will take you to your cell."

There is no way to convey the emptiness I felt as I followed the turnkey through the damp and narrow corridor. My cell was Number 1, of four that were reserved for dangerous criminals awaiting their date with the gallows. The turnkey opened the heavy iron door and I stepped into a small room, eight by twelve. The walls were whitewashed, and the high ceiling was domed. At the apex of the dome were two five-hundred-watt lightbulbs that kept the cell so bright it was painful to the eyes. The floor was unevenly paved with stones, and a window, two feet square, on the wall opposite the door, had a steel bar across it. It stood so high that even a tall man—I was six feet three— could not reach it standing on his toes.

Furniture was nonexistent. Along the wall was a folding cot that missed by three or four inches accommodating the length of me. To the right of the door, resting on a small wooden stool, was a dilapidated enamel basin, and next to it, on the floor, was a water pitcher of the same quality. In the space on the other side of the door was a large galvanized bucket that served as a toilet. There was no top to cover the bucket, which was emptied three times a week.

The guard returned as I stood there in a state of numbness, trying to adjust to these surroundings. He apologized for not having a pillow or a blanket to offer me. He said that it was after hours and the storeroom was closed.

I asked if he could turn off those blinding lights. He explained that the orders from the Attorney General were that the cell was to remain lighted all night, so that when he made his rounds every half hour he could be certain I was all right, that is, that I had not tried to take my life.

The light served one other purpose: it helped the prisoner keep track of the vermin—rats, spiders, and insects—that infested the cell.

I curled up on the cot, the light directly in my eyes. Even when I closed my eyes, the brightness was such that I could not tolerate the glare. The veins of my head throbbed, and I wanted to scream. I grabbed my hair with both hands and pulled as hard as I could, forcing myself to concentrate on the pain. It helped me to take a grip on my mind. I recovered my self-discipline. I sat on the cold and humid floor and began to meditate. I was aware that the door had opened and the turnkey was beside me, staring at me nervously.

"Are you all right, Mr. Fred?"

I smiled and assured him everything was fine. And for that moment, at least, it nearly was. Something in my spirit had been revived. When he left, I stretched out on the floor and moved slowly until I found a way to accommodate my body. I turned over on my stomach and slept.

The next morning I washed myself in the enamel basin and used the galvanized bucket. I did twenty pushups and walked around the room on the tips of my toes. Then I ran in place for ten minutes. I had determined that I must stay in shape and exercise. It was my best hope of keeping my sanity and self-control. I felt better, and my mood lightened. I can only wonder how I would have felt if I had been told that I was to live in that dungeon for four months and two days.

I was an innocent man in the custody of the English Crown, waiting to be tried by my peers, and I would live like an animal for the next 124 days. I would eat standing up, with the stench of my own excrement around me, and sleep on a bumpy stone floor. But it was too early yet to yield to self-pity.

In the morning I was brought to Captain Miller's office. He pointed to a chair facing his desk and I sat down. A convict brought us coffee and toast and closed the door.

"How do you like your new residence?" he asked, not sarcastically, but in a tone that indicated he did not expect a happy answer.

"It stinks," I said.

"I can do very little to improve things," he said. He looked at me carefully and said, "I have my own ideas about this case. But I would like to hear for myself. Did you have anything to do with this murder?"

In an odd way, the question encouraged me. I did not think he would have bothered to ask if he believed me to be guilty. "You have my word," I said. "I had nothing to do with the death of Oakes."

"From the moment I heard Oakes had been murdered," he said, "I could have predicted your arrest. I believe you to be innocent. Conduct yourself not only as a man, but as an *innocent* man. Be dignified. Be calm. Give yourself the best chance you can. Never forget they are out to hang you."

When I returned to my cell, I felt as if cold water had been poured slowly along my spine. In spite of myself, I felt helpless and frightened. I had no one to whom I could turn, no one to ask for help. The silence of the jail on Sunday grated on my nerves. Every inmate was locked in his cell until dinnertime. I sat cross-legged on the floor and attempted to analyze every angle of this predicament. I trusted my memory and had a gift of recall. I catalogued in my mind my recent conversations with Harold Christie and Harry Oakes, and the details of their complicated accounts.

Of this I was certain: I had last seen Sir Harry on March 29. Until I went to Westbourne with John Anderson on the morning we learned of his death, I had not stepped inside his home in two years.

In the quiet of the evening I suddenly heard music outside, voices laughing and talking. It was not far away. The sounds were coming from a nightclub nearby, in the Negro section. Life was all around me, free people having a grand time, without contemplating the fragile state of their freedom. I compared my fate to theirs. I felt an empathy with what they had come from; I told myself I was no better off than a slave of olden days. I had no will of my own, could go nowhere, see no one, do nothing without the consent of my jailers. At that moment, I envied the black patrons of that bar their freedom to sing, to dance, to drink, to love—to go anywhere or do whatever their hearts desired.

THE FRAME

THE similarity between a legal case and a theatrical production has been noted often. Even today, it is a common practice in many American police precincts to describe suspects as "actors." But, of course, the true stars of any courtroom drama are the attorneys. The gestures are theirs to make, the great lines theirs to speak.

A man on trial for his life, as I would be, has roughly the status of a piece of furniture. You are talked about, you are seen, you are ignored, but for the most part you stand there in a wooden cage while others decide your fate.

I believe I am qualified by experience to say that trials are not really about truth or justice. They are about winning, just as tennis matches are about winning, and not about the sureness of the stroke or the swiftness of the stride. The trial becomes a contest of will and ambition between the prosecutor and the defense attorney. Each feels an enormous pressure to win. Their egos require it. Their records demand it. At some point the defendant becomes a pawn in this match, and it is a foolish individual indeed who thinks otherwise.

Godfrey Higgs was white, in his early forties, tall, his hair worn in the 1920s fashion, parted almost in the middle and slicked back. Trained in Britain in the Inns of Court, he had been my lawyer from the time I arrived in Nassau. He was a corporate attorney and had not been in court more than a dozen times in his career. His greatest asset was his known honesty, a rare gift in Nassau.

The two of us sat tensely on either side of Captain Miller's desk. His eyes locked on mine, he asked if I would swear that I had not killed, or in any way been involved in the killing of, Sir Harry Oakes. I swore my innocence, and more. I told Godfrey that if at any time he had reason to believe me guilty, I would expect him to withdraw from the case. He gripped my hand and gave it a firm shake.

Yet I knew that Godfrey had to wrestle with his conscience before taking the case, one that would place him in a most awkward position. To save my neck, he might have to discredit certain witnesses, among them Harold Christie, with whom he served in the House of Assembly. They were political allies.

British proceedings in a murder case are totally different from those familiar to most American observers, except that in both countries a man is innocent until proven guilty. Under the U.S. system, the accused may be set free on bond. He is free to prepare his defense, live in the comfort of his home, lead a normal life, and attend to his business. He may talk to the press, and may discuss the charges against him with whomever he wishes. In short, he is considered a bona fide innocent being until his guilt has been established.

In the United States, a grand jury decides whether the prosecution has a justifiable case against the accused. If, after due process of law, the accused is found guilty by a jury of his peers, he may still appeal his case, potentially all the way to the Supreme Court, often while living as a free soul.

Under British law, no bail is allowed in a murder case. The moment the accused is arrested, he is in the custody of the Crown. No one but his lawyer may confer with him. No statements, public or private, are permitted by his lawyer under threat of disbarment.

Within days of his arrest, even hours, the accused must appear in a lower court to hear the charges against him. A magistrate sits alone and fulfills the role of the entire grand jury. After hearing the charges of the prosecution, he then decides whether the case should be dismissed, or the accused remanded to jail to be tried by a jury. Since there is no bail, the accused, who is presumed innocent, must languish for months in jail, a confinement almost guaranteed to have a shattering effect on his morale, his health, his finances, and his family.

The American grand-jury system diffuses power by putting it in the hands of representative citizens—the so-called jury of peers, honorable and honest people. This protection against abuses is nonexistent under British law, where the magistrate acts as judge and jury.

I should have found great comfort in the knowledge of how much British justice had contributed to our Western civilization since the days of the Magna Charta. Respect for law and tradition, what the English call fair play, was inherent in this system. But when you sit in a cramped and barren cell, musty with the smell of other men's fears, these are no longer abstract ideas, buried among centuries of parchment. They take on human form.

And in Nassau, as I well knew, noble principles were in the hands of one Eric Hallinan, who had been recently posted there as Attorney General. He was an ambitious man, a British civil servant whose promotion to a more important colony, after his four-year term ended in the Bahamas, would be assured by a dramatic courtroom victory. The Oakes case was made to order for Hallinan.

I ought to concede here that anyone who has been in prison, or accused of a crime, is likely to grasp at the "devil" theory: *Someone is out to get me.* This "someone" may be a devious prosecutor, a political or business enemy, an ex-lover, a spiteful relative. And sometimes, someone is. For the system of justice to fail, it is only necessary for one weak or corrupt official to lie or cheat.

My anger and suspicion were focused on Hallinan. If the Crown relied on perjured testimony or false evidence, the responsibility would be his. But I did not then, nor do I now, doubt that others of higher rank, and stronger influence, were willing to let me hang for a crime they knew I had not committed.

Directly after the murder, Melchen and Barker went through the pretense of investigating Harold Christie, a path the Attorney General saw no reason to pursue. Christie seemed to have nothing to gain from Sir Harry's death. And no one was eager to challenge the most powerful man in Nassau, the leader of the House of Assembly and the indispensable friend of the Bay Street Boys. Christie was unassailable.

Though questions existed about his actions as a houseguest on the last night of Sir Harry's life, Christie was quickly eliminated as a suspect. The list was not a long one. In less sensitive times, the police might have been tempted to drag the first luckless black man off the street, hang him, and close the case. Not now. There was already a young Negro in jail awaiting trial for a murder he had confessed to committing. A race riot the previous year had cost millions in property damage, and was still vivid in everyone's mind.

By simple elimination, I became the one person who could be safely accused, who could be hanged without dividing the island. I was a foreigner; I had quarreled with Oakes, loudly, more than once; I had married his daughter, years younger than I, without asking his consent; I had been less than discreet in certain public comments about the Duke of Windsor.

Besides those sins, I had offended the authorities by taking on unpopular causes: water for the blacks, fair treatment for the refugees from Devil's Island. Hallinan had tried, and failed, to convict me of breaking the laws of the Exchange Control Board, and these skirmishes had caused him some embarrassment around town. Perhaps his judgment and integrity were unclouded by his personal hostility toward inc. But he took pleasure, I thought, in watching me languish behind bars for four months and two days, with the prospect of facing the gallows in the end.

My arrest and trial—eventually to be described by a Nassau newspaper as "a tragedy of errors"—began on that morning of July 8, 1943, with Harold Christie's call to His Royal Highness, the Duke of Windsor. I have no doubt that Christie discussed with the Duke his decision to contact the Miami police, and seek the loan of Melchen and Barker.

In point of fact, the Americans were brought in not to assist with the investigation but to keep the local police out of it. After Hallinan briefed them at the airport, Colonel Erskine-Lindop was overheard to say, cryptically, "They understand what is expected of them."

The speed with which the Miami duo acted helped spread the impression of my guilt. The conclusion was hard to resist: to make an arrest so quickly, within thirty hours of their arrival, the evidence had to be overwhelming.

Fortunately for me, both men were ignorant of the British judicial system. They thought I would be tucked away in jail and, after a few days of whatever coercion or tricks of the trade might be needed, a confession would be extracted. Instead, they discovered that the moment I was arrested I became incommunicado, and held under the protection of the Crown. They had to alter their strategy.

The case against me would drag through the magistrates' court from early July until the end of August. The morning the hearing began, the gallery was packed. The front two rows were reserved for the many reporters who had flown in from the United States and Canada. The murder seemed to offer a respite to a press and public grown weary of the unrelenting war news. The case had all the ingredients of a potboiler: the setting was a tropical paradise, and the victim a man reputed to be one of the richest in the world; the accused was described as a swarthy fortune hunter, a playboy who had killed his father-in-law out of anger and greed, having duped an innocent teenager into marrying him. For the final touch, the ex-King of England governed the island and initiated the investigation.

The press thrived on rumor and innuendo, and this was a case that would generate many. The reporters reminded me of sparrow hawks, preying on helpless victims, consuming the carrion of human misery. They would hound me for the next decade, seldom looking at me as I was, but judging me by their own preconceptions.

By now I had been disabused of any notion that the process would be swift, or justice easily served. Each new day seemed to bring another disheartening turn.

Nancy learned of my arrest on the tenth of July, but flew to Bar Harbor, as I had urged her to do, to comfort her mother. On the thirteenth, two days before the funeral, she found that the family compound, and the family grief, had been penetrated by two strangers.

Captains Melchen and Barker.

After returning from the funeral, Lady Oakes took to her bed, and there, at her bedside, the visiting detectives insisted on telling their tale. While mother and daughter listened in a state of near hysteria, and lesser relatives were all but mesmerized, Melchen and Barker recited this narrative:

The killer, they said, had taken a stick from a pile of balustrades he found in the garage, and had then climbed the outside stairs to Sir Harry's bedroom and struck him down.

While the victim was still unconscious, the killer had sprayed his body with insecticide and set the bed on fire. The flames must have revived him, they continued, because, though mortally wounded, he tried to fight off his attacker.

They concluded that he must have been in terrible agony. Finally he was overcome, struck again on the head, and the fire started a second time. In the struggle, the heavy Chinese screen in the bedroom must have been knocked over; the killer had replaced it to mask the flames from the cars driving past. They said there was no doubt that the murderer was Alfred de Marigny.

Barker added that he had found fingerprints and handprints on the screen. He advised Lady Oakes, and Nancy, that "de Marigny had been there when the crime was committed. More likely, he did it himself."

It was a brutal picture, and a convincing one. Whose mind would not be poisoned by such a description?

Nancy, for one, would not succumb. Whatever else the future held for us, for that stubborn resistance I shall always be grateful. Later she would say, "One thing that is more or less unpredictable is human nature, and I cannot say that I have made a study of it. But from my knowledge of Freddie during the year since our marriage, the situation seems fantastic to me."

On one other point, Barker may have overreached himself. Melchen was astonished to hear his partner declare that they had identified my fingerprints. They had traveled together for two days, and he had failed to mention the recovery of a single positive print of anyone.

The finding of a distinct print should have been so significant that one would hardly forget to share such a discovery with one's partner. At that point they could place me on the road that went past Westbourne, but not inside the house. They were working on a motive—family arguments and financial need. They did not have the confession they wanted, or any prospect of obtaining one. They had no physical evidence. They had no case.

The story Barker told was so prejudicial, so unethical, so transparent, that one writer speculated that he had in mind something other than building a case. Could he have been laying, instead, the foundation for a blackmail scheme?

Disbelieving, but shaken by what she had heard, Nancy stopped off in New York on her way to Nassau and engaged the services of a colorful private detective named Raymond Schindler. Though she acted out of the best of intentions, and Schindler would provide reams of copy for the press, the move was not one that gladdened my heart or raised my hopes.

I was by now painfully aware of how desperate my circumstances were, and how active the prosecution had been. But in a small corner of my mind I wanted to be able to plan a future we could afford, on the slight chance that I survived.

Schindler's fee was three hundred dollars a day, plus expenses. Schindler was an Alfred Hitchcockian figure, a robust man with a taste for fine living. He was the kind of man, who, if you gave him an unlimited budget, would exceed it.

Schindler claimed to be the first investigator to "wire" an informant to obtain evidence, using a new device, the Dictograph, the forerunner of today's tape recorders.

His richest and best-known client was Anna Gould, the only surviving daughter of the railroad tycoon Jay Gould. It was never clear what specific services he performed, but he provided security at her estate on the Hudson River and performed investigations on request. In return, she paid him an annual retainer of $50,000 and allowed him to live, rent-free, in a lavish home on her property.

Exactly how Schindler would help my cause had been left open, but he did engage in my defense a distinguished fingerprint expert, Maurice B. O'Neil, who headed the Bureau of Investigation for the New Orleans police department. Schindler also brought with him a staff that included his brother and Leonard Keeler, the inventor of a new technology that he called the "polygraph" machine, or lie detector. No one knew for certain, including my defense team, what role these experts and their gadgets would play. But I suspect that their arrival kept the lights burning later than usual in the Attorney General's office.

I calculated that by the end of the trial Schindler and his entourage could cost me as much as $150,000, a point that led to testy conversations between Nancy and me. And contrary to whatever myths came out of the trial, the money was my own. Nancy did not have a dime in her own name.

My wife would not arrive in Nassau until the preliminary hearings were nearly over. On the first day, I sat next to Godfrey Higgs and surveyed the room. Most of my friends were there. George Thompson caught my eye, and a bright smile lit his face. The crowd seemed oddly jovial, like people in a theater, waiting for the band to tune its instruments.

Magistrate Fields presided. I had looked upon him as a friend. However, I was soon to count him among the many white Nassauans who considered that being against de Marigny would align them with the Oakes money.

During his lifetime, Sir Harry had been cordially disliked by most on the island for his arrogance and rudeness in general, and his ruthlessness in dealing with his employees. Yet he was feared and toadied to because of his wealth. In death, the aura of power remained, and few among the white community dared to jeopardize their possible gain by dwelling on the recurrent questions about his partner, Harold Christie.

Dr. Hugh Quackenbush was the first witness. He had replaced Ricky Oberwarth, who had examined me the day I was admitted to jail, and reported finding no indication of burned hairs on my person. He was then dismissed as the prison doctor and barred from the room where the body of Harry Oakes was autopsied.

Dr. Quackenbush was a pleasant man, trained in Canada, and regarded by the medical community in Nassau as just competent enough to take care of the hangovers of tourists.

He told the court that death had occurred around two in the morning, that he had found behind the victim's left ear four holes, about one inch apart. When probed, the holes went in an upward direction, were the diameter of a pencil, and penetrated the skull. When asked what could have made such holes, the doctor stated that he thought they had been caused by a blunt instrument.

Photos of the wounds and the skull were placed in the court dossier, and copies handed to Godfrey.

At least one previously undisclosed fact had been gleaned from the doctor's testimony. A thick, dark liquid was found in the stomach of the deceased, but had not been tested. It raised the possibility that Oakes had been drugged during the evening, rendering him unaware before his intruder attacked.

From the position of the clotted blood on his face—flowing upward from the ear over the bridge of the nose—the doctor concluded that the body had been moved. Another conjecture: death came almost instantly. He would not have risen from his bed to defend himself.

During the questioning, the doctor let slip one tantalizing piece of information: the plane carrying the body of Harry Oakes had left Nassau for Bar Harbor, Maine, only to be called back halfway to its destination. The coffin had been returned to the hospital and wheeled into a room with armed guards at the door. No one entered the room but Barker, Hallinan, Melchen, and Dr. Quackenbush. Hours later, the body was placed aboard the same plane and again departed on the journey to its final resting place. No explanation was given at the time for this bizarre sequence. For days we would ponder the meaning of it, sensing that here was one of the keys to the death of Harry Oakes.

In magistrate court, the evidence emerges in bits and scraps. There is a random quality to the testimony. Witnesses meander. The attorneys are probing, fishing, establishing points or raising questions they may wish to pursue or reinforce later. When two black policemen referred to the feathers attached to the victim's burnt and sticky flesh, reporters in the first rows stampeded to the phones. To their fertile imaginations, Oakes may have been killed in a pagan ritual involving the scattering of chicken feathers.

Of course, the history of the island was such that no theory could be rejected out of hand. Ritual murders, though rare, were in fact still performed by certain native cults in the event of misconduct with another's wife (not a likely fate for Sir Harry). Thus the voodoo connection was born. For several days the press published incredible theories on voodoo, and linked the death of Oakes to possible voodooism. What exotic and nonsensical reading that made.

We could track the difficulties of the Crown's case by the postponements Hallinan requested, stretching the hearings through July and into August. These delays were a source of annoyance to me. I looked forward to the trips to court as a way to break the daily monotony of my cell. More important, I still harbored a faint hope that the case would be dismissed by the magistrate, and I was growing impatient to be done with it. My innocence, the facts, the clumsiness of the plot against me all seemed so clear to my eye. Why could everyone not see them as sharply as I did?

My conferences with Higgs and his young associate, Ernest Callender, were a juggling act. I needed them as a connection to the life I had recently led, and to which I hoped soon to return. I needed them to stay alert and involved. But lawyers are in the business of warning you of the worst and the least that can happen, and these meetings often left me depressed.

I liked them both, and felt comfortable with Callender. He was a native of Nassau, what was then called a "high yellow," the son of an English mother who had married a native of British Guiana.

Callender had a deep and vibrant voice, and had yearned at one time to be an actor. He had worked briefly as a newscaster for the BBC, but in the end chose law as the more stable course. He studied in Britain for twelve years, and on his twenty-seventh birthday made his appearance before the bar in Nassau.

Higgs and Callender hammered away at what I should expect from the prosecutors. They would find the most damaging face to put on my actions, my background, my character. I would be painted as a seducer of women, a fortune hunter, a man motivated by greed and hatred.

For the first time I began to think deeply about the jury, people who would eventually judge me—decent people, I had no doubt, but for the most part products of the island's puritan religious base. I had gone through life insisting that I did not care what others said or thought of me, so long as I knew my stand was right or my actions harmless. In so doing I allowed gossip and rumors and pure fiction to go unanswered. On reflection, I can see that I might have helped myself with less independence, less indifference.

The basic outline of the case against me was taking shape in the magistrate's hearing:

Witnesses would testify to my arguments with Harry Oakes, how he had threatened me, and I him; how I resented being excluded from the family; what I said or didn't say to Lieutenant Douglas on the day of my arrest.

The details of our domestic life would be exposed, with emphasis on Nancy's age and health, the abortion her mother and father forced her to undergo.

My bank records would be brought into court and examined under a microscope. The balance in my account fluctuated; an overdraft or two was recorded. The implication would be that I was struggling financially.

The bombshell would be dropped, the introduction of a fingerprint of the little finger of the right hand, and the spot where it was found on the Chinese screen. Not exactly the abundant proof Barker had described to Lady Oakes, but, if genuine, enough to place me inside the smoke-filled bedroom of Sir Harry.

Timidity was never one of my faults. I gave Higgs and Callender my opinion of the testimony, offered suggestions on their rebuttal and on strategy, urged them to be more aggressive. I suppose the old prison adage is true, that every inmate becomes a lawyer.

Under the rules of the magistrate's hearing, in theory, the burden is on the prosecution, which had only to persuade the judge that a prima facie case against the accused existed. The defense rarely cross-examines, for fear of tipping its hand too early. I was eager to break with this tradition. It seemed obvious to me that every witness had been well rehearsed, the prosecution being secure in the belief they would not be grilled. I urged Higgs to spring such a surprise, and force them to react.

Higgs agreed. He would reserve that tactic for the big fish, Melchen, Barker, and Christie.

The money question was a tricky one. It was true that as I withdrew cash to make investments, I sometimes scraped the bottom of my checking account. But on the day of my arrest, I had on deposit five thousand pounds; my home, my sailboat, a new Lincoln, and my real estate in Eleuthera were fully paid. I was free of debt. I had assets.

Also, I had a substantial sum of money in a brokerage account in New York, the existence of which I could not readily disclose.

As a British subject, under emergency wartime regulations, I suppose my New York holdings should have been liquidated and the funds transferred to the Bahamas. To do so, of course, would have been to accept a huge loss, given the decline of the pound sterling on the world currency market. The British government was then supporting the pound to avoid a total collapse.

To maintain such an account, to move money in and out of a foreign bank, was illegal. Of course, so was adultery, but this fact didn't seriously hinder anyone intent on an extramarital dalliance, any more than the illegality of maintaining a foreign bank account stopped anyone from doing so who had the means and the desire.

To comply with the law—at least technically—my accounts were held in trust for me by a New York attorney. What others saw as my mysterious ability to afford the purchase of certain luxury goods caused me, once, to be hauled before the Exchange Control Board. I was acquitted, in part, I suspected, because the Duke of Windsor, given his own secret dealings, could not take the charges seriously.

At the risk of sounding self-righteous, let me make a distinction. The money I had banked and the stocks I had bought in New York were there before the hostilities, before I settled in the Bahamas. Right or wrong, I was protecting what I owned, not profiting from the vagaries of the war. Oakes, Christie, Windsor, and Wenner-Gren, I would eventually learn, were tunneling millions to the Banco de Continental in Mexico, trading in the money markets, laundering dollars that were looted from the treasuries of occupied countries, hedging their bets against whatever way the war went.

The more observant reporters and lawyers who followed the case from afar remarked on how courteous and respectful certain aspects of the proceedings were. The Duke of Windsor would be mentioned only once. The Attorney General would suggest that it was somehow unfair for the defense to attack the sincerity of Harold Christie.

And, while days would be spent on my finances, no inquiries would be made concerning those of Christie, Oakes, or the Royal Governor.

No one quite knew what to make of Harold's performance in the witness box. He repeated the story he had already told by then to the police and news agencies. But he was wooden, hesitant, stumbling in his speech. He gripped the railing in front of him so tightly that the whitening of his knuckles could be plainly seen. He kept mopping his face with a handkerchief already dripping with perspiration.

When Higgs rose to question the witness, Hallinan objected, and was overruled by Judge Fields. Godfrey led him through an exchange that was electric:

HIGGS: If Captain Sears were to say he had seen you in town the night of July seventh, what would you say? CHRISTIE: I would say that Captain Sears is very seriously mistaken and should be more careful in his observations.

HIGGS: I put it to you that Captain Sears saw you at about midnight in a station wagon in George Street. CHRISTIE: Was he certain? HIGGS: I put it to you. CHRISTIE: Captain Sears was mistaken. I did not leave Westbourne after retiring to my room that night... and any statement to the effect that I was in town is a very grave mistake.

HIGGS: Would you say that Captain Sears was a reputable person?

CHRISTIE: I would say so. Nevertheless, reputable people can be mistaken.

Harold Christie was on the stand for two days. He described, but could not explain, the smeared blood on his bedroom and bathroom doors, on his sheets and towels and around his water basin. He could not be sure if the doors that led from his room into Sir Harry's—through a bath and another bedroom—were closed or not.

He recounted his conversations the morning of the murder with Colonel Erskine-Lindop, his brother Frank, Madeline Kelly, Etienne Dupuch, the doctors Quackenbush and Fitzmaurice, then was excused and hurriedly left the courtroom. Yet he failed to recall any of his conversations with the Duke of Windsor.

He was one of the esteemed citizens of the Bahamas, and no one wished to say flatly that Harold Christie had lied. The question went begging: why was he so insistent that he had never left Westbourne, yet had seen, heard, or smelled nothing—the Three Blind Mice, with an allergy.

Nothing in Christie's account had incriminated me—or anyone else, except possibly Harold himself.

It was clear to everyone in the courtroom that the prosecution's case, and de Marigny as well, would hang on the validity of the fingerprint lifted by Barker.

The afternoon session started with Barker on the stand. He was calm and sure of himself, his words unhurried, the veteran witness at ease in this environment. Hallinan asked if the bloody marks on the walls and doors had been tested for possible fingerprints.

Barker said no, he had *powdered them and the prints had become blurred and unreadable.* On July 10, before noon, he had sent every print he had lifted to the RAF laboratory to be processed. Early on the same afternoon, he had discovered that one of the prints on the Chinese screen was of the tenth digit—the little finger of the left hand—of "the accused, Alfred de Marigny."

Hallinan immediately dismissed the witness, allowing the impact of that statement to echo in the room.

I whispered to Godfrey, "The man is a liar. I never saw that screen in my life." Higgs looked at me in silence, his face a blank. I could almost sense his thoughts turning to the original agreement we had made regarding my innocence.

The screen had been brought into the courtroom and placed to the right of Judge Fields. Higgs asked Barker to indicate in pencil where on the screen he claimed to have lifted the print, and to sign and date it. Barker complied, and a photograph of the lifted print, marked Exhibit J, was passed to the defense.

I knew the print was a fake, but how to prove it? The prosecution had no other way to place me in that room prior to the murder. Unless we could expose Exhibit J as a fraud, and prevent it from being admitted into evidence, my hopes would be as sand in the wind.

I was befuddled by the question of the fingerprint. As evidence, Exhibit J failed to meet a certain basic test. It was not the print in its original place, but a lift—a copy made by putting tape over the original and actually lifting it. There was no supporting photograph to show its origin, and it carried two curious moisture marks in the background.

Barker blamed the humidity for destroying all fingerprints of Christie and Oakes on the screen—both had moved it—but could not explain why my print, allegedly made hours later, should survive in perfect condition.

Of course, once lifted, an actual fingerprint is gone forever. There was no way to look at the Chinese screen and say "De Marigny's print was *there.*" For this reason, the lifting of a print had to be done in the presence of a witness, each lifted print numbered, and a record made of the place from which it came.

Barker broke most of the rules well established by the law and his profession. He had worked alone, although several of the local police were available, standing idle, while he searched for prints at Westbourne. In the end he was the one and only witness who could say that such a print came from such a spot. There was no one to support or contradict him.

Melchen, followed by a constable and a police corporal, trooped to the stand to recite their version of my interview at Westbourne. Melchen told the court that I had been taken upstairs on the afternoon of the ninth, at 3:30 P.M. He said I was examined for about an hour and then returned to the custody of Lieutenant Douglas around 4 P.M. That testimony was meant to be the last nail in my coffin. If true, my print could only have been left on the screen the previous night.

"He's lying," I whispered to Higgs. I was almost jubilant. "It was around eleven in the morning. I can prove it."

Hallinan cut short Melchen's examination. Higgs began to cross-examine the American detective.

"Are you certain of the time you led Mr. de Marigny upstairs?" he asked.

Melchen removed a notebook from his pocket and searched the pages. "Here it is ... all recorded. Three-thirty on the afternoon of the ninth of July."

Higgs studied Melchen for a long moment. He would let the matter of the disputed time pass for now, and lay the groundwork to impeach Melchen's testimony in another area. Casually he asked, "By the way, while you were with de Marigny upstairs, did you offer him a glass of water?"

Melchen scratched his head, looked at the ceiling, then said, "Very possible."

"While you were talking to de Marigny upstairs, did Captain Barker enter the room?"

"He could have."

"Did Barker ask you if everything was all right?"

"He could have."

"If I were to tell you that Captain Barker entered the room and talked to you after de Marigny had finished his glass of water, would you deny it?"

Melchen remained silent. Higgs insisted on an answer and Melchen replied, meekly, no, he could not deny it.

During the recess, Higgs asked me cautiously, "Fred, how can you be certain you were not in that room at the time Melchen said?"

"Easily," I said. "I was there in the morning, and Colonel Erskine-Lindop was with me. He can vouch for it. And Lieutenant Douglas noted the time in his log when we left the house. I am sure of it."

"I hope so," Higgs said tersely.

At the time, his pessimism seemed out of order. I believed the odds to be shifting in my favor. It was simple, really. Barker had sent the prints and lifts to the lab before noon. Melchen had changed the time he interviewed me so no one could suggest that he had used our meeting to obtain a fingerprint from me. Suddenly, I could hardly wait to return to court. We would expose the chicanery of the prosecution! Who could deny my innocence now?

Of one thing I was confident: Erskine-Lindop would not lie for them.

In a trial, your emotions swing wildly. One minute your hopes soar, the next your life seems consigned to Dante's Inferno. So far it had been beyond my imagining that human beings could so glibly swear on the Bible to speak the truth, and in the same breath perjure themselves with no apparent conscience, knowing, as they must, that they are putting a rope around the neck of an innocent man. What manner of people could close the books on one murder simply by committing another?

On August 31, Magistrate Fields brought in his finding: there was sufficient evidence to send the case to trial. All of this, I knew now, had been only the sparring. The life-or-death battle would begin in the fall, in October, when the case would be heard by the Chief Justice of the Supreme Court of the Bahamas.

Two days later, Basil McKinney sent word to me that he had talked with the caretaker from Lyford Cay, and his assistant, who swore that on the night of the murder a cabin cruiser had docked there around one in the morning. Two men went ashore and were driven away in a car that was waiting for them on the street. They returned an hour later, and the vessel immediately left. The weather was frightful, but they were able to obtain the name of the boat, and its registration number. Basil had urged Godfrey Higgs to see them immediately and take their statement Saturday or Sunday.

Another piece of evidence turned up about the missing watchmen from Westbourne. Basil had learned that they lived in the Pine Barrens on the south side of Nassau. He had gone there to question them, but their wives refused to talk to him. All he could get from them was that their husbands had gone fishing on Andros Island and would be back in a few days. They did not return.

Godfrey was pleased with these developments and knew how helpful they could be to us, but he objected to using his weekend to take a statement from the men at Lyford Cay. He was exhausted, he said, and planned to rest. He would contact the men and see them on Monday.

Suddenly, everyone had something to do and I found myself once again alone in my cell by sundown. I was despondent. I felt vaguely troubled that Godfrey hadn't interviewed the two men from Lyford Cay immediately. I even regretted that Nancy's friend, Raymond Schindler, was back in New York.

At dawn on Monday morning, the turnkey came to my cell with news: the two caretakers at Lyford Cay had been found dead. One, an old sponger, had drowned. The other was hanging from a tree.

That was the beginning of a series of unexplained deaths whose circumstances would fascinate mystery fans in the years to come. Not all were classified as murders. Yet, often enough to defy pure chance, someone would arrive to investigate the case, or claim to have information regarding the identity of the killer, and that person would shortly be fished from the bottom of a well, or found floating in a lagoon, or attached to a knife. Others were summarily deported. No one was allowed to get too close to the case.

I brooded about the lost opportunity, but I fought against any feelings of defeat. Reporters from around the world would be pouring into Nassau in October, and I believed that the interest in the case—the so-called crime of the century—would ensure a fair trial.

With the trial still three months away, I learned that four of the island's most important citizens would be among the missing. Axel Wenner-Gren had been tipped off that the FBI was planning to question him, and one night the *Southern Cross* slipped out of the harbor and sailed to Mexico.

The Duke and Duchess of Windsor sent their regrets; they would be visiting friends in New York, Washington, and Baltimore for the duration of the trial.

And Colonel Erskine-Lindop, the superintendent of police, who could verify the times of my appearance at Westbourne, had been suddenly transferred to Trinidad, and could not be recalled to testify.

For this news I was unprepared, unable to get my mouth to work. Instinctively, my right hand massaged my throat.

THE JAIL

VISUALIZE a play in which every member of the audience knows each character on the stage, some well, some by sight. But on any day, there is the chance that they will pass one another on the street. Such was the nature and intimacy of Nassau. And so the trial itself assumed an intensity few murder cases have ever equaled. My prosecutor, judge, and jurors would be known to me. With the exception of the reporters and the tourists drawn by the scent of the scandal, the face of Harry Oakes would have been familiar to anyone in that courtroom. They had seen him walking countless times along Bay Street, in his riding pants, high boots, and soiled jacket, hands buried in his pockets, a hat jammed on his head.

They knew me as well, although I was in many ways the most foreign among them, liked by the native Bahamians, respected as a yachtsman, farmer, and free spirit. My difficulties had been with the Bay Street clique and with the English civil servants I despised.

In the solitude of my cell, I was insulated from the fever that had grown around my arrest and trial. Quite simply, there had been no case to equal it in the history of the Bahamas, or in recent British jurisprudence. It was a case custom-tailored to the tabloid press of Britain and the United States, and no angle went unworked: There was great wealth; there were the tropical landscape and the vestiges of power. The speed with which the Duke of Windsor set in motion my arrest was matched only by his haste in leaving the island as the case came to trial.

At the core of the story was the "beautiful young heiress" whose husband was accused of murdering her father.

After the magistrate's hearing, I was returned to the jail in a pall of silence. I had hoped against reason that I would be released. Now another three months, at least, awaited me in the dungeon. I was allowed visitors now, and my friends tried to console me, pointing out that I was safer behind bars than on the street; whoever had killed Oakes might not hesitate to kill me, as well. Obviously, I found little comfort in this idea.

The news brought by my visitors was hardly more encouraging. George Thompson had been questioned and beaten by the police, when he refused to tell them what they wanted to hear. The police paid visits to anyone who had offered to testify on my behalf. Cars circled their homes; their phones rang at odd hours.

At least, Hallinan's office finally approved my request for a table and chair in my cell, and writing materials so that I might keep notes for my own defense. I would list the points against me and ponder them. Unless one totally ignored the testimony of my dinner guests, I was alone on the night of July 7 except for no more than twenty-five minutes. The prosecution had to convince a jury that this was sufficient time to allow me to learn where Sir Harry was sleeping, go there, sneak upstairs, surprise him, kill him after a struggle, splash an inflammable fluid around the room and stairs, start a fire, and escape.

No matter how absurd the accusations appeared to me, I was the one on a tightrope. Faced with months of confinement in a squalid and airless cell, I had to avoid giving in to cycles of negative or irrational thought. Fear and anger propel you. They give you energy.

I was baffled by the motives of Hallinan, by what I took to be his personal animosity toward me. I knew him as an Irish Catholic who went to mass every Sunday and took communion every Friday. I wondered if ambition fueled him, the knowledge that he had fallen into a once-in-a-lifetime case, or whether he was simply doing the bidding of the Duke of Windsor.

I remembered the looks he'd given me when our paths crossed at church. He and his family would pile out of their small British car, a Morris Minor, while I parked my Lincoln Continental. He was a civil servant who worked tedious hours for low wages. I tried to understand his resentment of me.

At that point, it was easier for me to see Eric Hallinan as my enemy, my persecutor, than Harold Christie. I felt the Attorney General's actions had been underhanded, at best, in hiring Adderley to lead the Crown's case.

I had a chance to confront Adderley outside the courtroom on the day I was remanded to trial. "At least you could have had the courtesy of sending me a refusal," I told him.

"I don't know what you mean," he said.

"You know exactly what I mean. I sent word through the police that I wanted you to represent me. You did not have the courtesy even to acknowledge my request before turning me down."

Adderley's puzzlement seemed genuine. "This is the first I have heard of it," he said. "Had I received such a request, professional ethics would have demanded that I see you in person. I assure you, this is the first I have heard of such a request."

In interviews he gave years later, Hallinan insisted that his own protocol would not have allowed him to interfere with my choice of counsel. Only two other men on the island had enough influence to see that the police lost the message in transit: Christie and the Duke of Windsor.

I had finally begun to see myself as surrounded by peril. The British had invented the "old-boy network." I had confidence in the legal skills of Higgs and Callender, but I worried that they would conduct my defense in a way that would not harm the image of the Bahamas, or alienate anyone whose favor might be Critical to tliem in the future.

The preparation of my defense was going forward. Experts

on fingerprint evidence were interviewed. A copy of the Chinese screen was being constructed. Higgs and Callender and their clerks were wading through the law books, looking for any cases where similar evidence had been argued.

The question was reduced to this fundamental point: Could a print be lifted from an ornate surface without including at least some of the background?

There were two basic ways to lift a print. The distinction in the two methods was a fine but crucial one. To reveal a print, the preferred method was to dust it with a special black powder, then photograph it, which left the print undisturbed for an indefinite time—under normal conditions. To *lift* one, transferring it to tape, removes the evidence from its source.

Barker's print was a fake, a plant, but my life depended upon the ability of my attorneys to unmask this fraud in court.

Meanwhile, I kept searching my own memory for clues that might explain why someone needed to end the life of Harry Oakes. I struggled to make sense out of conversations half-remembered, events half-seen. I kept returning to the showdown between Sir Harry and Harold Christie over the contracts for the new Allied air base.

I passed this information to my attorneys, and even discussed with Captain Miller how Oakes had been determined to build the airfield as a monument to his own patriotism.

He had given Harold an ultimatum and ordered him to move the matter quickly through the House of Assembly. Instead, Christie diverted the contract to an American company for a fat fee, which was to be split between himself and the Bay Street Boys.

Harry Oakes was no novice at playing poker. To send Christie into a cold panic, he needed only to ask for an accounting of their joint investments. He added that his attorney from Palm Beach, Walter Foskett, would fly down to audit the books.

My own conclusion was that Sir Harry had planned to

force Harold to sign over Lyford Cay to him, in settlement of any monies he may have misused.

These mind games were interrupted by word of my wife's arrival in Nassau. The thought of seeing Nancy was both euphoric and unsettling. One could only guess at the pressures she had endured: her father dead, her husband accused, the mind of her mother quickly poisoned by the police.

I was eager for Nancy to hear from me the truth of my innocence. Doubts and fears grow like a fungus in the damp darkness of a prison cell. I needed her. If she now turned against me, it would be a shattering blow to my morale and my case, a vote for my conviction.

I met her in Miller's office. I was not allowed to receive visitors without supervision, but the captain discreetly excused himself to get coffee. Nancy ran toward me and we kissed. Then she held my hands in hers and stepped back. "Darling, you look so pale, so thin," she murmured. "You must eat better. I shall see to it."

I wanted to laugh. Irrepressible Nancy. It was as if I had been staying in a boardinghouse, where the only problem was the unoriginality of the menu.

As she pulled away, I had my first chance to study her closely. She wore a flowery dress, a large straw hat, and white gloves, a gay ensemble meant, I assumed, to cheer my spirits. She radiated an air of confidence. In a visible way, she seemed to have thrived on the tragedy and scandal.

I sensed the deeper changes that had taken place in Nancy in the three months we had been apart. Wanting her independence from a strong and abrasive father, she had married a man she considered worldly, who was as proud and stubborn in his way as her father. Now her father was dead, her husband in prison, waiting to go on trial for his life, the most helpless among us. Nancy had flown to my rescue; she was in charge.

More clearly than she, I saw the very fine line she dared not cross. She had told her mother she intended to stand by me; her mother had said she expected no less. In taking my side, Nancy had to remain grateful and loving to Lady Oakes, loyal and respectful to the memory of Sir Harry.

That she had my interest at heart I never doubted; that the role excited her was also obvious. Nancy asked if I had read the newspapers and seen "some of the horrible things" that had been written about me. She seemed surprised to learn that my access to news was restricted. Still, she had a strategy for dealing with the press. Raymond Schindler would keep them entertained.

Soon we were bickering, as I knew we would, over the usefulness of the flamboyant private detective. Schindler had already made two or three trips to Nassau from New York, had talked with witnesses, annoyed the local constabulary, and drawn a few conclusions.

He took great delight in proving that the police were monitoring the phone calls from his hotel room. He did so by picking a name at random from the phone book and dialing the number. Before the other party could speak, he would bark out instructions on where to meet and when, and would add a mysterious comment or two: "You know what has to be done. This may be our only chance." Then he would hang up.

Arriving early by taxi, he would find a place where he could lurk unseen, and wait there until two police cars pulled up, a few minutes before the appointed time.

Schindler developed his own theories, but uncovered no evidence, to my knowledge, that was not already known to Godfrey Higgs. He did not testify at the trial, but did satisfy himself of my innocence and slipped information to the press that was favorable to my case.

Schindler spread the word that Nancy had hired him only after she agreed to an unusual condition: if, in his investigation, he found persuasive evidence of my guilt, he would be free to submit it to the Attorney General or the local police. Schindler used the story to demonstrate Nancy's faith in me, which was nice, but without value to me in the courtroom. If it had any positive effect on my treatment in the press, I missed it.

Nancy had hired Schindler to "get to the bottom of the case" and find out "who really murdered my father." Her tone was defiant. "Ray is going to turn around the bad publicity you have been receiving and see that the truth is told. He is very well liked by the newsmen, and I trust him."

It had not occurred to me that my problems could be solved by better public relations. Maurice O'Neil's testimony regarding the fingerprint evidence would prove helpful. The credentials of Professor Keeler were impressive, but his contribution was more on the order of parlor games.

The lie detector machine Keeler had invented was said to be superior to an original German model, but the results of such tests have never been admissible as evidence in court.

I gathered that Schindler's role, in the weeks leading up to and during the trial, was to inform Nancy of the latest developments and interpret the testimony for her. They would usually conduct these sessions over lunch or dinner with others of his staff, in the dining room of the Colonial Hotel, where Nancy put the bills on my tab.

(Years later, I called upon Raymond Schindler in New York, still looking for answers to the questions that lingered after the trial. My reception was a curious one. He occupied a one-room office in an old building next door to Grand Central Station. On the walls were framed articles that praised the "legendary detective" who had cracked the Oakes case wide open. Schindler had appealed to the Duke of Windsor to reopen the case a year later, to no avail, and he had no answers to give me, only theories I had already heard, and rejected. All the refreshment he offered me during my visit was a Coca-Cola in a paper cup.)

I might have seen the humor in all this, if the idea of hanging had not been so much on my mind. If the people in

Nassau, and elsewhere, who thought of Nancy as an innocent schoolgirl seduced by a continental swinger, could only see her now.

Of course, the press found her open, engaging, radiant. She was all of these and more, five-feet-five, with auburn hair and deepset eyes. She did not, however, live her life in a thimble. At ten she was attending a boarding school in Gstaad, Switzerland. Her education continued in London, at the French School for Girls in New York, at art school in Vermont. She was dating at fourteen, skiing in St. Moritz. She had traveled around the world with her father, a journey of sentimental motive, retracing many of the steps he had taken in the lost youth of his prospecting days.

I do not mean to be ungallant. But in the matter of our courtship, as we say in sailing, I laid off the pace. No one led Nancy where she did not wish to go.

Now the press had virtually adopted her, and these attentions she seemed to mistake for real friendship. Whatever uneasiness I felt was quickly put aside as she described Captain Barker's narration of the death scene, at the family home in Bar Harbor.

Barker spared them nothing. He paced the room, provided gestures, everything but sound effects, as he gave his version of how Alfred de Marigny had murdered Sir Harry Oakes. The widow in her bed, the daughter and cousins sitting beside it, listened in horror, the only other sound in the room the sobbing of Lady Oakes.

Some of those in the room, Nancy said, appeared on the verge of being ill. Barker went on to tell Lady Oakes that her husband had not died quickly. He had fought off his attacker, reached in vain for his automatic, staggered into the hallway, and been forced back to his bed. Blood spattered the wall. He was alive, but helpless, as the murderer sprayed an inflammable fluid over the bed—with an insecticide sprayer, he said—and set it on fire. "He must have died in terrible agony," Barker added, in one more gratuitous comment.

Great, wracking sobs rose from Lady Oakes. The story had exhausted her, and she waved a hand that clutched a wet, wrinkled lace handkerchief, a gesture that plainly begged him to stop.

But Barker had to hammer across his final dramatic point: "We found," he announced, "de Marigny's fingerprints, three or four of them, at the scene of the crime."

The slickness, the effectiveness of this presentation was marred slightly by Melchen, who spun around, stared at his associate, and blurted, "You *what?!*"

Barker ignored him, offered his condolences to Lady Oakes and Nancy, and led his partner out of the room.

I was depressed when the visit ended and Nancy had to leave, as well as sickened by the story of police mischief and saddened by the tragedy that now left a mother and daughter on opposing sides. And I felt apprehensive about whatever future we might have—if and when I was freed from my cell.

She was living a fantasy: the heroine standing by her husband, an heiress, the daughter of the richest man in the Bahamas, some said in all of the Dominion. And, although she had not a dime of her own, as time went by she would make every effort to live up to this self-portrait.

Summer was a stagnant time in Nassau, the heat as thick as glue, and there was no relief from it behind bars. August and September passed. The monotony was broken by the visits of the friends who were now allowed to see me: Basil McKinney, Oswald Moseley, and Durward Knowles, my fellow sailors and all natives of Nassau; de Visdelou; and the Trolles, George and Marie, at whose home I had first danced with Nancy.

No visitor better symbolized my predicament than Henri de Boynes, the leader of the Devil Islanders I had helped rescue and resettle. I smiled at the sight of him, at the reversal in our positions. He stayed a short time, meaning only to comfort me, and he did. As he left, he gave me a photograph of himself, on which he had written: "To Monsieur de Marigny, who alone and through his help permitted a miserable one to become a man once again. With respectful gratitude, Henri de Boynes."

That snapshot was among a handful of possessions and papers I saved from my life in Nassau, and held on to during the years of my wandering. It sits on my desk even today.

The hours passed on elephant feet. I had reached a point where the days were too long and the nights unending. Sleeping was a chore. I could not rest, could not stop thinking about the murder, the coming trial, and about what I now saw so sharply as a conspiracy to hang me. The only light relief from the gloom was still the music from across the road in the Negro quarter. I would stand on my tiptoes and peer out the tiny barred window at the top of my cell, trying to locate the sound. The music had become important to me, something to cling to in the midst of madness.

Despair is hard to shake. It clouds your outlook like ink from an octopus. I felt fettered, choked, my every move observed by my jailers. I could not comprehend how any human being would survive years of solitude in a cell.

I put myself on a schedule: a minimum of an hour each for meditation, exercise, and reading. I read every book on sailing I could get my hands on. I made notes on the trial, wrote out long questions for Higgs and Callender. I thought about the finding of the autopsy, that a so-called blunt instrument had caused the death of Sir Harry Oakes. Captain Miller drew me a diagram of the mastoid on the left side of the skull. He had also drawn, in blue, four small circles where the blunt instrument had penetrated into the victim's brain.

Miller asked me if I knew what mastoiditis was. I said I had a vague idea. He explained that when a person suffered an infection in that area, the operation was so difficult that the surgeon had to use a hammer and chisel to break through the thick layer of bone. For anyone to make a hole all the way through the mastoid, that person had to have almost superhuman strength. In any event, the thinner bones around the mastoid would cave in under the impact. To imagine that four holes, one inch apart, could be caused by any object or instrument in this location was beyond belief. Moreover, the ear was not even bruised.

I knew of no tool or device or weapon capable of causing such wounds—other than a small-caliber gun. If indeed a gun had been the murder weapon, that would explain why the plane carrying the corpse of Harry Oakes was called back to Nassau, and why the body was taken under guard to the hospital, where Hallinan, Melchen, Barker, and Dr. Hugh Quackenbush, who had performed the autopsy, were alone with the corpse for over an hour.

Testimony at the magistrate's hearing had shown that Quackenbush had been careless, if not incompetent, in his first examination of the body. He had observed only one wound, had put the tip of a finger in it, and had overlooked the others, which were hidden by congealed blood. He had raised the Duke of Windsor's hopes by tossing out the opinion that the death may have been "a suicide, disguised as murder."

But it had to be only a matter of time before Melchen and Barker realized that Oakes had been shot. They knew that the skull had not been opened, and that the bullets that killed Oakes were still there. They ordered the body brought back, and under their supervision the skull was cleaned out.

I turned the theory around in my mind. Why would anyone conceal the fact that the murder weapon was a gun? There was only one reason: If anyone could prove that Oakes was shot, Christie's last defense would be gone. He might not have been disturbed by the storm, the wind, the rain, or the smell of a smoking mattress, or even the odor of burning flesh. But if there were four bullets in Sir Harry's skull, how could Harold not hear four shots fired from twenty feet away, in a wood-and-stucco house that amplified every sound?

I believe it was Christie's dilemma that gave rise to the

story of the blunt instrument. No one has been able to explain what kind of weapon would create such wounds.

(Forty years later, amateur sleuths were still clutching at theories to explain the "blunt instrument." A writer from California visited my home, and said he had learned that a miner's pick was missing from the garage at Westbourne the morning after the murder. The romantic idea this implied, of a man who had made a fortune by finding gold, whose life had been ended ironically with a miner's pick, enthralled him. Later, I asked a forensic surgeon if this could have been the weapon. He replied that the first blow, much less four, would have crushed Sir Harry's entire skull.)

Of course, no matter how badly the investigation was bungled, there was no assurance it helped my case. We knew that the Miami detectives had fabricated the fingerprint evidence. Melchen had lied about the time, Barker about the print. But juries have a tendency to believe what the police tell them.

Higgs complained to Hallinan about the doctored evidence, and the campaign to prejudice Lady Oakes. The Attorney General replied, "I believe we have enough evidence to hang de Marigny. Failing that, I shall do everything in my power to crucify him."

It was not hard to read something sinister into each new move or statement connected with the trial. Erskine-Lindop had made no secret that he wanted to be transferred out of the Bahamas. But when the orders came through, the transfer was arranged on a weekend, so shrouded in secrecy that no one heard about it until he was gone.

Several years later, after he had retired from the force and settled in England, Erskine-Lindop was visited by a writer, Geoffrey Bocca, who was at the time researching the Oakes case. The colonel refused to speak about the trial or to provide any details of what had happened the night of the murder or in the months after my arrest.

So the question went begging: Who was so important that

his name needed protection all these years later? Why would an honest and reliable officer, as I knew Erskine-Lindop to be, lend himself to covering up the treachery of others?

The news that the Windsors were leaving seemed predictable. They had decided to take a long vacation in the United States, and would return, the press was told, after "the mess" was over. Windsor had run away from his duty as a king, and now he was running away from ... what? A fear that justice would or would not be done?

Both the Royal Governor and Harold Christie may have thought I knew more about their secret dealings with Oakes than I did. In the days when we were still talking, Sir Harry told me more than I cared to know about his partnership with Wenner-Gren in the Banco de Continental in Mexico City. I was aware of the money-smuggling scheme, and the fact that a sizable sum—I did not yet know it was more than two million dollars—would be held in trust for the Duke of Windsor.

Sir Harry, in fact, had suggested that Nancy and I join him in Mexico, where I would be given a management position with the bank. I spoke Spanish and had been his interpreter in previous dealings with the Camacho brothers in Mexico and the Trujillos in the Dominican Republic.

Our "feud" was mostly in Sir Harry's mind all along, but I suppose he did not take well my refusals of the jobs and other benefactions he offered. He could be bighearted in an impulsive way, but I understood what these offers were. They were attempts to hold Nancy close, and to have me in his debt. Sir Harry had something in common with the big governments that were so often the subject of his complaints. If you accepted his hospitality, he soon felt entitled to determine how you led your life.

I knew there was still a connection to be made somewhere, between Harry Oakes, Harold Christie, the Duke of Windsor, and a new, flourishing bank in Mexico. What it had to do with war and murder and my neck, I had not the slightest idea. Not yet.

At night, in my cell, I tried to analyze the case the prosecution would soon be bringing against me. It was like trying to lift a bale of hay onto a truck; it came apart in your hands.

Then there were the ominous signs, as I saw them, of a campaign to conceal the truth and sabotage my defense:

My message to Alfred Adderley, asking him to represent me, never reached him.

The two security guards at Westbourne had disappeared; the two caretakers at Lyford Cay, who reported seeing an unidentified boat docked at the cay the night of the killing, had been found dead.

Colonel Erskine-Lindop, who could verify that I had been taken upstairs at eleven in the morning, not at 3:00 P.M., as Barker and his witnesses swore, had been whisked away to a distant post.

Outside, summer was melting into autumn. As the trial drew nearer there were still, in more than a poetic sense, miles to go before I slept.

My days dragged on. I slept fitfully, if at all. No sooner would I shut my eyes than I was awakened by another nightmare. The evidence, the lies, even the image of the new Nancy were like a maelstrom in my head. In a recurring dream, I saw the final verdict:

The judge appeared, his head covered with a black hood and wearing a black cap, reading the sentence: *I was to be hanged by the neck within thirty days.* A scream of innocence stuck in my throat. I was like a ghost floating in the room and observing the entire scene. I saw myself in the box reserved for the accused, flanked by two policemen. When the judge finished talking, everyone wept, then began to applaud. The noise of the applause awakened me. I was drenched in sweat, my heart pounding. I thought I would be sick to my stomach. I could not close my eyes the rest of the night.

I reached a point where I actually dreaded falling asleep. I became fearful of the night, when I would face those demons that haunted my rest. The thought of being hanged remained dominant in my mind and returned to torment me. I tried to imagine how I would react when they led me to the scaffold, tried to imagine how it would feel. These would be the last yards I would ever walk. I told myself I would show no fear or cowardice.

A black hood would cover my head. I could feel the roughness of the rope around my neck. Then the trapdoor would open—would that be the last sound I would ever hear?—and I would fall into eternal space. Would the sleep of death be peaceful, or would my soul go elsewhere? I *saw* my body dangling, then cut down and placed in a coffin.

When I opened my eyes, I was again thinking, waiting, wondering: Would I walk out of this prison or be carried away in a coffin? Dying young, and for no reason, seemed the most miserable and pointless of fates. I focused my bitterness and hatred on Hallinan and Windsor. I remembered the tales of the Count of Monte Cristo, and imagined myself rotting in jail for years, until I could escape and destroy them, as Edmond Dantes had destroyed his enemies.

I prayed: May they all burn in hell.

Like death, tedium can cause one's life to flash before one's eyes. And so at night, tossing on the thin bed I had improvised, I thought about the vagaries of fate that had led me, step by step, to this time and place.

PART THREE

IN SEARCH OF NASSAU

MAURITIUS

THE world I knew as a youth no longer exists. To understand what happened later in my life, it is necessary to know what that world was like, to know the soil that shaped me.

My ancestors were Normans, sailors and even warlords who turned, in two or three generations, to bankers and farmers. In 1789, the French Revolution and the guillotine forced them to flee their ancestral lands in Normandy.

They escaped to Mauritius, then known as Isle de France, and settled on a land grant given to the family by Louis XV. There, in the middle of the Indian Ocean, five hundred miles east of Madagascar, they started the cultivation of sugar cane, which led to the prospering of the plantation. Mauritius proved to be more than just a sanctuary: it was one of the most enchanting places on earth.

Mark Twain visited the island and, in his book *Following the Equator,* published in 1897, wrote: "You gather that Mauritius was made first and Heaven was copied later."

What caught the writer's eye and pen were the virgin tropical forests, the waterfalls, rivers, and lakes. Mountains loomed above the coastline, and the reefs that girdled the white, sandy beaches formed lagoons of transparent water. Here swam the richest variety of tropical fish in the world. A three-thousand-foot dome in the center of the island was evidence of a huge volcano millions of years ago. It must have pleased Mr. Twain to learn that this unique place had been the home of the now-extinct dodo bird, a comic name, almost a figure of myth.

Into that exotic setting I was born on the twenty-ninth of March 1910. My island upbringing forever drew me to life by the sea.

My earliest recollection of childhood was of the large colonial house where I lived with my grandmother and two spinster aunts. I was led to believe that my mother had died when I was three. From that time I seldom saw my father. I had no memory of her, little knowledge of him. They were not discussed in my presence. Yet I felt secure in the home of an adoring grandmother, and at some point I stopped asking the questions that always had gone unanswered.

My days revolved around the black servants who had been a part of the family for generations. Emilie, my grandmother's age, was in full authority. Her daughter, Julie, was my milk mother and looked after me. Each morning, after taking classes from a priest, I was free to play with the children of the black servants who lived in a camp behind the house, near a fruit orchard. There, children laughed; dogs barked and tussled; cats watched; chickens, followed by their broods, roamed in search of food; roosters crowed; ducks, goats, and geese mingled into one heterogeneous family.

From their native Africa, the blacks had brought many superstitions. Voodoo was their basic religion. Nounou, the old, white-haired herb doctor, mesmerized us with tales of bats and flying cats and men turning into wolves during the full moon. They were called the *loup-garou* and they preyed on children, taking them to their caves and eating them alive. The years I lived on the island as a child left an indelible mark on my nature. Superstition became ingrained in me. I learned to ward off the "evil eye" and to trust no one but myself.

At the far end of the garden, at the back of the property, the Hindus lived and worked in the sugar fields.

They were a breed apart from the Negroes. Their houses,

their persons, their food, and their way of life were obsessively clean. They never kept animals around their homes, ate no meat, and drank no hard liquor. Where the blacks loved music and dancing for the fun and pleasure they derived from both, song and dance were rituals with religious meaning to the Hindus.

The man who most influenced my early life was Mahadev, the spiritual leader of the Hindus, a strong and mystical figure who lived alone in a white bungalow. His bed was a coconut-fiber mat on the floor. In a corner of the room was an earthenware jug with drinking water. Several smaller mats covered the rest of the room. He was tall and thin, his head shaven except for a long, braided topknot. He wore a white robe that covered his ankles, and always walked barefoot. Although his eyes reflected an inner peace, it was impossible to hold his gaze. He looked right through you.

On the day I first met Mahadev, he asked if I wanted to learn; I said a quick yes. He sat cross-legged on a mat, his hands on his knees. I did likewise, afraid to break the silence and disturb the holy man. After a long while, Mahadev said in a soft, deep voice: "You may learn the truth if you wish, because you are patient." We both got to our feet. He placed his hand on my head and added: "Patience is the first step towards virtue."

I visited Mahadev daily. I loved to listen to him talk. Death had always frightened me; he made it sound simple. He explained to me that one lifetime was the continuation of others, and there was no reason to fear what was inevitable. He taught me that one could have complete control over one's feelings, over one's body; but the mind controlled pain, pleasure, thirst, and hunger. I practiced daily and learned how to meditate.

At the start of summer, everyone in the camp talked about the "fire-walk" at the village, a short distance from the plantation. I mentioned it to Mahadev, and he offered to take me if my grandmother agreed. It was to be an experience I would never forget. We started for the ceremonial grounds before sunrise. There was a ditch about twenty feet long and half as wide, filled with red-hot charcoal that had burned for several days. The glare and heat were such that I could barely keep my eyes open. The participants were men who wanted to cleanse and purify themselves and exorcise their surroundings. They had spent the night praying and at dawn had bathed in a small stream that was sacred to them. They walked toward the village, singing and chanting and dancing all the way.

I would hear echoes of that music a quarter of a century later, on another island, in another hemisphere, in the shadow of my own death.

A goat was brought and tied to a pole, and the singing grew louder, the dancing more intense, as the onlookers joined in. A man wearing a yellow robe came forward. He carried a long knife. The crowd fell silent. With one stroke he separated the goat's head from its body. Blood spurted from the severed neck, and the men who were to walk on the fire rushed forward, dipping their hands into the blood and using it, like paint, to mark their foreheads. The singing started anew, but one could distinguish no words, only a melodious murmur. The men danced with mincing steps and followed one another toward the blazing trench. They stepped onto the glowing, smoking coals, and walked with the same deliberate motion to the other end of the trench. There they stood for a moment, facing the fire. Then they raised their arms and looked at the sky, beating their chests with their fists until they seemed to have reached the end of their strength. Their arms became limp and dropped to their sides. The men were purified. The ceremony was over and the crowd left the scene in dead silence.

I was speechless. When we reached home I found my voice, and asked Mahadev how men could walk on fire without being burned. He quietly explained that those people had achieved a level of discipline and self-control so high they could dominate pain completely. To a small, impressionable boy, these were acts of wonder.

My thoughts kept returning to what I had seen. I wanted

to learn from it.

My life on the plantation came to an end when I left the island for a Jesuit school in Normandy. Gone were the large and sunny room, my fine bed and furniture. Instead, I lived in a cubbyhole into which were crowded a narrow bed, one chair, a small desk, and a wardrobe, with barely enough space to turn around. The pallid light that infiltrated through a dirty window gave the room a sullen aspect.

Days went by with monotonous regularity, and study became my way of life. My schedule included Spanish, Latin, French, and English. Mathematics was a must. But the social change was traumatic. I had been transplanted from a tropical island, surrounded by warm and interesting people, into the arid atmosphere of a Jesuit school in frigid Normandy.

To compound matters, I was surrounded by boys who were clannish, and whose little groups were defined by that part of the land from which they came. Their objective was to make life miserable for others. Any simple discussion turned directly into an argument and ended in a fight. Sarcasm and irony were their tools. They laughed at my accent and made fun of my habits. They were unable to understand why I would exercise to the limit of my endurance, then retire to my room, sit on my folded legs on the floor, and meditate.

That first year was long and lonely and demanded painful adjustments. The six years that followed were carbon copies of the first. I was always at the top of my class—in discipline and hard work. For the rest of my life, I would react hotly to those I identified as society's snobs and bullies.

By the time I was eighteen, I had finished my secondary education and had passed the entrance exam for Cambridge University. It was time to return home to see my family.

The trip to Mauritius lasted two months on a mail boat that called on the Canary Islands, Ascension, St. Helena, Tristan da Cunha, Whalefish Bay, and Capetown. Can one imagine such a voyage today? It was of another century.

Once home, I was amazed at the changes that had taken place. Automobiles had replaced horses and carriages. Stone buildings had supplanted wooden ones. Trucks loaded with sugar bags rattled toward the harbor in a cloud of dust. People were everywhere. I found the noise startling, the activity exciting.

The central dome had mushroomed into a new city, and the rich growers lived there during the torrid heat of summer. My grandmother had followed their example and built a new summer house. Everyone was in full regalia to meet me. My aunts and all the servants waited on the landscaped lawns. My little milk mother, Julie, hugged and kissed me, clucking over how tall I was. Mahadev, in a starched white robe, held me close to him. The effusion of love and affection brought a lump to my throat. I began to cry.

During the days that followed, the euphoria of my arrival gave way to a disagreeable feeling that I was being held back, shielded, from something I could not fathom, or even guess. There were no invitations and no effort by anyone to introduce me to my peers.

I was not even invited to attend a party at my uncle's home for the fifteenth birthday of his daughter. It began to dawn on me that I had lived the life of a young hermit. I had never attended a local school, and my only friends were the children of the black servants on the plantation.

I knew very little about life, but I knew enough to recognize that I had become a social pariah, and I needed to know why. I chose a family gathering at my grandmother's home to press for an answer.

My uncle stood behind her chair, with my two aunts on either side of her, so stiff they might have been posing for a portrait. Pulling a chair close, I took my grandmother's hand in mine, and kissed her cheeks. Softly, I asked if there was a family secret that had been withheld from me, and if so, I begged her to withhold it no longer. "You know how much I love and need you," I said. "Dearest Grandmother. I beg of you, tell me who I am."

There was a long moment of silence. Then the words came as quickly as I could absorb them. My mother was alive. My father had divorced her on grounds of adultery three years after I was born. In a Catholic community as close as ours, a divorce had been unheard of, while adultery was regarded as worse than a crime—it was a damnation. A shadow of shame fell across our entire family. The scandal was such that my two aunts, who had been engaged to be married, had their engagements broken.

Everyone now desired to get a word in. Each new detail stabbed me deeper. My father had left for South Africa, unable to face the community who knew of his disgrace. My mother hastily married her lover and moved to France. She was excommunicated by papal edict, which was read during high mass on three successive Sundays. My aunts were joined by my uncle in explaining how much my father had suffered. I was told that he had avoided seeing me after the divorce, so fearful was he of being reminded that I was my mother's son.

Even as these words echoed in my ears, I could not help wondering how my mother felt, lying in her lover's arms. Did she feel any guilt about the three-year-old son she had abandoned?

But my confusion only deepened. I had heard only sympathy for my father—his loss, the pain he had endured. Not one word about the son who had been forgotten. I stood up, kissed my grandmother, and walked slowly out of the room. From then on, I resolved, I would need no one's compassion or pity. I would face the world without shame.

I went straight to Mahadev's quarters. He watched wordlessly, as I sat on the floor opposite him. Then he looked past me and spoke in a tone of voice I had not heard before: "Destiny pointed its finger at you the day you were born. You shall travel through dramas and witness tragedies. You shall know great love, passion, and joy. You shall know hatred and tears. You must know one to appreciate the other. When the wind blows you to the ground, you must struggle to your feet and fight. Only the strong survive. When finally you walk the length of the road, you will close your eyes knowing that you drank of the cup of life to the last drop."

We meditated for a long time. When I entered his room, I had felt bitter. His words cleared my mind and made me accept my family's lack of human feeling toward me. I walked back to the main house, knowing at last why I had been so isolated. No one in our social class cared to associate with the son of an excommunicated woman.

My father was back on the island, living at the plantation. I made up my mind to meet him as soon as possible. The next day I was shown into his living room. I had longed for the sensation of being held in my father's arms. Instead, he was distant, his handshake formal. We had an awkward lunch; the meager conversation was shallow. My father finished his cigar and offered to walk me to his factory, which was being repaired. The day dragged by until it was time for me to leave.

He stood on the veranda until the car drove from view. I had a last glimpse of him, a solitary figure who dwelt in the comfortable prison he had built around himself. I felt nothing.

I decided to remain on the island for the time being, and see what life had in store for me. I registered at the Royal College of Agriculture for a two-year course, and moved into a small house Grandmother had bought for me.

My cousin, Georges de Visdelou, was back from Europe and we began a lasting friendship. His family's wealth came from its magnificent sugar plantation. He had spent most of his youth in France, and had come home to visit before moving to London, where he was to take a degree in law.

Georges was a cynic who enjoyed shocking the local purists. He was untroubled by my family history. We were regulars on the courts at the Tennis Club, where I met many of his friends, notably a circle of lovely young ladies, most of them cousins of mine. In Georges they saw the scion of a powerful family. In me they saw someone with a shadow hanging over his background, which excited their curiosity. To their eyes I was forbidden fruit, never invited to their homes or parties. Georges simply laughed and convinced me that the advantage was mine: if they did not wish to associate with me outside the bedroom, then I had the better part of the bargain.

I was in his company, at the Tennis Club, the day I met the mother I had not known since infancy. It was a moment remarkable for its absence of drama.

Two couples came off the court and sat down at the table next to ours. Abruptly, one of the gentlemen came to our table and announced that a lovely woman wished to meet me. The next moment, I was introduced to my mother.

The encounter, the introduction, was as casual as if a waiter had merely taken our orders.

I felt neither joy nor pain. Under the circumstances of this unscheduled meeting, I wanted to feel more, to show more—some thunderclap of recognition. But I could generate nothing. There was none of the tension I had felt in the earlier meeting with my father. She was composed, and beautiful. She seemed matter-of-fact, and talked to me as one adult to another. There were no tears. The moment was filled with dignity.

She was leaving the next day for France, and gave me her addresses in Paris and Marseilles. She hoped I would travel there soon.

The events of the day had worn me out. I wanted to be alone that evening, and after dinner I sat on the terrace and began to sort out my feelings. I felt a sadistic pleasure at the thought of dropping in my family's lap the news of my meeting with my mother at the Tennis Club. I decided to wait until Sunday, when my father would be joining us for family dinner.

Finally the special moment arrived. Between the soup and the main course, I said lightly, "By the way, I had the pleasure of meeting my mother at the Tennis Club the other day.

I found her to be a stunning woman."

A chill descended on the room. I could see my father clench his fists; his voice was leaden and dry: "That woman you call your mother died the day she abandoned you and left me. I am shocked that you would speak to her. That must never happen again. You have a choice. Her or me."

I looked at my father with an expression of mock surprise. "I am certain," I replied, "that you do not mean what you have said. I was raised in a Jesuit school, a devout Catholic. I am certain you could not ask me to pass judgment on my parents."

Without another word, he left the table and walked out of the dining room. My two aunts followed him. I never saw or spoke to my father again, or heard any news of him until his death some twenty years later.

Shortly thereafter, Mahadev died of a heart attack. His death was a huge loss to me. Suddenly, I found myself like a boat cast adrift on the ocean without a rudder. Mahadev had once told me that each of our actions was written in the Great Book, and nothing could change our destiny. Those words, added to my Jesuit education, became crutches that allowed me to rationalize my conduct.

Under the tutelage of my cousin Georges, I was becoming a chauvinist and a hedonist. It was a trend made all the more troubling because I knew too little about people to see this behavior as faulty. I asked myself, why not follow the path to which life seemed to have led me?

Six months later, I left Mauritius, feeling deep in my heart that I would never again set foot on my native land. As the steamer sailed away, I had my last view of the imposing mountains and lovely beaches.

Whatever was ahead of me, I believed that a benign destiny guided my steps.

THIS WAS LONDON

IN the interlude before World War II, London was a paradise for a bachelor. Money, a good address, and a Savile Row tailor were considered the essential assets. I had gone there, joined by my cousin, Georges de Visdelou, to start a career in finance. We quickly obtained two of the three requisites, lacking only an assured source of funds.

In late spring, London was invaded by an army of young women, daughters of the well-to-do gentry. These families were prepared to spend large sums to see their daughters make their debuts and cap the social events by being presented at court. The sponsors required by these young ladies charged a substantial fee for room and board and arranging escorts for their wards. This delicate arrangement was usually undertaken by a titled family, who made up in connections what they lacked in cash. The task required subtlety, since the number of debutantes exceeded the supply of suitable males by a wide margin.

Any reference to these social activities would be unimportant, except that my circle of acquaintances included people whose paths I would cross, with mixed results, in later years.

At one party, Georges and I were introduced to Lucie Cohen and Lady Patricia Mackay, two leaders of London society. Lucie was a charmer, the daughter of Sir George Cohen, a financier whose neighbor was the Woolworth heiress, Barbara Hutton, then married to Count Reventlow. The Cohen home contained, among many luxuries, a private theater, where they entertained their friends once a month. That night the recital featured Richard Tauber, the famous German tenor.

I met a young man of roughly my age, Paul Meyer, the son of a Jewish banker from Berlin. He spoke French and English fluently and was enrolled in the London School of Economics. He suggested that I monitor the lectures given by the best brains in England. One of the lecturers was John Maynard Keynes, whose unorthodox theories of economics had evoked intense debate. I followed Paul's advice and we began to meet daily.

Meanwhile, Lady Patricia invited me to be her escort for dinner at the Reventlows. I looked forward to meeting the heiress who had made headlines when she was pursued around the world by the Russian prince, Alexis Mdivani, who succeeded in becoming her first (of six) husbands. The marriage cost her a million dollars in cash, not to mention a string of polo ponies, a private plane, and a sports car.

Barbara Hutton Reventlow was in her mid-twenties, but she looked oldish. She was pallid and had a concave chest. Her eyes were sad, with deep circles under them. She spoke with a low voice, and gave the impression that she was always on the verge of fainting. All of this was in odd contrast to her beautiful dresses and the small diamond tiara perched atop her hair.

But what I remember most about that night was being introduced by Lady Patricia to another guest, a towering Scotsman, Lord Ronald Graham. He invited me to lunch at his club later in the week.

Several years my senior, Lord Ronald had a subtle way of finding out everything about me, while revealing little if anything about himself. Halfway through lunch, another guest arrived. His name was Frederick Bosch, a handsome man in his thirties, who turned out to be a German diplomat.

The conversation turned to politics. I had not the slightest idea who or what they were discussing, but it was not hard to catch the frequent references to someone named David. Before the evening had ended, Bosch handed me a book. "A gift," he said, smiling. "May this book become your bible."

The book was *Mein Kampf,* written by Adolf Hitler during his year in prison following the abortive Beer Hall Putsch of 1923. The man and his Nazi party, then mushrooming in Germany, had become popular topics in England.

Lord Ronald told me to keep the week of Ascot open. He wanted me to be his guest at this most famous of British horse races. I thanked him and drove straight to Paul's apartment to seek an evaluation of what I had heard. A sad smile touched his face. He warned me to be careful of Lord Ronald and his friends. They were Nazis.

"I know how they operate," he said. "They need people like you. Graham will endeavor to recruit you. Be careful."

I had come to England innocent of the rumblings and undercurrents already spreading fear and danger on the country's edges. Germans were there, they were not unpopular, and many of the British liked the sound of the brand of socialism Hitler was peddling. It sounded almost clubby.

Paul saw the terror coming, and he had been urging his parents to leave Berlin and come to London or go to America. He could not hide his distress.

And so my circle widened. One party, one introduction, led to another. Strangers became friends, and friends became, well, not always what they seemed.

One season proceeded much like another. Georges announced his engagement to Diana North, the daughter of Lord North. I had become Lucie Cohen's frequent escort, which flattered me. I was proud to be seen with her. She was regal-looking, with class and breeding written all over her. One night she warned me never to accept an invitation from people I did not know. I thought she was being protective, until she added, "Avoid them like the plague. Imagine, you might wind up going to a ball with a girl from Manchester or

York. It could kill you socially."

It struck me then that she was a snob. Without realizing it, I had drifted in the same direction. I sat in my room that night and began to meditate. I had acquired so many tastes, I had forgotten the things that mattered. I wondered where I was heading. The so-called society life I had been so eager to invade had begun to grow tiresome and petty. At one party I was asked to inscribe a thought in the guestbook of a young debutante who was then the toast of London, and who typified everything that now seemed so shallow. Unable to resist such an opportunity, this sentiment leaped from my pen:

"To you, dear, love is always the same . . . Never another feeling, always another name . . . New patterns on the ceiling."

I closed the book and left the party.

I did join Lord Graham for the races at Ascot, a Crown tradition since 1711, celebrated in the lyrics of the musical *My Fair Lady*. And there he introduced me to the man who years later would have a hand in putting me on trial for my life.

Ascot was a remnant of elegance past, a four-day pageant for the British peerage and aristocratic rich. We survived the social preliminaries, and eventually reached the racetrack to see the finale. My host was excited. He had a mare in the first race and felt that her chances of winning were good.

The scene was spectacular, the men in gray cutaways and gray top hats, the women in flowery dresses and the latest fashion in chapeaux. Queen Victoria had been the one exception, wearing her usual signature headgear with dignity and elegance. As part of the opening ceremony, King George and Queen Mary arrived at Ascot by open carriage, with liveried attendants on the box, and a retinue of horse guards behind them.

To be in the royal enclosure and rubbing shoulders with the English nobility, in the presence of Their Majesties, gave me a sense of achievement. I could not keep my thoughts from drifting to Mauritius and the snobs who had refused me entrance to their homes.

I followed my host into the paddock, where the elite evaluated the horseflesh and one another. In the distance I spotted the Prince of Wales, surrounded by admirers and friends. I could not take my eyes from that boyish-looking, slight man who was then the most popular prince in the history of England. As we drew closer, his image came into focus. His complexion was pasty and his actions jumpy. He waved at Lord Ronald, who quickly walked toward him. They shook hands and Lord Ronald introduced us.

The Prince asked if I was French. I replied that I was from Mauritius and, in fact, was British. To my surprise, I felt no unease in talking to the heir to the British throne.

The Prince smiled. "Mauritius," he repeated. "My brother [the Duke of York] visited your island several years ago. He told me it was quite a beautiful place. Sorry I never got to see it." He shook hands with both of us and said, "I have to make the rounds." He moved away, followed by his aide-de-camp.

I wagered a hundred guineas on Lord Ronald's mare, and another hundred on a colt running in the Derby and owned by a friend of his, the Maharajah of Ragepippla. (There is no way to mention a maharajah without appearing guilty of name-dropping. No one, I assure you, can do so effortlessly.) The horse was named Windsor Lad. I won both bets at good odds, and picked up the check for dinner at the Savoy. Lord Ronald invited three of his lady friends, and our picture appeared in one London paper. I was surprised to find myself described as a "socialite and sugar magnate from the island of Mauritius."

In spite of my better instincts, I was learning to play the society game like a pro. The pace was brisk. Where it was to lead I did not know, and once in the flow of it, I did not care.

When I returned to London, I called on Paul Meyer, who had invited me to spend the summer vacation with his family in Berlin. We decided to leave in ten days. Paul seemed worried, almost lost. I knew he was facing a terrible ordeal because he was a Jew. It was beyond the scope of my understanding.

I returned home and pondered how I might help my friend.

It happened that I was to meet Lord Ronald the next day for lunch. He wanted to introduce me to Hans Bosch, a cousin of Frederich, who was stationed in Berlin. He gave me his card, inviting me to call on him whenever I visited Berlin. He would be pleased, he said, to show me everything Hitler had done for the German people. How he had unshackled the nation from the Treaty of Versailles that had enslaved Germany for twenty years.

Bosch added, casually, that once the Prince of Wales was on the throne, Germany and England could form an alliance that would protect the world from Communism. "Germany will control Europe," he said, "and England's navy will rule the seas."

I dropped by Paul's apartment the moment I left Bosch. He was already starting to pack. We walked into his study and he closed the doors. I repeated what Hans Bosch had predicted, but Paul could only shrug his shoulders. He had other concerns. "We shall be in Berlin the day after tomorrow," he said. "I must convince Father and Mother that it is time to leave. The elections are coming. I cannot figure Hitler sitting in the chair of Bismarck. But if he becomes chancellor, Europe will have to deal with the devil itself. It is madness. No one cares. The French are worried about the quality of their wine, and the British complain about the weather."

"Where does the Prince of Wales stand?" I asked, my curiosity quite real.

"He is dangerous," he said, "because he is weak, and yet they love him. He is a dense, cocky, and arrogant little prig. He is more German than Hindenburg."

We spent the night talking. The days leading up to our trip passed quickly, and we left for Berlin. The German capital was in a state of nervous tension. Politics seemed to be the only topic of the day. I neither spoke nor read German, and thus was able to enjoy my stay.

Paul's family lived in what turned out to be a mansion.

His father was in his fifties, plump, with a crown of gray hair around his bald head. His mother was petite, charming, blond, and blue-eyed. Their daughter, Edith, who was slightly older than Paul, was a replica of her mother. The Meyer family were most attractive, and everyone made certain that I felt completely at home.

One of the other houseguests was a Chilean Jew named Jaime Weinstein. He was Mr. Meyer's age, tall, almost emaciated, with dark eyes that reflected intelligence and kindness. We found ourselves alone in the sitting room after dinner. I had noticed that his English was poor and his French worse. I spoke to him in Spanish. It was as if a ray of light had illuminated the room. He smiled and we chatted. He asked endless questions about Mauritius. I turned the conversation around and learned that he was a bachelor, an investor in charge of large funds from many Jewish groups throughout Europe and South America.

He asked me if I was Jewish, and I said no. **But** I was interested in their history, and what they had suffered. I had been touched by the story of Masada, where the entire colony had chosen death rather than slavery under the Romans.

He frowned and looked at me intently. "You should be careful in Germany these days," he said. "For the Jew, days of rough roads are ahead. Maybe for their friends also."

Quickly he changed the subject. "Are you working in London, or are you going to return to your island?"

I shook my head. "I shall never go back there again. I am finishing a course at the London School of Economics."

Weinstein handed me his card and said, "Don Alfredo, on your way back to London, drop by and see me in Paris. I am at the Hotel Meurice. I have there my home and my office. Maybe I could interest you in working for me."

I was flattered. We parted that evening with my promise that I would call on him in Paris.

The Meyer family made every effort to make my stay with

them agreeable, in spite of the tense atmosphere. A few of their friends joined us on quiet picnics at the lakes around Berlin, and Edith led me on a tour of the many museums. Paul refused to go out, lest we encounter the kind of unpleasant scene that was becoming so common.

"I never realized that it had gone this far," he told me. "Edith is blond with blue eyes, the Aryan type. It will be safe for her to show you around. I won't be missed." I felt sorry for my friend. Circumstances had brought fear to his soul.

After a week we left Berlin and visited Austria, which was gay and happy, regardless of the heavy Nazi influence taking root there. Italy was charming in spite of the Fascists. Italians will always be Italians.

We stopped in Paris for a reunion with another friend of mine, Marc Levy, and his sister, Sara. I had met them when I spent a few months in France, visiting my mother and attending classes, before moving to London. I had never known a person who was Jewish, not on Mauritius, and not in boarding school, until I met Marc and Sara. It was Sara who taught me about the history and traditions of this religion, and I was fascinated.

In the company of the Levys, the gloom faded. No one needed to say aloud what so many were thinking, that there might not come, soon, a chance to be so carefree again.

All around us, people were forced into making decisions that were, quite literally, matters of life and death. I would learn years later that Marc's entire family had been arrested when the Germans occupied France, and shipped off to a concentration camp. They were never heard from again.

At the end of the summer of 1936, Paul returned to Berlin. I decided to visit Jaime Weinstein at the Meurice Hotel, in Paris.

OUT OF EUROPE

OVER the next several months, I traveled all over Europe and I saw the immediate future. Its name was Adolf Hitler. The newspapers were filled with stories of Hitler's victory in the German elections. He was no longer a figure of comic relief. Governments were going through a period of schizophrenia, unsure whether they would soon be doing business with the Nazis or going to war against them. In the end, the business of Germany *was* war.

I would have an early brush with the dictator's armed camp. My work would justify my traveling inside Germany, but it was friendship that gave the trips a purpose.

I had been hired by Jaime Weinstein to manage his investments in the metals market, working out of the offices of a brokerage house in London. Reluctantly, I explained that I knew nothing about that type of business. He smiled and assured me that my education would be a quick one.

He insisted that I accept an advance of one hundred pounds, money I hadn't sought and didn't really need. I was living well on a trust fund my grandmother had provided. Weinstein insisted. "Consider it a loan," he said. "You shall repay me with your first commission."

And so I did. I discovered then that I had passed a kind of character test. He had, in the same manner, helped launch the careers of a dozen or more young men. I was the first to repay the loan.

The complexities of a new job left little time for social

activities. Still, I stayed in touch with Lord Ronald Graham, whose political contacts I sensed could be useful in the months ahead.

Paul Meyer was back in London, burying himself in his textbooks. He saw nothing but terror ahead with each step that Hitler took as Chancellor of the Third Reich. His father's refusal to leave Germany had robbed him of hope. His mother and sister insisted on remaining with Mr. Meyer. Paul was fatalistic: "We are trapped. At the end of the semester I shall return home and do my utmost to get them out."

Lord Ronald was intrigued about my working on the stock exchange. He dropped several hints about picking up a good "inside tip," and I promised at the right time to let him know. It was an old tactic that always paid dividends. Let someone believe that he can make easy money through you, and you own that person.

The same news that depressed Paul Meyer caused Lord Ronald and Frederick Bosch to rejoice. At celebrations with their friends, the champagne flowed and toasts to Hitler rang out. I was disturbed by the number of British aristocrats who were always present. Members of the best families were in awe of the author of *Mein Kampf,* who had, without firing a shot thus far, transformed a beaten and occupied nation into a new threat to the balance of world power.

Once a week I journeyed to Paris to confer with Weinstein. I mentioned the inquiries of Lord Ronald Graham, and wondered if it might not be wise to allow him to invest through me and permit him to make a profit. "Who knows," I said, "we might need him sometime." Weinstein agreed, on the conditions that Graham never know where the money was invested, and that it should be a onetime transaction.

I began to buy lead and zinc. I bought for my employer's account, and, with my commissions, traded for myself as well. I informed Lord Ronald that I could help him now with a tip on a sure thing. He wrote out a check for one thousand pounds, and accepted my condition that no questions were to be asked.

I poured myself into studying the market. It had become my whole life. I slept with lead and woke up with zinc. Those two items were moving slowly but steadily. My profits were growing.

I accepted an invitation to accompany Lord Ronald and Frederick Bosch to attend a Nazi party rally at Nuremberg. Both assured me that it was going to be a spectacle beyond the realm of my imagination. Since our route to and from Nuremberg had to be through Berlin, I would have the opportunity on the way back to see the Meyer family and try to persuade them to leave Germany.

Weinstein encouraged me to go. Paul was pessimistic: "Father is at heart a Prussian. Nothing will make him move."

The streets and hotels of Nuremberg swarmed with people. Soldiers were everywhere, some in gray field uniforms, others in brown, and more in black and silver. Lights flooded the squares, and around the rim of the sports stadium, hundreds of swastika flags fluttered in the light winter wind. The discipline of the crowd was impressive. Everyone knew where to sit, when to stand. Paramilitary groups acted as ushers. It was a chilling sight. I thought about the politicians who still doubted that Germany was preparing for war. Either those were combat troops we saw parading through town, or the Germans just liked to go for long walks in columns of four.

The rally had been going on for four days. Tonight was the finale, and Adolf Hitler was to speak. An empty chair awaited him in the middle of the stage. To his right and left were the Party's higher-ups: Hess, Goebbels, Goering, Streicher, Himmler.

A dead calm had settled over the immense crowd. Hitler emerged from behind the podium and climbed lightly up the steps. I was disappointed by his looks. He was short, his uniform ill fitting.

Unlike the others, he wore no medals, except for the Iron Cross. Nothing about him suggested the aura of a leader. The hair plastered across his forehead and the mustache the size of a postage stamp had already made him a prime target for cartoonists.

He raised his right arm. The crowd went wild. Still, the military spirit so ingrained in the Germans kept them in perfect formation. A transformation that amazed me now took place. Hitler's whole personality changed as he spoke. The force of his expression, the conviction in his speech, were hypnotic. That silly little man towered over that vast assembly. Some twenty years later, when I lived in Cuba, I felt the same atmosphere, the same hypnotic power of the speaker, when my curiosity drew me to the rallies of Fidel Castro.

As Hitler swept the crowd into his act, I found myself shouting "Heil!" with the rest of them, without realizing I was doing so, and in spite of the contempt I felt. Worse yet, I had no idea what he was saying.

My two hosts remained in Nuremberg after the rally. I stopped off in Berlin to visit again with Paul's parents. What I found shocked me even more. SS men, in their stark black uniforms, spread fear wherever they went. Youths dressed in khaki shirts, with a swastika on a red armband, patrolled the streets and avenues. They shattered the store windows of Jewish merchants, and chased from the streets anyone who got in their way. They marched to the sound of the military music ("Today we rule Germany, tomorrow the world"), and in the light of flaming torches. The bacchanal went on all night, punctuated by gunshots or the screams of someone being beaten.

The Meyer home looked like a morgue. It was a house without laughter. Gretel, the elderly maid, was the only servant left. Windows facing the street were broken, the rocks and broken glass still scattered where they fell.

Mr. Meyer had aged since I saw him last, but his stubbornness had faded not at all. "We are Germans," he said. "I am a German like my father and his father before him. I am proud to be a German. I fought for my country in the Great War in 1914. I shall not run like a rat from a broom closet. Germany will never permit a pogrom."

My heart ached for this old man, so German, so willing to risk his life and those of his family, for his pride in a country that no longer recognized him.

In their home the same painful choices were being debated as in almost every Jewish home: whether or not to leave Germany, and when. Mrs. Meyer felt that to do nothing was to invite tragedy. She wanted Edith to return with me to London. Edith would not defy her father's wishes.

There was little I could do by staying in Germany. I returned to Paris to tell Jaime Weinstein of the dilemma of his friends. He shook his head, and paced the room for a long time in dead silence. Abruptly he said, "One day soon, Meyer will be picked up by the Gestapo. The bankers will be high on their list. If they just take him and leave the women behind, with God's help we might do something for them." He looked straight into my eyes. "I count on you then, Don Alfredo."

Back in London, I called on Paul and tried to cheer him. Instead, I was the one who grew depressed when he told me he had decided to return to Berlin. He felt that he alone could change his father's mind.

A few days later, I drove my friend to the airport. Neither of us spoke. The pent-up emotion, the dangers of the trip, choked us both. My friend, who had been gifted by the gods with looks, intelligence, and a kind heart, was leaving everything behind to return to hell.

At the gate to the plane, we hugged each other tightly. I sensed that I would not see him again. Looking at him through the tears that rolled down my cheeks, I said, brokenly, "Whatever happens to you or your father, I swear that I will do anything in my power to help your mother and Edith."

Paul shook my hand, then turned and ran to the waiting plane. He did not look back.

Soon after Paul's departure from London, I left for Scotland by train, along with several young British aristocrats. We were all to be Lord Ronald's guests at a grouse shoot. As we rolled across the beautiful countryside, I admired the English custom of respectful silence when locked in a small place with other people. The only conversation took place at the bar or during meals in the club car.

I already knew that my fellow passengers believed in the justice, or at least the inevitability, of the Nazi cause.

Graham's castle was an imposing relic, square, with four towers, one in each corner. The wide moat had been dry for many decades, but a still-working drawbridge led into the immense, paved courtyard.

He had promised his guests a surprise. On the last day of the shoot, around noon, the *Gypsy Moth,* the private aircraft of the Prince of Wales, flew in, piloted by His Royal Highness. The Prince was in high spirits.

I was the only one in the group who did not seem familiar to him, and Lord Ronald stepped in. "You remember Alfred de Marigny," he reassured him. "You met at Ascot. Fred is one of our close friends. He went with us to the rally in Nuremberg."

The Prince relaxed and we shook hands. That evening, politics dominated the conversation. Lord Ronald talked about the rally in rapturous detail, and of a later meeting with the leaders of the Nazi party. It was crucial for the world economy, among other reasons, he declared, that England and Germany remain friends.

The wine and liquor flowed, and the mood was fraternal. The Prince of Wales rose to offer a toast. He spoke with pride of the worthy German blood that ran through his veins.

"There is no need or purpose," he said, "in going to war for the benefit of foreign powers, and by this I mean France, the Communists, and international Jewry." A roar of applause greeted his words. "We need a strong friend as an ally . . . the same nation that helped us get rid of Bonaparte. An alliance with that power, and its leader, should be the cornerstone of our foreign policy."

It was an amazing speech, and one that remains engraved in my mind to this day. The Prince left the next morning, and I was not to see him again until our paths crossed in Nassau twelve years later.

By late 1935, his father, King George V, had fallen desperately ill. The Prince of Wales succeeded to the throne on January 26, 1936, and ruled for ten and a half months, all the while calculating how to make a twice-divorced woman acceptable as his queen. Instead he succeeded in creating a constitutional crisis, and the man who was briefly King Edward VIII abdicated before his coronation.

I read with interest of his visit to Germany and a private meeting with Hitler in 1937. He had become close friends with Joachim von Ribbentrop, once Germany's ambassador to Great Britain, later the Foreign Secretary, who was hanged as a war criminal after the Nuremberg trials.

As the Duke of Windsor, his marriage to Mrs. Wallis Warfield Simpson took place in Cannes, at the castle of Cande, in a ceremony witnessed by his German friends.

After war was declared, he turned up in Franco's Spain. There he became the focus of German intrigue, and rumors flourished of a serpentine plot that would result in Windsor replacing his brother on the throne and making an accommodation with Germany. Winston Churchill stepped in and sent his personal emissaries to meet with the Duke in Portugal, and alert him both to the dangers of his present position and to the need to move quickly in finding a secure base.

I might not have kept track of these events, except that Churchill resolved the matter by offering the Duke the post of governor of the Bahamas, an impoverished collection of islands in a remote corner of the globe. *Sic transit gloria mundi.* There we would meet again, for the last time.

Two remarks, I thought, crowned the debacle of the short reign of Edward VIII. The first was when he telephoned Mrs. Simpson, in Cannes, at the home of Herman Rogers, where she had taken refuge. According to the *New York Times,* in a January 1939 issue, when he told her of his decision to abdicate, she asked, 'TJavid! Can't you at least remain Emperor of India, even if you are no longer King of England?"

The second was when he advised the Queen Mother that he would abdicate if he was not allowed to marry Mrs. Simpson. The venerable queen answered with great poise and calm, "My son, then abdicate, because if such a thought is in your mind you are unfit to rule the British Empire." Nor did she leave any doubt about when he could return from exile: "On my death."

It was hard, and getting harder, to turn one's mind back to business. London was in a state of near hysteria; the stock market had soared and fortunes were being made. Lead and zinc had risen to twenty-five pounds. I cashed in Lord Ronald's futures and handed him a check for thirty thousand pounds. He thanked me heartily, and then exploded in a thunderous laugh: "Alfred, you have put me afloat for another year."

In Germany, Hitler was fulfilling his vow to rid the Reich of the Jews. Weinstein had learned that Mr. Meyer had been arrested and that Paul had been shot and killed in a scuffle with the Gestapo. In the confusion, Edith and her mother were able to slip away. I offered to leave immediately for Berlin and try to locate them.

On my part, there were no feelings of being noble or unselfish or even of the risk that might be involved. I was motivated by a concern for these kind and innocent people who had befriended me.

I was excited to be involved. I would have the exact feeling years later when I lived in Cuba, and helped a family to escape from Castro's punishment. Every revolution has its slogan to excuse its crimes. During the French Revolution it was "Liberty, fraternity, equality." Castro simply sent his victims to "El Paredon" (The Wall).

That evening I called Lord Ronald and told him I was to be in Berlin a few days on business. I asked him to contact Hans Bosch and advise him of my arrival. The money I had made for him was already paying dividends.

Berlin was crawling with SS men. Hans put a car and a French-speaking chauffeur at my disposal, and I spent the afternoon driving through Berlin in a Mercedes with a swastika flying from a small antenna on the right fender. I asked the chauffeur to drive through the neighborhood where the Meyer family lived. The homes were all large and opulent. Many of them had an ominous yellow flag hanging over their front doors. I asked what the flags meant, and the driver replied that the homes formerly belonged to Jews who had been evicted, and their homes impounded by the government. I sat back and tried to act relaxed and indifferent.

The next day I told Hans Bosch that I was trying to collect a debt from a young Jew I had met in London. I gave him Paul's name and address, and there was an instant flicker of recognition on his face. "That is old Simon Meyer's home," he said. "A very rich banker. He was arrested for tax evasion, his home impounded. If my memory is correct, he had a son who tried to resist, and was shot by the police. That was a quite recent affair."

I thanked Hans for his courtesy and asked if it would be possible to visit the Meyer house. "I am curious to see how those bastards lived," I said.

He scribbled a note on the back of his card and handed it to me. "Give this to the driver," he said, "and you may visit the home of every dispossessed Jew in town, if you like."

Later that day, I rang the doorbell at the Meyer address. The Gestapo had taken over the house, but old Gretel was still the housekeeper. Out of the hearing of two guards, I told her I had returned to try to get Edith and her mother out of the country. She whispered their hiding place to me: 32 Von Molk Street, in the town of Rathenow. I was to ask for a Dr. Ludwig.

I dismissed the chauffeur, whom I wasn't sure I could trust, and from the hotel took a taxi to the train station. Rathenow was a small industrial town, at which four trains stopped daily.

It was early afternoon when I reached my destination. The streets were deserted. Almost everyone worked at the various factories on the edge of town. Von Molk Street was close by, and I easily found the address Gretel had given me. Like all German towns and villages, Rathenow was immaculate. It was surprisingly quiet, and I noticed a complete absence of SS troopers.

Dr. Ludwig lived in a solid brick house with a vegetable garden on both sides and flower beds in the front. I rang the bell several times before a maid appeared and spoke to me in German. 'Wo *sprecken Deutsch,* " I said.

A moment later the doctor was studying me from head to toe. "I am sorry, Herr Doctor," I said, "but I speak only French and English."

"I speak both. What can I do for you?"

I explained that I was trying to locate Mrs. Meyer and her daughter. I gave him my name and added that Gretel had provided me with his address. He said nothing. "Mr. Jaime Weinstcin and I are their friends," I said. "We are trying to get the two ladies out of Germany."

His eyes bored into mine. Silently he got up and left the room. He returned ten minutes later and seemed out of breath. "Please come," he said.

I followed him through the back door, down a narrow path that led to a neighbor's garden, and then to a huge wall. Dr. Ludwig unlocked a wooden gate in the wall, and I found myself in the garden of a convent. A nun was waiting for us. She took us through a long passage, up a flight of stairs, and into a small vestibule, where we were asked to take a seat.

We had been sitting only a minute or two when an inner door opened, and there stood Edith. She ran toward me and embraced me, with tears rolling down her cheeks. We could not utter one word. It took several minutes for the three of us to regain our composure, to get out the hard words about their father and Paul, and how and why I had come.

Edith said, "Alfred, I prayed for many days and nights. When I saw you, I knew my prayers had been heard." The wife of Dr. Ludwig was a cousin to Mrs. Meyer. The good sisters had offered them shelter; there were now twenty Jews living in the convent.

We did not have much time. I opened the camera I'd brought with me, and took several photographs of each. I got their fingerprints and signatures, their dress and shoe sizes. I placed the film and the notes in a compartment in the camera case. I told them I would be back in Paris the next day, and would contact them as soon as forged documents could be prepared for them.

I caught the last train to Berlin that night, and connected with the express to Paris.

Jaime Weinstein was waiting when I walked into his office the next morning. I gave him every detail of my trip. "There are no alternatives," he said. "Don Alfredo, you know if you are caught it might mean death or a Nazi jail. I do not know which is worse."

I nodded that I understood, but wanted to continue. "First we must get Edith out," he said. "That will take more preparation, due to her youth and her heavy German accent. Her mother should not be as difficult. Did you get the articles I needed?"

I handed him the items I'd hidden in the leather camera case. Piece by piece, he inspected them, then laid out his plan. I was to reenter Germany, using my real passport. Edith and I were to leave as a newly married couple, Mr. Robert Dupuis, born in Paris, and Jeanne Dupuis, of Metz. That would explain her accent, and why she had to enter France at the Saar, where nearly everyone had a German accent. The wedding certificate would show that we had been married thirty days ago, the normal time for obtaining a passport from the government.

I was to leave France on the first of September and go to Cologne, where I would visit a Franz von Speck, a Gentile friend and business associate of Weinstein, who would be expecting me. Edith and I were supposed to have stayed at his home during our honeymoon. That would explain why our passports did not have the police stamp required for hotel guests.

He also gave me ten thousand marks for the good sisters. His secretary had packed one of the suitcases with clothes, including shoes and even an overcoat for Edith.

Everything was ready within forty-eight hours. My passport, as Robert Dupuis, was flawless. Edith's, as my wife, was no less perfect. The marriage certificate was adorned with a gold seal and a tricolor ribbon, and held together by a wax seal embossed with the arms of the city of Paris.

On the first of September, Weinstein accompanied me to the rail station. I said *au revoir* and swung aboard the train.

The trip went smoothly. I slept until we crossed the border. There a guard looked at my British passport, stamped it, and waved me through without checking my luggage. An hour later I was having breakfast with Mr. Weinstein's friend, Herr von Speck. He read the letter addressed to him, and received me warmly. Around noon, he drove me to the station, reassuring me that I could count on his cooperation.

Berlin was lovely that evening. The weather was brisk and the moon full, which I took as a favorable omen. I registered as Alfred de Marigny in a small hotel by the station, and told the manager I would be leaving early the next morning. At nine, I was on the train rolling toward Rathenow. The trip seemed to take an eternity.

I left my suitcase at the station and carried Edith's luggage to the Ludwig home. The doctor greeted me at the door, and we went directly to the convent. I believe the prospect of seeing her daughter taken to safety was no more exciting to Mrs. Meyer than the sight of Edith dressed again in fine clothes. The parting was difficult. I promised her that within a few days I would return to bring out her mother. But now we had to concentrate on the journey just ahead of us. I schooled her on the details of our cover story, upon which our safety depended. She recited for me the names and dates and addresses. I added that if any question arose, I would do the talking.

I gave the sister the envelope containing Weinstein's gift. Mrs. Meyer fought back tears, but smiled. "Darling, I shall be with you in a few days," she told Edith with conviction.

We walked to the train station, where we had almost an hour to wait. We picked out a bench in the empty waiting room, and I took Edith's hand in mind. Only then did I notice the wedding band. "I see one of them fitted your finger," I said.

She did not respond. There was nothing I could say to relieve her tension. I told her to make an effort to smile and appear happy. We were supposed to be on our honeymoon.

Finally she smiled and touched my cheek.

We arrived in Berlin during the dinner hour, and passed through Frankfurt in the middle of the night. We had some six hours to wait for the connection to the Saar. We were both exhausted, mentally and physically.

We left our luggage at the depot and walked up and down the immense platform to stretch our legs. By two in the morning, Edith was hungry. The restaurant at the station was open all night, and we passed more time over cold roast chicken and salad. I bought a German newspaper and Edith read it, translating the news for me.

Dawn began to break and, finally, at eight in the morning, the train arrived, belching smoke. It was the last leg of our trip to the French border.

As luck would have it, we had caught what appeared to be a milk train, which stopped at every station and took three hours to cover a hundred miles. Edith was restless and miserable. I told her to put her head on my shoulder and sleep and, even if she was awake, not to move until we reached the border. She fell asleep almost instantly.

A couple of hours had slipped by when two uniformed officers appeared at the door of the compartment. They spoke to me in German. I placed my finger to my mouth and nodded at the sleeping Edith. One of the officers smiled and asked, in French, for our passports. I handed him the documents. His companion noted the lack of a hotel stamp, and asked us where we had stayed. I explained without hesitation that we were on our honeymoon and had been the guests of a family friend, Herr Franz von Speck, and I gave his address in Cologne. The guard stamped both passports. One of them asked if I had German marks in my possession. I had a few, and was told to keep them.

The two officers left. Thirty minutes later we crossed the border into France. Edith grasped both my hands and said softly, "God bless you, Alfred."

For the first time since I had known him, Weinstein was excited and showed it. We drank champagne, and Edith beamed with happiness. The next morning we began to plan the rescue of Mrs. Meyer. There were other problems to overcome. To begin with, it would be difficult for me to carry two suitcases without the risk of having them opened. Weinstein decided that a woman in his office, who was not Jewish, would travel with me to Berlin and take a room at the Enden Hotel, as Mrs. Meyer would. I was to carry to Rathenow the English-made clothes she would need for the trip to Berlin. Mrs. Meyer had saved a few pieces of jewelry and would wear them. She needed to maintain a certain appearance, since her English passport was in the name of Lady Berkley, with visas for Italy, Spain, and France. Dozens of entries and exits covered the pages.

The bags were from Harrod's and again indicated a reasonable amount of wear. She would stay in Berlin for two days, then take the train to Stuttgart and cross the border at Basel. I was to take her safely into Switzerland. The woman from Weinstein's office would remain in Berlin until Mrs. Meyer's arrival from Rathenow, at which point she would return to Paris.

Mrs. Meyer was an attentive pupil. I gave her a substantial sum of money in marks, pounds sterling, and Swiss currency. When she checked into her hotel in Berlin, she looked quite opulent, wearing her pearls, rings, and earrings. The hotel staff greeted her with bows, and she quickly disappeared into her room. The next morning, Weinstein's employee left for France.

That afternoon we boarded the train for Switzerland. Mrs. Meyer's British passport went unquestioned, and soon we had left Germany behind. I checked her into the Grand Hotel at Lausanne, and returned to Paris. Weary and drained, I slept all the way to the French capital. Deep in my soul, I felt a mixture of great happiness and sorrow. I had kept my promise to Paul. Still, a sadness filled my heart at the thought of my friend's fate, a death that was meaningless, the end of a young life full of promise and ambition.

I remained in Paris long enough to see Weinstein. The same day I was on my way to London.

The stock market had gone up and down. The contracts for lead and zinc had reached the unprecedented price of thirty pounds. I liquidated my stocks, and in one stroke of the pen I was a rich man.

There was nothing to keep me in England. The idea of leaving Europe was growing more attractive by the day. America had always fascinated me as a place where the land was vast and open, the people hospitable. I could never forget the library a generous American, Andrew Carnegie, had given to us in Mauritius so that we could keep abreast of the world. I had spent the best hours of my childhood there.

To see Andrew Carnegie's land now seemed essential to me.

COMING TO AMERICA

I knew that I was leaving behind the Old World, in every sense, that summer of 1936. I crossed the Atlantic on the SS *Normandie*, the flagship of the French Line, the most luxurious ocean liner afloat.

The *Normandie* was a city on the sea. The first-class cabins were opulent, each decorated by a French artist, with a separate bedroom, living room, and bath. But my lasting memory of the voyage was not the luxury of the ship, but the rough texture of a friendship formed there.

A day out of port, I strolled through the various decks and ended on the top promenade, where the lounge was a popular retreat. A couple was already at the bar, the woman blond and very attractive. Her companion was almost as tall as I, with broad shoulders and a big, mocking smile. He studied me for a moment, then spoke: 'I'll roll you for a round."

I was startled, but not annoyed by the challenge. The barman brought the dice, and he won. I ordered a sherry. He was drinking Pernod. We introduced ourselves. She was Martha Gellhorn. His name was Ernest Hemingway.

"Frenchie, I shall give you another chance," he said.

I raised my hand. "I am a very light drinker," I said, declining.

Later, the couple in the cabin next to mine saw us together, and asked me to invite my new acquaintance to a cocktail party. My curiosity was aroused. I wondered what could interest them in a fellow I had pegged as a bit of a ruffian, perhaps a promoter of sports, a horse breeder or bookmaker. His conversation was pointed, his jokes salty, his manner brusque. I decided to ask him what he did for a living. Martha laughed with great delight.

"Don't tell me you never heard of Ernie?"

"Any reason why I should?"

"Have you read *The Sun Also Rises?*"

I felt my face redden. I looked at Martha, then at Ernie. He was watching me with a delighted grin. I slapped my forehead with my hand. "Of course. Ernest Hemingway!"

"The great writer," Martha laughed, finishing my sentence. We were to become close friends and remain so to his death. His granddaughter, Margaux, and one of my sons, Philip, were baptized on the same day in Havana. I became her godfather.

The next afternoon we competed in a skeet-shooting tournament, which I won with a borrowed Belgian gun. Ernie finished third, behind a Spaniard, and once we had adjourned again to the bar, he rebroadcast the match.

I kidded him about being a great talker, and he retorted, "A great lover, too."

I proposed another wager, a round of drinks, on which of us was the better in that area. It amounted to which one could tell the bigger lie about his first sexual experience. I won.

He paid for the round. I had the feeling that this silly game sealed our friendship. Twice in the same day I had bettered him. Hemingway loved winners. He had a macho personality and could accept nothing less from his friends.

I was on deck early when the *Normandie* entered New York Harbor. From a distance, in the morning mist, I could see the Statue of Liberty, holding aloft the torch that the New World had lit in the soul of mankind. All of downtown Manhattan seemed to awaken to our arrival. Sirens came alive, tugboats swarmed around the enormous hull of the liner. The sounds of the city reached out to us, trucks rumbling along the dock, car horns honking.

Customs and Immigration awaited the passengers in an immense room. The level of noise was strange to me. No one walked. Everyone was in a rush. I was relieved to find a taxi to take me to the Waldorf-Astoria Hotel.

Hemingway called in the morning to ask me to meet him at the office of his lawyer, Maurice Speiser.

I had taken a genuine liking to Ernie. He was a character, wonderful to have around, always drawn to the center of the stage, always prepared to talk about himself. I noticed that he was addicted to Pernod, a miserable French drink that over a period of time can have an adverse affect on the mind.

"In Paris, all artists and writers drank Pernod," he said. "It was fashionable. So I developed a taste for it."

He told me about his early years, when he had had to scramble for a living. To earn food for his wife and son, he was a sparring partner to Georges Carpentier, the French champion who fought bravely in a loss to Jack Dempsey.

His eyes had a faraway look. "It was *la vie de boheme*," he said, "to its last detail. I was broke, trying to sell short stories, magazine articles, without success. Mind you, those were tough times. I had a young wife and my son Bombie [Jack] to support."

He left his family to write, living like a hermit in a village in the south of France, hardly leaving his room until he had finished twenty short stories. He caught the train to Paris to deliver them to a publisher, and on the train he bumped into a friend he had not seen in years. They talked and drank, and when the train reached Paris they hurried to a bar at the station to continue to celebrate their reunion. The train pulled out with Ernest's stories right where he left them, in his seat. "Never saw them again," he said. "Best stuff I ever wrote."

I decided on our first meeting to retain Speiser as my attorney.

I marked him as a shrewd judge of people. "Ernie is an engima," he told me, out of Hemingway's hearing. "Breaks every rule in the book. One minute he is kind and almost gentle, the next he may sock you in the jaw and call you a son of a bitch."

I would see that side of him in the better barrooms of New York. Liquor did not bring out his best. He would pick a silly fight with some idiot, and flatten him with one punch. Then he would pick up the poor slob and invite him to have a drink. Everyone was amused, except possibly the fellow who had been slugged.

Speiser had negotiated a movie deal for his next book, and when the papers were signed, Ernie invited me to his home in Key West. The house was empty, his wife having gone north to visit her mother. It was the beginning of summer, and I looked forward to sunshine, citrus, and the sea.

Ernie was in his element on Key West. We went out in his thirty-five-foot cruiser, the *Pilar*, and fished for marlin. Hemingway landed a big one, and everyone in every bar along the Keys knew about it. He downed many drinks, and retold many times the same story. A few days later we left for Havana. The journey across the Gulf Stream was dreadful, the small boat rolling and pitching without mercy. I felt relieved to see Morro Castle, and we met calm water in the lee of the island.

Hemingway had secured rooms at a Chinese hotel downtown, which turned out to be a fleabag. But he was a friend of the owner and liked the location, a block or two from the Floridita, where he camped all morning, drinking frozen daiquiris.

Havana was a beautiful city, nearly unspoiled, very old and pleasantly dirty. Cubans were vagabonds. They seemed to live on the street day and night. They loved loud music, and when they lifted their glasses it was to toast wine, love, and money.

Most of the Basques living in Havana were refugees from Spain. They hated Franco and could never forgive the bombing of Guernica, the holy city, which had been razed by the Luftwaffe as a demonstration of the effectiveness of terror bombing of civilian targets. The Basques wanted to preserve their religion, traditions, culture, and language, whose roots are lost in antiquity. They loved Ernie, who wrote moving stories about their province and had stood beside them during the Civil War.

On our last night, he took me to the Basque club, the Centro Basco, in an old building at the entrance of the Malecon, along the seafront. Red wine flowed from wicker-covered jugs, and the stories flowed as freely, until a silence crept across the room. Hemingway stood, and one by one his companions rose with him. I looked around to see a dark-haired woman walking toward us with the grace of a queen, completely sure of herself.

Ernie reached out to her and she took a seat beside him, across the table from me. Her red blouse gave fire to a striking face. She wore large hoop earrings and no makeup. Her black eyebrows formed an arch over her nose, which made her look hard, yet the moment she smiled, her expression changed and the seriousness melted away. The eyes turned soft, full of warmth.

Hemingway introduced us. Her name, Pilar, instantly struck a chord; he had named his boat after this woman. The three of us walked back to the Chinese Hotel. Ernie said good night at my door and walked with Pilar toward his room.

As we rode the choppy waves out of Havana, he told me that they had met during the Spanish Civil War. She was a leader of the Republicans, a patriot. "I wanted to marry her then," he said. He turned his head from me and spoke into the wind, as if talking to himself: "We didn't, of course. That was the way the chips fell."

When the time came to leave Hemingway, in Key West, I felt sad and lonely in a way I had not felt since childhood. His casual way of living appealed to me mightily. I hated regimentation, and never could picture myself seated behind a desk. The most beautiful tiger in the zoo is always well fed, but is still behind bars. I had no ties to shackle me, no home, no family, no country of my own. Ernie's friends, the Basques, a simple people with roots close to the soil, sensed in me the nature of a gypsy. Many years later, if I met an old Basque friend in Mexico or Miami, I was greeted as "El Gitano (the Gypsy.)"

I would not see Hemingway again for a leisurely visit until after my trial, but we kept in touch through Speiser. I learned that he had obtained his divorce, married Martha Gellhorn, moved to Havana, and finished a new novel, his biggest yet.

When the book was published, in 1940, one connection was not difficult to make. The black-haired beauty I had met in Havana was the Pilar of *For Whom the Bell Tolls,* the heroine of the Civil War, a woman Spanish men were willing to follow to the death, the woman who "made the earth move" when she and the novel's hero, Robert Jordan, made love in the famous sleeping bag.

Speiser also enjoyed keeping me up to date on the adventures of the new Duke of Windsor. On one visit to his office, he greeted me with a pile of newspaper clippings he had saved. I regarded the British monarchy as an archaic system that could never be transplanted, but the American press tried. The New York papers could not get enough of the Royal Family's soiled linen. One day the Duke was fawned over, the next ridiculed.

On the third of June 1937, six months after the abdication, days after her divorce was final, the former King of England and Wallis Simpson were wed at the Château de Candé The *Times* reported that the honeymooners were traveling with 225 pieces of luggage, including 185 steamer trunks. In Italy, Mussolini placed his personal railway car at their disposal. The Windsors visited Austria and finally returned to Paris.

I had no reason to think we would ever meet again, but my interest in the Duke was heightened by my awareness of his political leanings. On occasion, these were also noted by the press.

On October 13, *The New York Times* carried an account

of a dinner honoring the Duke and Duchess, given by von Ribbentrop. Also present were Heinrich Himmler and Hermann Goering, Hitler's adjutant, and other officials of the German Foreign Office. Ten days later, Hitler himself received the Duke, after making him wait one hour. Of his decision to see for himself the Third Reich's industries, and social institutions, the *Times* noted:

The Duke is reported to have become very critical of English policies as he sees them, and is reported as declaring that the

British ministers of today, and their possible successors, are no match either for the German or Italian dictators.

Shortly after, von Ribbentrop, the new ambassador to the Court of St. James's, when presented to their majesties, gave the Nazi salute three times, as is becoming when saluting a sovereign, shouting each time, "Heil Hitler." The Duke, in his travels, continues to give a modified Hitler salute (halfway between a wave and extending his arm).

Nothing I read surprised me. I had no illusions about the man I had known as the Prince of Wales. It was hard, but by no means impossible, to penetrate the mythology that had grown around him. He was perceived outside England as the sweet prince, a romantic figure who had placed love above a crown. Even in Nassau, removed from the war, feeling useless but clinging to the trappings of the kingdom, he commanded a certain sympathy. Except for the occasional hints and innuendos in the press, the myth helped conceal for a long time his pro-Nazi instincts.

Of course, in these matters I find it hard to be impartial, much less charitable. I saw him as a man of unending doubts, who felt deprived of the power and wealth to which his birth and training had pointed him. No figure in history had more excuses made for him, before and after he shirked the responsibility for which he had been groomed since birth.

How far away London now seemed, and the spasms of the

British monarchy. In New York, my love of sailing gave me an entree to Long Island's clubby society circles. This was Gatsby country, and the life seemed to revolve around the exclusive Piping Rock Club, where the cost of membership alone was then $75,000.

Every weekend the activity moved to one or another lavish estate, where guests sat beside the tennis courts most did not play on and the swimming pools they did not swim in.

I met Paul Shields, then the head of the New York Stock Exchange, but better known to me as a champion sailor and the father-in-law of the actor Gary Cooper. In a year or two I would be competing against Shields in international races.

The home of Alfred Vanderbilt boasted an indoor Olympic-size swimming pool, heated in winter, as well as an indoor tennis court and an exercise room with a masseur, barber, and manicurist. This was forty years before the era of home gymnasiums and "pumping iron."

One weekend resembled another; only the homes were different, each one more palatial than the last, the lawn greener or the hedges higher. As a houseguest of Coster Schermerhorn and his wife, Ruth, I walked into a room where a group of men were kneeling and sitting in a circle on the floor, sipping cognac and playing what I soon learned was craps. Though I had never played, I knew of the game. It had been introduced to the States in New Orleans, a century before, by one of my great-uncles, Bertrand de Marigny, who, like his father and grandfather, was buried in the Cathedral of St. Louis in that city.

Coster was a pleasant-looking man in his late forties, a senior partner of the brokerage firm Fahnestock and Company. His friends called him Schemie. Ruth's family, the Fahnestocks, had founded the firm. She was a stunning blonde, with green eyes full of life. She spoke to me in perfect French.

The Schermerhorns were among the earliest settlers from Holland, who came to New York when that patch of land was called New Amsterdam. I arranged to invest my funds with

Coster and, to my eternal regret, entered into a disastrous love affair with his wife.

Our romance started with a phone call, hers, and a drink in the bar of my hotel. What followed seemed inevitable. The adventure that afternoon opened for me a Pandora's Box, and I was soon to find myself in the center of a maelstrom that was to begin the chain of events at the end of which I would find myself in the Nassau jail.

One day Ruth appeared at my door and announced that she had told her husband "everything," had asked for a divorce, had agreed to give up custody of her daughter. And she told me she and I would be married as soon as the papers were final.

All of which was news to me. Not a word had passed between us regarding her plans, or mine. I was still discovering America, and had allowed myself six months of leisure before settling down to business. There was no room for Ruth on my schedule.

My honest anger was no match for her tears. She could not believe I would reject her after she had just proved how much she loved me, had walked out on her husband, and was prepared to give up her child.

I did not know how Schemie had accepted the news, but I was dumbfounded. I was filled with dread. But she had touched a raw fiber. Deep inside myself, I could hear the same words my mother must have spoken when she decided to leave her home, her religion, and her only son for the man she loved.

The next day, a "blind" item appeared in the gossip column of Cholly Knickerbocker (the pseudonym of Igor Cassini). A Long Island socialite, he wrote, was divorcing her husband to marry a Don Juan from Mauritius. That evening, Walter Winchell repeated the same news on his network radio broadcast.

In New York, the press continued to educate me. No one was certain of my origin. From story to story, they moved me from Mauritius to South Africa to France. Ruth was a rich socialite, then an heiress. With each article her wealth grew.

I was in the process of acquiring two things I least needed: a reputation and a wife.

Maurice Speiser told me that it would take ninety days in Reno for Ruth to establish a residence in Nevada and obtain her divorce. He suggested that I get away for a while, take a trip to Nassau, and relax by the sea. He painted Nassau with rainbow colors. I decided to follow his advice.

PART FOUR

ISLANDS IN THE SUN

If one will sit on his doorstep and wait, he will see the corpse of his enemy pass by.

CHINESE PROVERB

PIRATES' ISLAND

DESCRIPTIONS of Nassau have often made it seem a combination of Tahiti and the Barbary Coast. An unspoiled tropical haven was the fantasy many pursued, but it concealed a brutal, cutthroat legacy. My first sight of the island is as clear to me now as it was then, in that balmy spring of 1937. The woman I was apparently engaged *to* marry had left for Reno to get her divorce. The steamer *Mungaro* docked around nine in the morning. Tourists poured out of the belly of the ship to be greeted ashore by a crowd of blacks in colorful attire, talking, laughing, busy at doing nothing, each a potential guide hustling a client.

I followed the motley crowd to the Prince George Hotel, a short distance down the harbor. An old-fashioned, single-story hotel, it had been the first in Nassau in the days of rum-running. In the main bar, tradition required that the first rum punch be provided free to the tourists off the boats.

I drifted to a table overlooking the channel between the mainland and Hog Island. The water stretched as far as the eye could see, a multihued expanse of emerald green, deep blue, and ribbons of white. The dark shadows of small clouds hurrying in front of the sun gave the picture movement and kept it alive. This beautiful sight reminded me of my home, far away. It brought joy and sadness to my heart.

Nassau and the other islands of the Bahamian archipelago had a long history of robbery, cruelty, and murder. Christopher Columbus discovered the islands in 1492, and they were awarded by papal grant to Spain; only pirates ruled the archipelago until it was taken over by the British in 1629. But the administrators sent out from London were ignored, or worse—one was roasted on a spit.

In 1710, Captain Woodes Rogers, the first Royal Governor, arrived, pardoned a thousand pirates, and, on behalf of King Charles, gave them small plots of land. The piracy didn't really end, but some rules were established.

It was to the Bahamas that many British loyalists fled after the American Revolution. The colony would become self-governing by the end of the eighteenth century, with an elected House of Assembly and a Governor General appointed in London.

The loneliness of the Out Islands attracted these early British settlers. Here could be found barren stretches of limestone and pink, sandy beaches. Miles of coral reefs protected them from the Atlantic waves, and formed lagoons rich in fish.

Nearly devoid of vegetation, these islands were uninhabited except by a handful of escaped slaves who survived on what the sea had to offer. The pilgrims from the American colonies established settlements among the Out Islands, and to their dismay, small groups of blacks drifted toward them in search of food and work. They terrified the whites, who had come from a land where a black man was an oddity. Still, they needed the Negroes to do the back-breaking farmwork, raising crops out of shallow craters and nonexistent soil. To relieve their fear that the races would mingle, producing an inferior breed, they adopted a form of apartheid. Under no circumstances could a black remain in the settlements after sun-down, under penalty of being shot on sight.

Strict enforcement of the rules assured the Out Islands of two distinct groups of inhabitants: pure white and pure black. The latter were proud people and, whatever their standard of living, they felt superior to the mixture that soon evolved in Nassau. A few white families controlled the business on the island. The mulattoes, who were many, held jobs as lawyers, schoolteachers, and civil servants. And the Negroes worked as domestics and small shopkeepers.

By the middle of the nineteenth century, Nassau was a poor and insignificant fishing village. Those who lived on the Out Islands had nothing.

One night a storm washed up the wreckage of a ship. It was as if the Sesame doors had swung open before their eyes. Under salvage law, everything on the ship became the property of those who found it. To make certain there would be no one left to file a claim, they summarily killed the captain and any crewmen still alive, and threw their bodies into the sea.

The ship's carcass was picked clean. The lumber itself was valuable in a place where trees were at a premium. It dawned upon the settlers that shipwrecking could be the industry they had never had. They lured their prey with fires set on dangerous reefs. When the new moon and bad weather became their allies, they moved to the lower end of the bay, there to hide and wait, armed with knives.

Every man, woman, and child took part in the gruesome performance. The wait could be long and the nights empty.

Once the ships broached the reefs, tearing their bellies with a thundering noise, the scavengers raced to the beach, screaming and brandishing their knives, intent on butchering the half-drowned victims who had managed to scramble to dry land. After the men had left, the women checked the dead and finished off any who were still breathing. The children emptied their pockets and stole their coins and rings.

When the storm passed, it left a beach littered with death. The bodies were dragged back into the water, where they were carried off by the tide, to be eaten by waiting sharks. The cargo was hauled ashore, loot for the winners. Lifeboats were treasured. They were suitable for fishing. The skeleton of the ship was dismantled and put to use. Everything disappeared.

In a matter of hours, a calm returned to the island, the

stench of death and all traces of the slaughter having been washed away by the wind that cleansed the air and the sea breaking on the reefs. It was as if nothing had happened. Life went on. The wreckers digested their plunder and prepared for the next round. No regrets, no sense of wrong, no guilt. It was simply a new and more efficient way of doing business.

This morbid practice became an industry of such dimensions that the maritime nations complained bitterly to the International Lighthouse Service. They appealed to have fixed lights placed along the coastline to enable the skippers sailing those waters to establish their positions safely.

Nassau's merchants reacted as expected. They dispatched a delegation to London, and protested to the Colonial Office that such measures would deprive the Bahamians of their just means of existence, starving their wives and children.

This objection was ignored, and the deliberate wrecking of ships came to an end. Nassau and the Out Islands once again knew bitter poverty. They fished for food and survival.

Now certain forces combined to change the rules once more. War broke out between France and Germany. The isolationists were having their way in Congress, and America would not declare war on Germany until 1917. Meanwhile, the U.S. had passed the Volstead Act and the country had gone dry.

Overnight, Nassau became the international capital of bootlegging. The Florida coast was almost uninhabited, and shipping liquor to the mainland was a simple affair. All one needed was a boat. Every trip meant big profits and the money filled many pockets.

The pickings were easy but, alas, short-lived. Organized crime moved into Florida and chased the Nassau boys back to their island. They accepted the new conditions, having no choice, and settled down to supplying liquor to the gangsters. The profits were more modest, but steady and reliable. The local merchants began to look toward a future ripe with promise.

Soon another, unexpected streak of luck came their way. Sponges had become valuable and the sandy bottoms of the bays were covered with them. A new industry emerged in Nassau.

The large fleet of small boats formerly used for rum-running now became carriers of a legal freight. The new cash flowed into the hands of a small and powerful clique, which became known as the Bay Street Merchants.

Bay Street was the main artery, five blocks long, lined by stores and small shops dedicated to fleecing the tourists. The road hugged the Nassau coast from east to west, snaking past the tropical gardens of the British Colonial Hotel, to a barren, rocky stretch near the golf club where Cable Beach began.

Whites and mulattoes had settled on the eastern end of the island, which was bathed year round by a cool prevailing breeze. Down the road were the Bluebeard Tower and the Yacht Club, the latter of which made up in history what it lacked in elegance. The governor of that period, Bede Clifford, had befriended Edward VII when he was Prince of Wales.

The governor loved sailing. He introduced in Nassau a sailing sloop that initiated the Corsair class. He then petitioned the King to grant a royal charter to the Nassau Sailing Club. His Majesty not only accepted the petition, but gave to the newborn Royal Nassau Yacht Club a gold challenge cup. The winner of the King's Cup would receive as a memento a small replica of the original.

From the center of town, one could see the Negro section, halfway up the ridge, a couple of hundred feet above sea level and rising to the top of what was known as the Hill. Groves of fruit and shade trees kept the area cool and free of mosquitoes. On the highest point of the Hill squatted the Nassau jail, once a fortress.

To the west of town was Government House, an old wooden colonial building with verandas, and a garden abloom with hibiscus and oleander. The British had intended it to be the home of the resident governor. No one in his right mind could have imagined that one day it would turn out to be the home of the ex-King of England.

Government House overlooked Victoria Square, adorned with a life-size statue of Her Majesty, Victoria, known to the natives as Aunt Wikki, who freed the slaves. The business district started here. The courts of justice were to the south, with government offices to the left and the police station on the right.

The sudden influx of money from liquor and sponges was wisely used to refurbish the entire street. Buildings were repaired and repainted. Others added a second story that became the offices of lawyers, doctors, and moneylenders. The ground floors were reserved for the shops that catered to the occasional tourist, offering French perfume, Irish linen, and English china. All the stores were the property of the Bay Street Merchants.

The new Royal Bank of Canada gave the street an aura of stability. It was flanked on one side by the old Prince George Hotel, and on the other by the picturesque Sponge Market, which filled the air with a pungent ocean smell and attracted tourists with a taste for the exotic.

In 1938, one walked past Chinese and Greek restaurants and a bakery, and around the Botanical Gardens, to reach the British Colonial Hotel. It was a splendid example of the bastard architecture so popular by then in Florida, a blend of Spanish design and local guesswork as to what a hotel in the tropics should look like.

Bay Street snaked along a barren, rocky stretch near the shoreline. The golf course was a few miles away. The view from that end of Nassau was startling, a vista of tall trees and greenery. This was the entrance to Cable Beach. The road cut through the golf course, with the clubhouse and tennis courts on the sea side and the links all the way to the ridge on the other. To the left of the golf club stood Westbourne, a rambling, two-story building that had been recently purchased by the Canadian millionaire Harry Oakes.

Fate apparently had decreed that Nassau go through cycles of abundance and calamities. The election of Franklin Roosevelt to the U.S. presidency was followed in 1933 by the repeal of the Volstead Act. The bottom dropped out of the liquor business, a setback soon coupled with a blight that wiped out the sponges. Nassau faced a depression reminiscent of the days when shipwrecking was abolished.

In times of emergency, someone invariably rises above the rest of the people to become the savior of a nation or state. In the case of Nassau, that person was a local real-estate genius and a man of strong vision: Harold Christie. He was not one of the Bay Street Boys. He was the owner of a small tourist agency, and that was all.

He had, however, great faith in the future of his island. He also had an abundance of gall and savvy. As weeks went by, the situation became appalling. Unemployment soared as business disappeared. Harold chose that very moment to invite the Bay Street Boys to his office. He needed few words to explain to the merchants that Nassau had nothing to sell to the world but a mild climate, a beautiful sea, and lovely, subtropical surroundings. He told them that those assets never had been exploited.

As a salesman, Harold had the gift of believing everything he heard himself say, even if he knew it to be untrue. He urged them to adopt a long-range plan. They had ridden the roller coaster of rags and riches, and the results had been disastrous. He convinced them that they had no choice but to accept his advice.

Christie outlined a marketing plan for the tourist trade. He divided them into three categories: (1) those who came for the day; (2) the working people who scrimped and saved and came for a holiday; and (3) the group that counted—the wealthy. They bought land and built vacation homes. They spent months at a time on the island and returned year after year, bringing guests who in turn joined them as part-time residents. These would provide a steady income to the merchants.

Christie could not suppress a smile when he explained about his special third category. These were the beautiful people, the wealthy men and women of the East Coast who were in search of fun and merriment.

Christie had shown them a road to fortune and, at last, a stable base for the development of the island.

He traveled to the playgrounds of England, Canada, and the United States, and to the banking centers of London, Toronto, and New York, selling his message. And they came in waves: the British, including Frederick Sigrist, who designed England's most modern fighter plane, the Spitfire; the Canadians, beginning with Sir Frederick William Taylor, the president of the Royal Bank of Canada; and the Americans, such as Mr. Lynch of the investment firm Merrill Lynch, Pierce, Fenner and Beane.

Harold and his partners purchased land cheaply from the natives and sold it to the newcomers at a substantial profit. His influence grew daily. He was no longer asking for Bay Street's support; he was issuing orders.

He was elected to the Governor's Council. He was now, by virtue of that membership, the Honourable Harold Christie, forty-seven, a bachelor, the new godfather of the Bay Street Boys.

And so the opening of one network led to another. The younger Americans fell in with such Nassau-born playboys as Brice Pender, who owned the Pepsi-Cola distributorship on the island. He lived in a handsome cottage on Cable Beach, worked hard and played hard, and had several marriages behind him. His friends were wealthy in their own right.

Christie had lured them away from their other spas, in such places as Spain and Portugal, with promises of an expanded golf course, the finest fishing and water skiing, good but inexpensive liquor, and casino gambling. He confided that Nassau would shortly have an airport, as well as commuter boat service to New York and Miami. He had not the faintest idea how to fulfill those wild promises, but he knew that the playboys wanted fun and cared little about the details.

Soon Pender's friends were buying land near his own on Cable Beach, and Harold helped them in the construction of their cottages. That part of the island became, of course, the American colony. In pursuit of the sweet life, they set the pace. They played golf for high stakes, drank too much, and awakened with hangovers in beds they shared with wives or girlfriends who were not always their own.

In that circle, marriages never lasted long. The wife of one season would return the next as the mistress of a friend of her ex-husband. It was as if no rules existed in Nassau, no etiquette, no interference. It was, for those who indulged in it, a life of endless self-pleasuring.

I would never belong to that set, or any other. I spent most of my hours working, taking my leisure on the water. These were not my closest friends. Their world was not mine. But when my character was open for examination by all, it was against this social setting that I would be identified and judged.

Every dollar Christie made in sales or commission was invested in Lyford Cay, a garden spot at the extreme tip of Nassau. The cay hung off the road into the sea as an afterthought of nature.

Here Christie owned fifty acres of sand dunes, which cost him little to buy, but a fortune to develop. It had beaches and the eternal white, green, and blue water on three sides. Harold had plans to turn that sandy area into an exclusive and palatial club for the very wealthy. He had piped in fresh water from town at a tremendous cost, covered the sand with a carpet of grass, and landscaped the rest with coconut and fast-growing casuarina trees. Masses of flowering plants added color, and along the beach, sea grape trees protected the sun worshipers from the midday rays.

A couple of docks were under construction, and a marina was on the drawing board. The only thing lacking to bring the dream to reality was access to unlimited sums of money. Harold's expenses always won a footrace with his earnings. He was gambling everything on Lyford Cay and the future millions he was sure the property would bring him.

While Harold Christie worried about the future of Lyford Cay, Harry Oakes had arrived in Palm Beach, Florida, in late 1934. A stranger to that part of the map, he checked into the largest hotel in town with his wife, Eunice, and his five children. His first objective was to retain a lawyer who would reassure him about his status with the Internal Revenue Service. Taxes were an obsession with Oakes.

The hotel manager recommended a firm a few blocks away. Without an appointment, Oakes walked into the office and told the receptionist he wished to speak to the senior partner. The young lady took one look at the little man wearing a checkered suit and a shirt and tie of the same pattern. His hair was uncombed and his shoes were dirty. She politely told him to wait.

Those were the wrong words to say to Harry Oakes. He hated to be kept waiting. As half an hour passed, his complaints grew ruder and more heated. The partners were still at lunch. The poor secretary suggested that a junior member of the firm was available.

Oakes carried his anger into the office of Walter Foskett, a diplomatic young man who agreed with Oakes as he cursed Foskett's bosses. On the spur of the moment, Oakes invited him to lunch. By the time they returned to the office, Foskett was in business for himself, as the personal attorney to Harry Oakes in the United States. He had, literally, hitched his wagon to a gold mine.

In time a rivalry would develop between Foskett and Christie. Foskett saw him first, but Christie worked faster. The moment Harold heard that Harry Oakes, discoverer of the

Lake Shore Mines, had arrived in Palm Beach, he arranged to meet him there. Oakes and his wife went back to Nassau with him, at Harold's expense.

Oakes appreciated a good listener, and Harold was one of the best. Christie learned of Oakes's phobia about paying taxes of any sort: how he considered them a form of legalized robbery; how he had left Canada to find a place where he could live without the threat of crooked politicians eager to rob him.

Christie was too clever to delude himself that Oakes was a pigeon. And Oakes knew instinctively that Harold was a promoter, a fact that did not offend him. They were, in fact, an extremely compatible pair.

Harry's interest grew as Harold explained the riddles that had to be solved to place Nassau on the map as a tourist center: an airport had to be built, the hotels refurbished, the golf course enlarged, new sources of water developed.

The timing was right. Oakes, having been idle for several years, had become restless. His ego required some kind of activity. Of course, the ego of man is not necessarily to be feared. Large egos accomplish large deeds. Oakes could see himself becoming the power in Nassau. He told Harold he would wind up his affairs in Palm Beach, and return with his family in two weeks. He left it to Christie to arrange for his residency papers and, later, his Bahamian citizenship.

Of course, Oakes took it for granted that everyone he met wanted to get a hand in his pockets. He could easily count those who did not: his sister, Gertrude; his wife, Eunice; Bill Wright, his old mining partner. With other relatives, his children, clergy, anyone else, he kept up his guard.

His nature was a puzzle, even to him. He was an educated man who chose not to reveal himself. Scorn and arrogance were his shields.

Oakes ordered Christie to find him the best house on the island, and with that he was gone, leaving as though ending an argument, not a negotiation. Christie could not hold back a smile. He knew there was to be a new force in Nassau, and he was to guide that force to his advantage.

All of this, and more, I would learn piece by piece over the next two years.

The first door I knocked on after I left the cruise ship was Harold Christie's. I went there with Basil McKinney, whose name I had been given by friends in New York. Basil was a member of the Royal Nassau Sailing Club, and was a bit of a rebel, although he came from conservative stock. His father owned the town hardware store and was a member of the House of Assembly.

When I expressed an interest in looking at property on the islands, Basil insisted that Harold was the one to see.

His appearance was not what I expected. He had a large head with red, kinky hair, a pink face, a flat nose, and thick lips—his features were almost Negroid. A thick neck settled into wide shoulders. I was most struck by his eyes, which were green, beneath bushy red eyebrows. They gave him a look that was piglike, but I reminded myself that this unimposing specimen had the boundless imagination to revitalize the Bahamas.

Our visit was cordial, and Christie arranged for a boat to take me on a tour of the Out Islands the next day. The one I was most interested in seeing was Eleuthera, a two-day sail.

I left Nassau in the company of Captain Burnside and his deckhand, Curtis Thompson, whom for no apparent reason the captain always called "George." Within hours after leaving port, Captain Burnside went below and passed out with his arms around a bottle of gin. He was to remain in that condition for most of the trip.

George sailed the boat, caught fish, dived for lobsters, did the cleaning and cooking. I admired his dexterity. He was about twenty-five years old, five-feet-eight, wiry, and very strong. His eyes were bright, his nature wonderful. He laughed a great deal, showing his pearl-white teeth. George was proud of his pure blackness. Even his gums were black.

We docked in Eleuthera, a ribbon of land sixty miles long and no more than two miles wide. George led me to a bluff overlooking a village called Governor's Harbor. The land sloped gently away to the beach and was lush with shrubs and trees. Over decades, George told me, dead leaves had collected in potholes and served as mulch for the soil. "Mr. Fred," he said, "anything you plant in those potholes will grow. And there is fresh water on this side of the ridge."

On the northern end of the island lived the descendants of the settlers who had once turned shipwrecking into a profitable business. "There are no conches here," said George, "not like in Nassau."

I asked him what he meant by "conches."

"A conch is a shellfish that crawls in clear water on the sandy bottoms. It is good eating. But one conch shell is never the same color as another. There are no two alike." He was clearly referring to the white and mixed-race professional and merchant classes of the island.

A white widow named Mrs. Blodgett, and her family, owned the land along the beach, two hundred acres of it. When fresh water was needed in the Negro village, their women walked miles and paid a penny a dipper for it.

I knew that I would buy this land. I thrilled at the thought of having something I could call my own. Destiny, and George, had led me here. I could envision the house I would build atop the dune where I stood.

I asked George if he would like to work for me and supervise my construction at Governor's Harbor. He replied that as much as that would please him, he could not. "I am the slave of the captain," he said.

"A slave? Of that drunk? You can't be serious."

He explained that he was in debt to Burnside for ten pounds, ten shillings (fifty-five dollars), and had no hope of paying him off, on a salary of two pounds (ten dollars U.S. at that time) a month.

I opened my wallet and handed George twenty pounds, saying he could repay the captain and tell him to go to hell. I hired him to manage my house, when I built one, and my property, when I bought some. I opened a credit line at the Bank of Canada so he could draw his salary, ten dollars a week, plus an allowance for clothing. He was a free person now.

When I left for New York, he drove me to the dock, and I could see tears in his eyes. From that day on, George Thompson became my shadow and right-hand man. Years later, when I had to fight for my life, the police threatened George and did all they could to make him lie, and perjure himself. True to his word, he stood by me, a friend and a brave one.

I had planned to stay a week or two, but instead had lingered through most of the summer. Ruth Fahnestock's divorce was nearly final. I left Nassau to meet her in Reno, where, according to custom, Ruth stood on the Virginia Street bridge and hurled her old wedding ring into the river. Then we reentered the courthouse to be married, with less than maximum enthusiasm on my part, on November 28, 1937.

I had fallen in love, all right, but with an island. I was eager to return to the Bahamas. I told myself that I knew this soil, these people. I felt a connection here to something in my soul.

GUILTY OF MARRYING NANCY

SHORTLY after my return, I completed the purchase of the land on Eleuthera—whose name was the Greek word for "freedom"—and built a bungalow at Governor's Harbor. Not that Ruth was pleased. Nothing that had to do with the islands, with that way of life, pleased Ruth.

She disliked the people, the heat, the isolation, the absence of fashion. She disapproved of my friends and resented my dogs, a white bull terrier pup and a pair of Belgian police dogs, gifts from Basil McKinney. Least of all did she like the time I spent sailing. This was her constant complaint. In the beginning, I tried to humor her, pointing out that she was my wife, while the boat was merely a concubine. Even as I spoke the word, I liked the sound of it. And so I named my boat the *Concubine,* in the process raising a few eyebrows at the stuffy Royal Nassau Sailing Club.

The sea was my escape from a marriage that all too soon became intolerable. Ruth was insecure, demanding, and jealous. I knew her moods well. She would go into a rage, pick a fight once we were home, arouse her own passions, and then want to make love.

Once she went into hysterics after claiming that I had paid too much attention to our hostess, a young widow, at a dinner party. Soon after that, while I was away on business, Ruth drowned two of my dogs. Prince, the Belgian male, ran into the woods and was saved by George Thompson.

I knew then that my wife was a sick woman. I flew her to New York to seek psychiatric help. While we were there, I discussed the range of our problems with Maurice Speiser, and knew there was but one answer. Ruth agreed to a divorce, persuaded in part by the prospect of no longer being burdened by British currency laws. Speiser called it a "divorce of convenience."

Though for several months we lived off and on in the same house, our divorce was final in April of 1940. It might have ended there, except that Ruth, having returned to New York, was enraged by the news that I had married Nancy Oakes. She was half-mad with jealousy. She wrote a vicious and distorted letter to Lady Oakes, and the prosecution would pounce on her accusations to inflate its case against me.

None of us knew it then, but 1939 would be a turning point in the history of Europe and Nassau, if not the world. Germany and Russia signed a peace treaty in August, leaving Hitler free to invade Poland. There was an influx to Nassau of people either fleeing the coming bloody upheaval, or in search of a safe place to spend their money.

Among the newcomers, a few were to play a role in the desperate times I would encounter in the years just ahead.

A Mrs. Effie Henneage, whose husband was assigned to the War Office in London, rented a cottage near Harold Christie's home.

A Mrs. Gudewill, a wealthy widow from Canada, arrived with her two daughters. The younger, Marie, a gorgeous redhead in her late teens, would marry Baron George af Trolle, the personal secretary to Axel Wenner-Gren. Marie and Nancy Oakes would become best friends.

The Frank Goldsmith family came from the British upper middle class. He was a member of Parliament, his wife was French, and their teenaged sons would create their own identities. Teddy won recognition as an ecologist, while Jimmy, the younger, became what used to be called a business tycoon.

Whatever the trend, an exception was Dr. Ricky Oberwarth,

a Jewish refugee from Germany. Pleading, pathetic letters had been pouring into the Colonial office from Jews throughout Germany, but nearly all were ignored. The Bahamas relaxed its prejudices only in the case of doctors, who were sorely needed on the Out Islands and in the public charity hospital.

One immigrant was not exactly unknown to me. My cousin, Georges de Visdelou, had left London without optimism. "The French have their Maginot Line, which is a joke," he said. "The English navy is the best, but her soldiers train in street clothes for lack of uniforms, and drill with broomsticks instead of guns."

Although often depicted as a bon vivant, Georges was an intellectual, a cartographer who had been accepted by the Royal Geographical Society after publishing a book about the discovery of Mauritius by the Portuguese. He had written incisive articles about the coming war.

It did not trouble Georges that others failed to appreciate his serious side. Shortly after he landed in Nassau, he began a torrid romance with a teenaged New York beauty, Brenda Frazier, whose face would one day adorn the cover of *Life* magazine. She was visiting her grandparents, the Frederick Taylors.

That year, no one on the island was in cheerier spirits than Harold Christie. Not only was business booming, but his friend and client, Harry Oakes, had returned to Nassau as a baronet. He had spent six months in England, and had contributed to several charities, including half a million dollars to a London hospital. He was knighted on the birthday in 1939 of King George VI.

What arrangements took place before the fact, I cannot say. But Christie was eager to take credit for the achievement. On the day of the announcement, I joined him in a champagne toast to Sir Harry and Lady Oakes.

"So," said Harold, his look triumphant, "what do you think of me now?"

I laughed out loud. "Oakes was knighted, not you," I said.

"Agreed. But I was the kingmaker."

I heard from Christie his version of how Harry Oakes had defected from Canada and moved to Nassau, as I would later hear it from Sir Harry. As best I can reconcile the two accounts, this is what happened:

Oakes was angry and bitter when Harold found him in Palm Beach, uncertain where he would now settle after feeling betrayed by Canadian politicians. His grievances were both personal and financial, and the object of his greatest scorn was Richard Bennett, the Conservative Prime Minister. He offered his magnificent house in Toronto as a guest residence for the Duke of York and his family during a visit to Canada, and Harry was furious when Bennett declined the offer.

He lost his temper, and the Prime Minister had him thrown out of his office, a security guard on each side.

No one humiliated Harry Oakes in such a manner—not when Oakes was paying three million dollars a year in assorted taxes. This was the kind of man he was: he built a private golf course in Niagara, but every time he played, he found himself flailing sand in the same bunker. Most golfers would have changed clubs or tried another strategy. Harry brought in a bulldozer and had the bunker leveled.

From what he said, and what I observed, Harry's sympathies were more with the conservatives than the liberals. But in the election of 1930, he made a special contribution to the Liberal Party in return for a promise to appoint him to the Senate.

Unhappily, the Conservatives won. Soon he was slapped with a quarter-million-dollar tax bill—on land and parks he had donated to the public. As he saw it, he was being penalized for trying to do good works. Bennett had not exactly found the way to Harry's heart.

The whole subject of taxation could move him to apoplexy. But more than that, he did not like being gouged. When the Minister of Mines informed him that his taxes were going up, even as other industries were being exempted, Oakes reacted exactly as he had threatened to do. He left the country.

When Christie described to Oakes the charms of Nassau, and the absence of taxes, he had made his most important sale, and his richest convert. And if the climate in July and August was unbearable, Harry had a dozen houses in three or four states, as well as Canada and England, where his family could seek relief. It was the perfect merger of money and ambition, of time and place.

Sir Harry returned to Nassau with Lady Oakes and the children at the end of summer. I met Eunice for the first time when I was invited to tea at the house they called The Caves, a mile from Lyford Cay. She was a robust woman, some six inches taller than her husband, with a complexion like rose petals. One might have described her as elegant, if not for her Aussie accent and a rowdy kind of laugh. As for Harry, knighthood hadn't changed him. He wore a plaid shirt that matched his socks.

I found myself wanting to like this short, barrel-chested man with a mop of red hair turning gray. There was no pretense about him. He held his head always erect, and he was, I think, a handsome man. There was mischief in his eyes, but in an instant they could become frozen and hard.

Something about his house puzzled me. The lawns were lush and manicured, but there were no trees or bushes within a hundred feet of the house. Harry had cleared the land, having decided that trees attracted mosquitoes and bugs.

That day I met for the first time their eldest daughter, Nancy, then fifteen, a lanky girl with lovely auburn hair and a freckled face. We could not have exchanged a dozen words.

When the Duke of Windsor arrived as Royal Governor of the Bahamas in August of 1940, the Duchess refused to stay in the official residence. She was unable or unwilling to abide the mildewed smell of the furniture, or the peeling walls whose color had been bleached by the tropical climate. Harry Oakes offered them the use of Westbourne, a lovely old house on

Cable Beach, next door to the golf club, until the repairs were complete.

Having the ex-King of England as a guest in his home was a kind of repayment for Oakes. It washed out the insult of when the Prime Minister of Canada refused to use the Oakes mansion in Toronto to host the Duke of York.

I found Oakes and his family interesting, but in truth they did not rate very high in my thoughts. I had made a commitment to Nassau, was pleased with my investments, and was trying to stem the bleeding from a bad marriage.

Sailing was my therapy. Basil suggested that I join the Royal Nassau Sailing Club and compete in the King's Cup Regatta, which dated back to the reign of King Edward VII. The boats taking part in the races were American-designed sloops of the Pirate class. My application was accepted, and I purchased a sloop in urgent need of repairs.

A local carpenter refurbished the boat, with lumber brought in from Miami. I sent off to the States for immediate delivery of a set of sails, and in no time the Pirate was in the water. With Basil as crew, I began to practice in earnest.

We had won the first two races of the regatta, leading up to the King's race, which Basil assured me we would win. However, he added, it was the custom to allow the governor of the island to finish first.

"The **hell with** that," I said.

"I think the way you do"—Basil nodded—"but Fred, you must know, if you win it is going to start a ruckus."

"Who cares?" I shrugged.

I looked forward to clinching the cup on Sunday. That afternoon the commodore of the club and the president of the racing committee dropped by my house. They had been informed, they said, that my mast was not regulation because it was hollow. Angrily, I told them such a charge was insulting and unworthy of them. I suggested they contact the carpenter who built the mast to determine if it was hollow. They refused. I then suggested that they bore holes into the mast to inspect its core. This they reluctantly agreed to do.

"If the mast is hollow," I conceded, "you are in a position to boot my ass out of the club, disqualify my victories, and forbid me to race again in the King's Cup. But, gentlemen, if the mast is not hollow, you must give me a letter of apology." I kept my voice calm but firm.

The three men huddled and whispered among themselves. The commodore finally turned to me and said, "The letter of apology is out of the question."

My butler opened the door to let them out. I immediately drove to the office of Godfrey Higgs, a man I considered one of the few honest lawyers on the island. He listened with a frown creasing his forehead.

"They have you exactly where they want you," he said. "If you resign, the governor shall win, as it is done every year. If you insist on racing, someone will foul you, and the racing committee is sure to vote against you. Take my advice, return their lousy trophies and resign from the damned club."

I followed his advice. I should have listened as well to Basil, who urged me to keep a lower profile.

But I could not resist the urge to get even with the crowd who ran the Royal Nassau Sailing Club. I became a member of the Nassau Yacht Club, which existed only on paper. The commodore, Roland Symonette, had obtained a charter from the International Star Class Yacht Racing Association, which qualified the club to host an international regatta every other year.

There were a total of three Star Class boats in Nassau, one belonging to Symonette, one to the chief pilot of the island, Captain Harry Knowles, and the third so decrepit as to be not worth counting. The club's headquarters turned out to be the large terrace of Captain Knowles, and the Stars were moored at the end of a long dock across the street from his home.

I soon discovered that the youngsters who hung around the captain's dock were born sailors. Durward Knowles, the eldest son of the captain, and several years my junior, was the prototype of a sailor, and a very modest young man. They accepted me as one of them.

At our first meeting, I announced our plans. We were going to add six new Star boats to the fleet, and I would provide them. The first four Basil and I found in New York. A fifth, built in California, I gave as a personal gift to Durward Knowles. In 1945, he sailed it to victory in the World Series, off the southern coast of California, and went on to win almost every race of consequence on the Atlantic Coast.

The sixth was my own, made by Purdy, the boat I called the *Concubine*. She was my great love, the first possession I ever truly lived to enjoy.

Now Captain Harry's dock was full—in fact, we had to enlarge it. I spent every spare moment on the water, sailing, working to improve. There *is* no modest way to say that I was soon recognized as the best sailor in Nassau. Basil and I competed at San Diego, the Great Lakes, and Long Island, with some success. Every weekend we held a regatta. We had no royal charter, but we were an authentic sailing club. Almost without exception, our members neither drank liquor nor smoked; they were the cleanest bunch of young people I had ever met. Only one problem arose, and it was another strike against me: I was not aware that my new friends were Plymouth Brethren, a very strict religious sect the Royalists had brought along from New England when they migrated to Nassau.

Sunday was God's day. Church in the morning, then religious meetings in the afternoons and prayers into the night. I had changed all that with the gifts of Star boats, and sails and prizes, regattas every weekend. The younger generation lacked the fervor of their elders, who considered me a sinner, a devil's spirit who had seduced their children from the path of God. I had made the kind of enemies who last a lifetime.

A year or more had passed when I saw Nancy Oakes again,

at an engagement party for Marie Gudewill and Baron Trolle. Was it my imagination? Every time I turned around, Nancy was there. We talked, drank champagne, and clicked our glasses. She looked very mature for her age.

Marie took me aside and warned me that Nancy had a crush on me. "Be careful. What she wants, she usually gets." I was flattered by the attention, perhaps more than I would admit. I did not take the warning seriously, yet I was startled to find that Nancy could list the sailing races I had won. She knew the number of the license plate on my new car.

A month after Marie's party, I flew to New York to see a doctor for the stomach pains that continued to trouble me. Nancy, who had returned to the French School in New York, found out what hospital had admitted me, and called my room, asking if I could have visitors.

The next afternoon she walked through my door, looking more beautiful than I remembered. Every day I was hospitalized, Nancy came to visit, bringing flowers or fruit or newspapers. After a week I was free to leave. The doctors decided my condition, whatever it was, could be treated with medication and a strict diet.

Before I returned to Nassau, Nancy made me promise to attend Marie's wedding on Long Island, in the summer of 1941. She said she would see me then, and with that she gave me a long, passionate kiss on the mouth. I remembered her friend's warning and smiled.

I was certainly not indifferent to the charms of Nancy Oakes, nor was I unaware of the gap in our ages. But I accepted our encounter as an innocent one. I did not stay in touch, even forgot about the wedding of Marie and Baron Trolle, and moved on to other matters. Some involved Harry Oakes.

Lady Oakes had retreated to their place in Maine, as was her custom, to escape the summer heat, and Sir Harry was alone, bored, restless, cranky. He would stay a day or so at The Caves, then a few nights at Westbourne, or in his suite at the

British Colonial Hotel.

It belabors the obvious to say he was a funny old bird. Now and then he would stop by Captain Harry's dock to watch us clean and repair boats. He liked this kind of activity, but it was unknown to him, requiring as it did a high degree of teamwork.

I sensed he was lonely and invited him to dinner, or to drop by for breakfast. He was clearly troubled. He feared, above all, that the colonial government could not be trusted—that they were about to impose some sort of income tax. Another worry gnawed at him: if something wasn't done soon to improve the lives of the blacks, a terrible rebellion was coming.

Nassau was a tinderbox, waiting for a match. I asked George Thompson what he had heard, and he said, soberly, "Those conches are going to have their necks cut if they don't start paying a livable wage. For them, the poor are less than animals."

Oakes had already begun to think about leaving the Bahamas. He dropped by to tell me that Maximino Camacho, brother of the newly elected president of Mexico, was arriving in a few days to visit Nassau as a guest of Axel Wenner-Gren. Then an odd thing happened. Two days before the arrival of his guest, Wenner-Gren left the island in the middle of the night aboard his yacht, the *Southern Cross*, destination unknown.

While the island buzzed with rumors, Sir Harry drafted me as an interpreter and to help entertain the visitors. Camacho arrived in a private plane, accompanied by two bodyguards, a masseur, and a barber. I was astonished by his resemblance to Oakes: both seem to have been cast from the same mold.

That night, after leaving Sir Harry at The Caves, I drove Maximino to the Prince George bar. Every city has a favorite place where people like to congregate for lunch or dinner, and drinks before and after, to watch, to talk, and to cut deals. New York has its "21" Club, Havana had the Floridita, and Nassau had the bar of the Prince George Hotel.

Basil McKinney had corralled several young and shapely

tourists, and when we joined them I could see lust and desire in the eyes of the Mexican. Much later, as Camacho entered his hotel elevator with three of the young ladies, I knew I was saying good night to a happy man.

When he left the next day, he called me his *compadre,* and extracted from me a promise to visit him in Puebla, Mexico, where he was the governor.

One month later, I was in Mexico. Maximino met me on the steps of the governor's mansion, and showed me to the guest house, which had sleeping accommodations for twelve. Dinner was at eight, and I did not realize until then that it was in my honor.

Had I known what was coming, I could have done gladly without the honor.

In the middle of the dinner, a bodyguard came to the table and whispered to our host. The electrical workers were striking. Maximino jumped to his feet, his face livid, and said, "Don Alfredo, come and see how I settle a strike."

The bodyguard handed him his gunbelt and he buckled it around his waist. He hurried out of the room with me and a few other guests in tow. A cavalcade of perhaps a dozen cars, filled with guardsmen, raced with sirens blasting along the darkened avenue to the electric company headquarters, where flags of black and red hung above the building, indicating a general strike.

Maximino stepped out of his car and demanded, "Who is the leader?"

One man came forward. "Colonel," he said, "I am in charge here."

Maximino looked at his watch and said, loudly, so those in the immediate area could hear, "I give you thirty seconds to put the switch on and *remove those damned flags.* "

"That I cannot do," the union man replied. "Colonel, you know I can't do that."

Still looking at his watch, Camacho called out, "Twenty

seconds! Ten ^econds! Five!" In the next instant he removed his gun from its holster and shot the man between the eyes, spattering the workers standing behind him with fragments of the leader's skull and brains. A ghostly silence followed.

The governor looked around and pointed to another striker. "You are now the head of the strikers," he said. "You have thirty seconds to pull the switch and give light to the city."

The man said loudly, "Yes, my colonel. Right away." He ran toward the building, and a moment later the lights went on. The flags were lowered and the strike ended. We walked back to the cars without a word.

"Don Alfredo," Camacho said, "now you have seen how to break a strike."

"Indeed," I replied.

On our return to the mansion, dinner continued as if nothing had happened. The next day I watched Maximino play polo, and then I was on my way back to Nassau, relieved to be at a distance from my impetuous murderous host. The furthest thought from my mind was that I would ever again need his hospitality, or his protection.

The talk in Nassau was still of Wenner-Gren, and the stunning reason behind his departure in the middle of the night. He had been blacklisted by the British government as a suspected Nazi agent. Everything he held in the islands—the Bahama Trust Company, his home on Hog Island, his bank accounts—was seized by the Exchange Control Board.

I had gotten to know John Gaffney, who had arrived a year earlier to head the ECB. He could not resist leaving me with a teasing thought: "He was going to be arrested, and only two people besides me knew of it—Harold Christie and the Duke of Windsor. Who do you suppose tipped him off?"

And there he left it, smiling, canary feathers fluttering from his lips.

The sudden flight of Wenner-Gren was bad news for Christie and the Duke—but perhaps not as bad as it would have been if he had stayed. There is no doubt that he would have been questioned not only by British Intelligence but by the FBI, and the answers could well have implicated his partners in the money-smuggling network in Mexico.

If that close call encouraged Oakes to act on his impulse to leave Nassau, then Harold Christie had other, equally pressing concerns.

Against that backdrop of war and intrigue, the social season was in full swing. Nancy Oakes was to make her debut at a Christmas ball given by her parents in the ballroom of the British Colonial Hotel.

Walking into the bar of the Prince George one day, I heard my name and, turning, found myself looking into Nancy's laughing eyes. She was a woman now. First, she scolded me for not appearing at Marie's wedding. Then she forgave me, on the condition that I act as her escort to the ball.

We bantered as I stood at her table, her bemused date looking on. I told her I was sorry, but I had made plans with friends to go duck hunting. She said her heart would be broken. I said I doubted her heart broke so easily.

Nancy tricked me into cutting my trip short, sending a fake telegram under Christie's name, and in the end I did appear at the ball. And that night we fell in love.

Nancy wore a green silk dress that made even more vivid the luster of her hair. She opened the ball by dancing with her father. When Sir Harry returned to our table, Nancy grabbed my hand and led me to the dance floor. "Now," she said, "I am all yours."

We danced for hours. After dinner we walked along the path to the seawall. The night air was thick with the scent of jasmine. We sat on a bench and embraced like teenagers—which, of course, one of us was. In the weeks to come, we water-skied and had picnics on the quiet beaches east of Nassau. I napped in the shade of a sea grape tree, my head in Nancy's lap, her hands touching my hair.

We celebrated New Year's Eve of 1942 at the Trolles, and

Nancy and I saw the first sunrise of the new year. In front of us, the sea was calm. The stillness of the dawn was broken by the cawing of birds and the chirping of crickets in the grass. All nature seemed to call to us. We kissed, and Nancy said softly, "I pray that this new year will be the beginning of many, many more we shall spend happily together, forever."

Nancy returned to New York to finish her studies. I missed her, but turned my attention to the Bacardi Cup race in Havana, scheduled in mid-January. I renewed my training at a relentless pace. Racing in the Gulf Stream was not a joke, and demanded great preparation for both the boat and crew.

At almost the last moment, as I was to leave for Havana, politics intervened. Godfrey Higgs called to advise me that I had been summoned to appear before the Exchange Control Board to answer questions about my finances. In brief, they wanted to know where the money had come from to support my life-style—the Star boats I had donated to the Nassau Yacht Club, my new Lincoln Continental, my first-class plane tickets to New York.

In short, I was accused of violating the currency regulations. Higgs was beside himself, trying to impress on me the seriousness of the charges.

I had neither the time nor the temper for such foolishness. Godfrey wanted me to plead guilty and accept a fine. I refused. I knew the English civil-servant mentality, and I had no desire to fall into their claws.

I asked him for a large manila envelope and stuffed it with paper, then scaled the envelope and scrawled across it in red ink: "Affidavits re Expenses, Presents, etc., etc." The letters were large enough to be read across a room. I asked Godfrey to hold the envelope for me.

The questioning would be conducted by the Attorney General, Eric Hallinan. Other members included the chief of police, the colonial secretary, the treasurer, two minor officials, and John Gaffney. They reported to the Royal Governor, who stood away from the conference table, smoking his pipe, watching the proceedings with an air of detachment.

After Hallinan read the charges against me, and began to explain the rules, I interrupted him. I freely admit that my defense was audacious, risky, and not in the best of taste. I asked Higgs to hand me the envelope I had given him earlier. I held it briefly and let it fall to the table. Forcefully, I said that I had not spent or transferred a dime more than the limits established under the regulations. And in the envelope was my proof. I received substantial gifts, I said, from lady friends in the States, women who were in some cases lonely and unloved, who chose this means to thank me for my company.

I said I would gladly provide the affidavits to support this claim, and I apologized if this explanation shocked their moral sensibilities.

Everyone present was hanging on my every word. When I finished, a long silence followed, broken by an occasional nervous cough. Just as Hallinan rose to challenge me, the Duke of Windsor spoke up. He had a faint smile on his face, which was really his usual expression, but in this instance I thought it was a reaction to the embarrassment so evident in the room.

He spoke in a slow and distinct tone: "It is clear to me that Mr. de Marigny has no reason to invent a story of such a delicate nature. His statement explains to my satisfaction how he obtained the articles in question. He has offered affidavits to document them, and I see no need to doubt his word. The meeting is adjourned."

Back in Godfrey's office, I answered his curiosity by emptying the envelope. It contained nothing but blank pages. "I'll be damned," he said. Then he leaned toward me and said, "Now listen to every word I am telling you. The Duke saved your neck. For reasons I am unable to fathom, he helped you. But do not be misled. Today you have made serious enemies. You made Hallinan look like an ass. One slip, and he will get you. You must watch your step."

Had my frivolous story touched some nerve in the Duke of Windsor? I had no hint. But I would come to regret the ways, small or large, that I insulted or offended him, and the contempt I took too few pains to conceal for the class into which I had been born.

I arrived in Havana with three days to prepare for the races. We finished rigging the *Concubine* and looked forward to challenging a field of first-rate sailors, among them such world-class competitors as Adrian Isclin, Harry Nye, and Harold Halstead. Luck was on our side and we won the Bacardi Cup easily. Now my name would be listed among those of the great champions, and I returned to Nassau feeling temporarily godlike.

Among the letters of congratulation awaiting me was one from Nancy. She suggested coyly that instead of spending all my time with a "Concubine," I should fly to New York and spend time with her.

My heart told me to go, my brain urged me to stay away. When I asked his advice, de Visdelou had a fit. "You are free," he bellowed, "free as the wind. Why should you start this silly romance with Nancy? Where will it lead? I know, I know, you are going to tell me the same old story: that you are lonely, you want to settle down, have a family, all the security you have not had since you were three years old.

"Please, Fred, think with something besides your groin."

I didn't listen. I felt I had fallen in love with Nancy. She was different from anyone I had known before, like a young filly who needed taming. I wired her that I would be in New York the first week in May.

She wired back: "Hurry. My birthday is the seventeenth. I shall be awaiting you with love and kisses."

I rationalized the trip by telling myself it was time for another medical checkup. I made an appointment with my doctor and checked into the Lombardy Hotel on a Sunday night, the tenth of May.

Nancy walked into my room carrying a small suitcase,

which answered a question neither of us had directly raised. She rushed toward me and we kissed and clung to each other. That embrace lasted far into the night.

It had not occurred to me that my medical examination would be anything but routine. But the results of my tests were troubling, and my doctor quickly called in another specialist in endocrinology. They feared that I had cancer of the pancreas, and a decision was made to perform an exploratory operation.

The next day I entered St. Vincent's Hospital. The surgery revealed no signs of cancer, but my insides were a mass of adhesions. I spent the next week in a special bed, the kind used for burn victims, enabling me to be turned every thirty minutes to prevent the adhesions from forming again.

Once again, Nancy's daily visits were my consolation. On Saturday and Sunday she never left my bedside. I could not have asked for more devotion from anyone.

She was the classic "poor little rich girl," and about this I knew I should have no illusions. On the other hand, while I was ill, Nancy had given me the affection and devotion I craved. She was, in a sense, as alone as I.

If her complaints seemed petty, they were no less real to her. She was ashamed of her parents, of her father's crudeness and her mother's tackiness. She saw her friends living in a world of elegance, and she made me feel that I alone could introduce her to that world.

I was released from the hospital on her eighteenth birthday. She asked me point-blank, "Why don't we get married?"

Words spilled from my mouth that had no obligation to my brain: "Of course. I shall do everything I can to make you happy."

My mind was set. I had convinced myself without a struggle that we were to be married.

The moment I left the hospital, I bought an engagement ring, and a friend arranged for the license and found a judge in the Bronx to perform the ceremony in his chambers. Nancy was ecstatic. Neither of us mentioned her parents until it was time to share our news. Perhaps I should have been concerned about their approval. But my position was simple: I had married Nancy, not her father and mother.

Nancy waited until we reached Palm Beach before she called home. Her father did not seem surprised. "How much money do you want?" he asked. Nancy assured him that she needed nothing from him. Then she handed me the phone, and Sir Harry invited us to continue our honeymoon in Bar Harbor. Lady Oakes's reaction was at first tearful, then she composed herself and begged us to accept her husband's invitation. She would have a guest cottage ready for us.

We went shopping for a wardrobe for Nancy, and she tried on each item, shoes, clothes, coats, and jewelry, as if the experience were entirely new to her. She glowed with excitement. I was entranced by her exuberance.

Our visit to Maine was unexpectedly pleasant. Sir Harry was on his best behavior. Lady Oakes had at times a drippy eye, but seemed to be bearing well the thought that Nancy was now married. Sir Harry went out of his way to be considerate. He took us to visit his birthplace, and to Moosehead Lake to meet his brother and sister.

When we returned to Bar Harbor, I gave him a copy of a document my attorney had drawn, signed by me and notarized. In this document I renounced any monies Nancy had or might inherit, from her parents or any other source. Furthermore, I gave up the dower rights I held under Nassau laws.

Oakes read the words slowly, then asked if he could have a copy. "This is your copy," I said. He smiled, folded the papers, and placed them in his coat pocket. "I am glad you did that," he said. "Somehow I expected it of you."

I remarked that I had not asked the same renunciation of Nancy. He laughed and we went for a walk.

Nancy's idea of marriage was more or less an extended holiday. She decided she wanted to visit Mexico, whose art, music, and dance entranced her. I agreed to extend our honeymoon for another month.

Harry made the arrangements through Maximino Camacho, and I should have expressed my misgivings right then. A year had passed since I saw him execute a man with a bullet to the head. But for one of the few times in my life I kept an opinion to myself. I put that scene out of my thoughts. At that fragile stage of our relationships, I did not want to spoil Sir Harry's business or Nancy's pleasure.

We had dinner one night with Maximino at the mansion in Puebla, and the evening was without distraction—if one ignored the bodyguards armed with submachine guns, and the attack dogs growling in their pens.

We went on to Mexico City and spent several days there. It was a mecca for refugees from Europe during the war. Wenner-Gren had sought asylum there, and was joined by ex-King Carol II of Rumania and his longtime mistress, Magda Lupescu, as well as a cluster of Vichy Frenchmen and a number of older Englishmen, who were peacefully enjoying themselves while London burned.

In Taxco, I had rented a small cottage, and it delighted Nancy to explore the narrow streets and small shops around the cathedral square. Our amusements came to a sudden and distressing end. She developed typhoid fever and I rushed her back to Mexico City, and had her admitted to the Anglo-American Hospital, where the best available doctors could care for her.

I telephoned her parents in Maine, and Sir Harry arrived the next day, followed at the end of the week by Lady Oakes. Nancy's condition had worsened. By the time they arrived, I had given her two transfusions of blood. Fortunately, we had the same uncommon blood type. The fever subsided, but a few days later Nancy begun to suffer from a form of trenchmouth on both the upper and lower jaws. An American dentist was flown in to treat her. He told Oakes and me that Nancy's gums were diseased, almost gone, and the bones exposed. She was going to need extensive surgery. Given her age and vanity, it was ghastly news, and I kept it from her. She had enough problems with her head being shaved, as was customary in typhoid fever treatment in those days.

After six weeks, Nancy was able to leave the hospital. We moved to a hotel in Cuernavaca owned by Axel Wenner-Gren. Her mother and father followed, but Sir Harry soon became restless. He suggested that he and I take a trip north and return to Mexico City by train. He assured me it would be a rewarding experience for both of us.

While Lady Oakes and a nurse stayed with Nancy, we flew north to Hermosillo, a town on the west coast, and from there took a train to the capital.

During the trip, Sir Harry opened up to me. His wife was adamant about not returning to Nassau. He did not know the reason. He was planning to liquidate his holdings in Nassau and move either to Mexico or Santo Domingo, where he thought there was a real opportunity to make use of his vast energies.

He told me about his life as a prospector and his fights with the Canadian officials over taxes. He mentioned how good it felt to take his revenge by purchasing a title from the British crown. "I showed those bastards I didn't need them," he fumed. "They thought my money was fine, but they had no use for me. They hurt Lady Oakes's feelings and I had to show them."

He expounded on his adventures with the Lake Shore Mine. He was bitter about the bankers who had tried to squeeze him out of his find. "Prospectors break their backs discovering the gold, and the bankers rip the profit from their work," he said. He laughed when he told me that the local merchants of Lake Shore had more faith in him than he had in himself. They had grubstaked him, he had paid them back in company stock, and they had all become rich.

"We needed a road from the mine to the highway about a mile away," he said. "We had no rocks anywhere. So I told the boys to use the ore from the mine to build the damned road." He roared. "I bet I could get a million dollars in gold out of that road today."

Shortly after our return from the train trip, Harry and Lady Oakes left Mexico. Harry shook my right hand and then held it in both of his. "Take care of Nancy," he said warmly.

Nancy had a series of operations on her jaw and gums. She would need even more, but for now she could talk without making whistling noises, and eat like a normal person.

We spent another month in Mexico, allowing Nancy to recuperate, and then went to stay with her parents in Palm Beach, where life took another odd tack. Lady Oakes had arranged separate bedrooms for us. Nancy stalked out of the room and screamed at her mother, who tried to explain that in view of Nancy's health she felt she would be more comfortable sleeping alone.

I stayed out of the argument, but I wondered what she would think when she found out that Nancy was pregnant. A few moments later my luggage arrived.

I was apprehensive about telling the family that Nancy was expecting. My premonitions about their reaction were correct.

Their lawyer, Walter Foskett, and his wife came for lunch the next day, and Nancy chose that moment to announce casually that she was going to have a baby. Sir Harry banged his fist on the table and walked out of the room. Lady Oakes began to cry. Mrs. Foskett led her out of the room, leaving Foskett, Nancy, and me to sit in uncomfortable silence.

That evening at dinner, Oakes was nice to the point of suspicion, his fit of temper apparently forgotten. After dinner, he told Nancy she had an appointment at the hospital the next morning, with a gynecologist. I did not know his motive then. But such a visit certainly seemed in order.

The next day, the doctor emerged from the examining room and addressed himself directly to me. He recommended, to my surprise, that the baby be aborted. But his words did not, as far as I could tell, surprise Sir Harry or Foskett, who were waiting with me. He said he did not feel that Nancy was strong enough, after her illnesses, to carry a pregnancy to term.

I walked into the hall to breathe some fresh air. Nancy joined me a few moments later and asked me what had happened. I told her that the doctor wanted her to have an abortion. She said nothing.

We drove back to the house. I was on edge. I told her that we should go to New York to see some respected doctors who could tell us what to do. Then I left her alone and went for a long walk along the beach. The ocean breeze and the sound of breaking waves had a calming effect, but my mind was swimming with doubt and apprehension. The omens for this marriage could hardly be described as favorable.

Dinner that night was the worst meal of my life. Sir Harry finally broke the silence after we had dessert. He invited me to play pool with him. As I followed him into the billiard room, he seemed almost jovial and patted me on the back. "Frenchic, you and I think alike," he said. "We both have a hell of a temper, but that's a good thing. Once we get it out, the pressure goes down and everyone can relax again."

Nancy came in while we were playing. Her hair had grown back, and to me she looked lovelier than ever. She was wearing one of her new dresses, and asked me to take her out to a nightclub. Before Sir Harry could object, we left the house and drove away, relieved to be free of the heavy weather of that place.

I should have recognized the forces that tugged at her. She wanted the promise of a normal life, the chance to dance, to explore, to have a child. But her pain was persistent, the treatment slow and harsh, the pace of her recovery unclear.

In the morning, Nancy was visibly disturbed, beset by second thoughts. The weight of the medical opinion, and the concerns of her parents, were more than she could resist. She had decided, she said, that the doctors were right. She must have the abortion. There was really no choice.

What was left of my Catholic training asserted itself. I could not be the sympathetic husband. We exchanged sharp words, then spent most of the day not talking.

Finally, I told Nancy to have the abortion if she wanted; it was her decision. In disgust and resignation, I signed the necessary medical release. I saw the issue then as a moral one ... and a test to see who controlled my young wife.

Nancy went to the hospital a day later. I felt unwell myself, and my doctor checked me into the same hospital to undergo tests for intestinal distress. We had rooms on the same floor, a few doors apart.

The tests were negative and I was resting in bed, reading a magazine, when my door burst open. There was Sir Harry, fuming, his fists raised. He looked out of his mind.

"You sex maniac," he screamed. "You had to get a room here so you could rape your wife. You are a dirty son of a bitch, and I'm going to have you horsewhipped."

I looked at him in absolute astonishment, and said nothing. "Well, what the hell are you doing in here?" he demanded.

"None of your damned business," I told him calmly.

"Get out of that bed and get the hell out of here," he ordered.

"Listen, and listen well to what I am going to tell you," I said. "Screw you. I take no orders from you or anyone. Get the hell out of here before I lose my temper and throw you out."

If he made the slightest move toward me, I knew I was going to have to fight him. I was prepared to do so. I might have taught him a good lesson, but he let his arms drop, turned, and walked quickly out of the room.

The next day I left the hospital, drove to the house, took my luggage, and left for Miami and then on to Nassau. In what had become a familiar pattern, time would resolve that clash and pave the way for the next. Lady Oakes would leave for Bar Harbor to spend the summer. Nancy and I would patch things up, and hope that the difficult days would be soon behind us. She would spend her summer in Vermont, and that would give her health and our own feelings time to mend.

That was the rough road we traveled to July of 1943. And now the body of Sir Harry Oakes had been returned to the earth of his native Maine, and my fate was about to be decided in an airless courtroom in Nassau.

THE TRIAL

I shaved my beard and mustache the morning of the trial. I had pioneered the bearded look among the young men of Nassau, but now was not the time to alienate the jury with my unconventional ways.

George Thompson brought me a dark gray suit, a white shirt, shoes, and a tie. I dressed early and met Godfrey Higgs in Captain Miller's office precisely at nine o'clock. We drove the short distance to the courthouse, my first trip outside the jail in three months. It was a delight to see trees and flowers, people milling about, children playing, life still going on. I had taken these things for granted, and now they meant more to me than I could ever have dreamed.

I was brought back to reality when the car stopped at the courthouse. I followed two policemen inside, and there, perched on a three-foot elevated stand, was a cage. Yes, a cage. With the kind of bars one might see in the zoo to protect the onlookers from a dangerous creature, a cage for a wild animal. I was put on exhibition, flanked by two constables.

I knew little about the law then, although I would consider myself to be reasonably well self-educated by the end of the trial. I believe the very sight of the prisoner in the dock had a prejudicial effect on the jury. It was the equivalent, in the American system, of bringing in a defendant manacled hand and foot. I faced the jury through my bars.

At least I had a commanding view of the entire courtroom. There was not an empty seat to be had; the well-to-do whites had sent out their servants at dawn to hold a place for them. Nancy smiled at me from a back row; she would testify later, and therefore could not stay.

My attorneys, Higgs and Callender, sat at a long table in line with my cage. Adderley and Hallinan sat next to them, fiddling with papers. The lawyers wore black robes and white wigs. The judge's high bench loomed over the lawyers' table at a right angle. The crier's place was below the judge.

All was quiet until the crier's voice broke the silence: "Oyez! Oyez! God save the King."

The entire courtroom rose to its feet as Sir Oscar Bedford Daley made his entry. He was dressed in a scarlet, fur-trimmed robe and full wig. He was a short man with what I thought was a kind face. He had been Chief Justice of the Bahamas since 1939, and had been knighted in 1942.

Reporters from the wire services and the leading newspapers of Britain, Canada, and the United States sat at a special table in front of the spectators' gallery. Their daily cables had whipped up the public appetite for one of the great murder trials of the twentieth century.

The court registrar read the indictment: "Marie Alfred Fonquereaux de Marigny, you are charged with murder under Section 335 of the Penal Code, Chapter 60; particulars of the offense being that during the night of the seventh and eighth of July 1943, at New Providence, you did murder Sir Harry Oakes, Baronet. Are you guilty or not guilty?"

As forcefully as I could, I replied, "Not guilty," and the words echoed in my ears.

All the preliminaries were behind us. The trial had begun. The date was October 18, 1943, a Monday, three months and a week since my arrest.

The jury was sworn in, with James Sands, a grocer, well known to me, as their foreman.

The Crown called its first witness, Harold Christie, and there was a tangible stir and hum of voices in the room. His testimony in the magistrate's hearing had not gone well, but if there was one truth generally accepted, it was that Christie had been the last witness to see Harry Oakes alive, and the first to find him dead.

The rest of the truth was what the case hinged upon, and Christie's nervousness as he entered the witness box was apparent to all. He stood, as was the custom, and gripped the rail in front of him as if he were on a heaving deck. I could only wonder what the jury's impression would be. To give the proper weight to his evidence, they would have to decide whether his were the normal jitters of any witness, compounded by the brutal death of a friend, or whether he had something to conceal.

Hallinan led Christie through the now-familiar ground: the dinner the night before, sleeping through the storm and the attack, awakening only to swat some mosquitoes; discovering Sir Harry bloody and burned; trying to clean his face and, believing him still alive, lifting the head and pressing water to his lips.

Christie's answers were frequently rambling, but Hallinan let him go on. He volunteered the information that his driver had brought his car around at about nine o'clock that night, parking it near the country club. He did not see it until the next morning, he said, since he had remained in Westbourne the entire night. He stressed this last part of his statement as if he anticipated other questions to come. The emphasis was lost on no one.

He described the condition of the room, and the frantic calls he made—omitting again, curiously, the calls between himself and the Duke of Windsor.

Godfrey Higgs rose to begin his cross-examination. No one was more curious than I as to how he would proceed. He had been reminded—warned—by Hallinan that Christie was not on trial.

He began gently enough, and drew from Christie an admission that Sir Harry had made at least two significant offers to me: the gift of a home, and a thousand acres of land to use and develop. I had declined both, as Harold testified, around February of that year.

I understood what Godfrey was doing. He had established, through Christie, that my relationship with Oakes was not one of uninterrupted hostility, as the Crown would contend.

No one on the defense team had yet figured out why Harold was so insistent about having been in the house during the murder, or why he was so touchy about the location of his car. But Higgs decided to probe.

Q. You know Mabel Ellis, Sir Harry's housemaid?

A. Yes.

Q. You know that she says that you always left your car outside Westbourne when you came there. Is that correct?

A. I did not always leave my car outside the main entrance.

Q. Did you leave your car there on Tuesday night?

A. Yes. On the northern end of the tennis court, a little east of Westbourne, nearer to Westbourne than to the country club.

Q. You know that Mabel Ellis says that on Tuesday night, the sixth of July, you left your car immediately outside the entrance to the southern court?

A. Mabel Ellis is incorrect. It was to the east of the main entrance. The courts are about three hundred feet away.

Q. You know that Mabel Ellis says that on Tuesday morning you drove up to town with Sir Harry Oakes?

A. I do not remember that. I am sure that I went alone and went to the Executive Council. If Mabel Ellis says I went with Sir Harry in his car, she is saying what is not true. I am positive of this because I was in a hurry. I had to be there at ten o'clock.

Higgs paused and waited while Christie fumbled with the handkerchief in his breast pocket and mopped his face. He was on the scent of something, and decided to push on:

Q. Do you remember if you got there on time? A. I believe so. It meets at ten o'clock. To the best of my recollection, it met at ten o'clock that day.

Q. And yet you say you left Westbourne between nine-fifteen and nine-thirty?

A. I said I did not remember exactly. I remember that I was in a hurry because I was late.

Q. If you did not have a watch, how did you know what time it was?

A. I may have seen a clock some time before.

Q. Do you think your recollection is better than Mabel Ellis's?

A. I could not say that.

Q. Have you a good memory sometimes?

A. Sometimes.

Q. Did you not stop at your house on the way?

A. I may have. I usually stop to pick up papers for Council.

The point of the questioning may have eluded some. But Higgs was testing Harold's memory, if not his truthfulness, and the jury was not likely to miss the unevenness of his recall.

Godfrey moved easily into another area. Harold admitted that he and I had talked on the last morning of Sir Harry's life, Wednesday. He denied that I had invited him to dinner, denied telling me that he was having dinner with Oakes.

Q. Would you say that the accused was lying again if he said you told him that you were staying with Sir Harry Oakes that night?

A. Yes.

Q. Why are you so positive of these two facts?

A. I should hate to do an injustice to the accused, but I did not tell him that. I did not know myself that I was going to dine with Sir Harry.

In the most subtle way, Higgs had undertaken to break down Christie's account of his activities on the night of the murder.

Q. When did Sir Harry invite you to dine that night? A. About eight o'clock.

Q. When did Sir Harry invite you to sleep there? A. He did not invite me. I had slept there on Sunday and Tuesday nights.

Q. When did you decide to sleep there?

A. After dinner. There was nothing that I had to do in town, and I had an appointment in the morning.

Q. I put it to you that you had planned to stay at Westbourne on Wednesday night.

A. Had we dined at the Prince George, I probably would have slept at home.

I was unsure that Higgs had anything more in mind than making Christie as uncomfortable as possible. But his use of the phrase "I put it to you" was a signal to the witness as well as the jury. It was the equivalent of a swordsman saying *en garde* to his opponent.

Q. You phoned your man Gibson during dinner?

A. Gibson phoned me while I was at dinner, and it was then that I told Gibson to bring my car.

Q. Why did you want your car?

A. I always want my car with me. ... I particularly wanted it that night because I was going on a trip the next morning.

Q. So it was during dinner that you decided to stay at Westbourne?

A. Yes.

Q. Did you instruct your man Gibson to leave your car at the country club?

A. I did.

Q. Why?

A. Because I wanted to conserve my gasoline, and if it had been brought over to Westbourne, there was a good chance of my car being used.

There was a titter of amusement in the courtroom. If that reply was true, it meant that Christie had gone through a rather elaborate manipulation just to save gas.

Q. When was there a good chance of your car being used?

A. There were guests at Westbourne and there were suggestions of going to the Prince George, or possibly some other place.

Q. Was it not the suggestion that dinner be had at the Prince George?

A. We could have gone afterwards.

A CONSPIRACY OF CROWNS

Q. Wasn't Mr. Hubbard's car there, as well as two of Sir Harry's?

A. Yes.

Q. Why were you, then, fearful that your car would have been used?

A. In the circumstances, there would have been every possibility of my car being used if it had been there.

Q. All would have been handy? Is that your best reason?

A. Yes. I was going on a trip the next day, and might not have had enough gasoline. Gasoline is rationed.

Q. Did you know how much gasoline you had in your car?

A. No.

Q. If you did not know, you were not in a position to say whether you would have had enough for the next day in any event?

A. That is correct.

Q. No one at Westbourne knew your car was there?

A. Not that I know of.

Higgs walked to the defense table, picked up a copy of the official record of the magistrate's hearing, and flipped through the pages. He then read Christie's testimony to the effect that he had left his car at the club, as he had done many times before, because he wanted to conserve gas for the next day, and because the country club was the logical place to leave the car.

Q. What do you mean that the country club is the logical place to leave the car?

A. It was the logical place because there was a watchman there and none at Westbourne.

Q. Then you left it there for security?

A. I did not think of that at the time.

Q. Why are you so especially careful to say you did not want to use the car *that* night?

A. I said I wanted to conserve my gasoline, and if my car was brought to Westbourne, there was a possibility that it might be used.

What was happening to Christie had to be as clear to the jurors as it was to me. If he had been wired to a meter that registered pulse or blood pressure, the needle would have shot straight up each time Higgs asked about the car, and how available it was.

He had milked that subject for all he could, and now the questioning turned to Harold's description of the house the night of the murder. I knew what he was driving at: he wanted some kind of confirmation that Christie was not in the house at the time Oakes was killed.

Again Godfrey read from the preliminary record, quoting Charles Hubbard, one of the dinner guests, as saying that he noticed Westbourne "all lighted up" when he passed it at eleven-thirty, after driving Mrs. Henneage home.

Erie Stanley Gardner would later write that he clocked Harold Christie's silence before he answered. It lasted twenty seconds, a length of time so dramatic in a courtroom that it might be compared to a television anchorman staring into a camera, suddenly struck dumb. Harold seemed to be nearly in pain. He said he would not deny that the lights in the house were on; he himself was in his room, reading. Of course, the lights were off when the mosquitoes woke him. He thought he might have been asleep longer the second time than the first.

Q. Were they the only two occasions when you awoke that night? A. Yes.

Q. Did you leave Westbourne at any time that night? A. I

did not leave Westbourne any time during the night of July seventh, or until the next night of July eighth.

Standing in the dock, in my cage, I was still unsure what Christie was hiding. He could not have killed the old man himself, of this I was certain. In such an event, he would surely not have been so insistent on having remained so near the death scene. But there was another possibility, which was that he feared evidence would be produced that implicated a hired killer, in which case his leaving could have been seen as clearing the way for the intruder.

Now Higgs guided him again through the testimony of Captain Sears:

Q. I put it to you that Captain Sears saw you at about midnight in a station wagon in George Street.

A. Was he certain?

Q. I put it to you.

A. Captain Sears was mistaken. I did not leave Westbourne after retiring to my room that night ... and any statement to the effect that I was in town is a very grave mistake.

The trial adjourned at five o'clock, and Christie was back in the witness box the next morning. It was noted that he was wearing a freshly pressed white linen suit and white shirt, as he had the previous day. Within minutes his clothes were drenched with sweat. Higgs moved on to the events of Thursday morning, the eighth of July. Christie recalled that he rose and went directly to the veranda from his bedroom. He did not have a toothbrush with him that morning, and he did not remember if he had gone to the bathroom.

Q. You know that Mabel Ellis, the housemaid at Westbourne, says that you and Sir Harry usually were dressed before you had breakfast?

A. If we were going out early, we dressed; if not, we probably would not.

Q. Why did you not dress for breakfast on Thursday morning?

A. After I had discovered the body?

Q. Before you discovered it. Were you going out to have breakfast?

Once again, Erle Stanley Gardner bent his arm and checked the second hand on his wristwatch. Thirty-seven seconds ticked off before Christie answered: "Sir Harry rose at daybreak and he usually could be found looking out over the water."

Q. You were planning to go out that morning?

A. At ten-thirty.

Q. If you had smelled the smoke, would you have gone directly to Sir Harry's room?

A. I knew nothing until I entered Sir Harry's room that morning.

Q. When you went in, was the smell of burning intense or not?

A. Not particularly. I would not say extremely intense. I did not smell it when I went by the porch.

One could sense the tension in the courtroom rising as Higgs now turned to the physical condition of the body. Once more, Higgs read from the court record. Christie had said the body was not exactly flat on its back. Also, it was slightly diagonal to the mattress, but not much.

Q. You lifted his head and shook him. Which arm did you use?

A. I used my right arm and lifted his head and shoulder.

Q. Did you notice any blood coming from him?

A. No.

Q. You then got some water out of the carafe?

A. Yes. I do not remember whether it had a stopper.

Q. What happened to the water when you put it into Sir Harry's mouth?

A. It appeared to go down his throat. It went into his mouth.

Q. Why did you touch the body?

A. Why did I? Well, if you walked into a room and found your best friend in that condition, what would you do? I thought he might still be alive. The body was not cold, it was warmish, and Dr. Quackenbush will confirm that.

The question had at first seemed to startle Christie, the irrelevance of it, and he answered with a touch of cockiness. But I knew from his reaction that Higgs had scored a major point. He had been waiting for the right moment to introduce into evidence the grisly photograph of Sir Harry lying across his bed. Taken by the official RAF photographer, it was a full-length view, showing in sickening clarity the bloodied head and scorched body. Higgs turned the picture around, gave it a final lingering look, then handed it up to Christie, who reached for it with a hand that visibly trembled.

Q. Does that look like the body of a man who is alive?

A. No, it does not, but the body was warm. I did everything I could, hoping there might be life. I asked Mrs. Kelly and my brother to get a doctor.

Q. Yet you called for the servants?

A. I called for the most immediate help, which would be the servants.

Higgs held out his hand, and Christie gladly returned the photograph, which was then passed to the foreman of the jury. All of the jurors craned their necks, almost in unison, waiting their turns to view the dead Sir Harry.

Q. You then went to the south window and called for the watchman?

A. Yes.

Q. You say you had some hope?

A. I had some hope, yes. I was panicky and I called for the nearest assistance.

Q. What help did you hope to get from housemaids and watchman?

A. I called them because they were nearest. I then called Mrs. Kelly.

Q. You never did phone a doctor, did you?

A. No. I asked Mrs. Kelly and my brother to get one.

Christie was shouting his answers now, so sharply that the people milling about on the lawn of the building could hear clearly, without having the words repeated by those stationed beneath the windows.

Q. Was not Sir Harry's mouth clenched tight when you gave him that water?

A. No. I was able to get the glass between his lips.

Q. And the water went into his mouth?

A. It appeared to.

Q. Did you notice any burning spots on the bed?

A. No.

Q. Yet you went through other rooms to see if there was any sign of fire?

A. There was smoke in the room, and burned spots on the door.

The jurors were now leaning forward in their seats. This was the first direct reference to the fire, which remained one of the bafflements of the case. If the fire had been meant to destroy the house and the evidence, why had it been set so carelessly that it failed to spread, or cause more significant damage? Or was it a device to mislead the investigators?

Q. In searching for signs of fire, I believe you went into the adjoining room to the east, into your bathroom and into your bedroom?

A. Yes.

Q. Why did you go into your bedroom?

A. To see if there were any sparks, or if there was anybody in there.

Higgs turned to the jury and, with his profile to the witness, drew out his next question with delicious irony: "But you had been in your bedroom all night, Mr. Christie?"

Again there was an agonizing delay as Harold shifted his weight and finally blurted out his answer: "Yes!"

Q. Did you, then, expect to find fire or someone lurking in your room?
A. It was logical to look there, which I did.
Q. In a room in which you had slept all night?
A. Yes.
Q. You got a towel and wiped Sir Harry's face?
A. I did.
Q. You think you wet that towel in your bathroom?
A. I think I did, but I am not positive. But that is my impression.
Q. Did you soak it?
A. I would not say I soaked it. I wet the side of it.
Q. Which side of it?

With that, Christie literally threw up his hands in a gesture of exasperation. "For God's sake, Higgs. be reasonable. I don't remember which side of the towel."

Ignoring the plaintiveness of that cry, indifferent to whether he was creating sympathy for the forlorn figure in the box, Godfrey continued in the same calm, plodding tone:

Q. And then later you wet that towel again? A. I am not positive whether I got another towel, but I thought I used the same one. Q. You did this in order to try to revive Sir Harry? A. Yes.

Higgs returned again to the stack of photographs on the clerk's table. He leafed through the pile and removed one, taken from the left side of Sir Harry's face. With a quick, almost taunting motion, he handed it up to Christie.

Q. Would you say that face has been wiped?
A. I say that this face had been wiped. I would say that water had been put on the forehead and on the face.
Q. That picture shows blood flowing from the ear across the face and over the nose?
A. It does.

When the jury received the photograph moments later, they saw a line of caked blood so distinct and straight that it might have been drawn with a red pencil. The line was perhaps a quarter-inch wide, and it ran upward from the bottom of Sir Harry's left ear to just below the left eye and over the bridge of the nose. It was simply not possible, if one accepts the law of gravity, for his head to have been in a level position after the fatal wounds were inflicted.

Q. Would that suggest to you that Sir Harry had been lying facedown on the bed?

A. Yes.

Q. But you did not find Sir Harry that way?

A. No. I did not find Sir Harry that way. When I first saw him, his face was straight up, not completely but partially.

At that point the Lord Chief Justice broke in, asking, "After you lifted it, how did it get into this position?"

"It might have fallen into that position shown in the photograph," said Harold, uncertainly, "after I had raised his head and put a pillow under it." The Lord Chief Justice shook his head, slowly, from side to side. The jurors watched him intently. Whatever the implications, Sir Oscar did not like them.

It was fairly clear by then that Higgs had succeeded in reducing Christie's thought processes to pulp. He was asked about the bloody smears both on the inside and the outside of his bedroom door. He thought he might have made them, but wasn't sure. He then changed his mind three times.

Responding to another question from the Lord Chief Justice, he said he remembered leaving his room by the north door. Higgs pointed out there were no bloodstains discovered on that door. Harold corrected himself: it must have been the center door into the middle bedroom.

Finally, he asked permission to change his answer again: he went through the north door first. He may have returned through the middle door.

Higgs decided that he had nothing further to gain by pursuing Christie, and with a nod to His Honor, he announced that he had no further questions. To Harold's obvious chagrin, Hallinan exercised his right to reexamine the witness. His questions dealt only with the issue of the feathers: they were scattered over the body and bed when he first entered the room; none were being blown about by the electric fan on the floor.

Christie was excused. He stepped down slowly and gingerly, as would a man with a bad back.

Through the courtroom buzzed that distinctive sound which indicates, at once, confusion and skepticism on the part of the spectators. I shared their reaction. The only difference was that my life was at stake, and their concern was what to have for lunch.

Higgs had so effectively demolished Harold Christie that Adderley took the unorthodox step of advising the jury that it may disregard his testimony. He added that their case would stand without it.

Clearly, nothing in what Harold said, or suggested, right or wrong, had been damaging to my defense. He had, in fact, pointed suspicion at no one except himself. Godfrey's objective was to discredit the prosecution's case wherever he could, and so far he had succeeded beyond our expectation.

Later, meeting in Miller's office, I still differed with him on strategy. I was much less inclined to give Christie the benefit of the doubt I had accorded him in July. The pieces were forming a pattern in my mind: Sir Harry's bitter belief that Christie had double-crossed him on the contract to build the new air base; his preparations to move to Mexico, or even Santo Domingo, removing his wealth from the Bahamas and leaving Christie's investments, and his future, in serious jeopardy.

I wanted Higgs to attack Harold on these points, and to raise questions about the financial alliance between Harold, Sir Harry, and the Duke of Windsor.

It was a battle I would not win. Higgs flatly refused. "Alfred," he said, "my job is to win your freedom, not to convict Harold Christie. And after the trial, one would like to think you will leave here without having to fear for your life."

Eric Stanley Gardner, analyzing the trial as Perry Mason might have, thought Christie had come off rather well, that his inconsistencies were understandable, given his personal trauma. But the jurors, as they contemplated the testimony, were perplexed. After examining the bloody and gory photographs, it was bizarre to think that anyone could have thought Sir Harry still alive, or would have made even a casual attempt to cleanse his face, or had found him in the position described.

But Harold Christie, as no one needed to remind me, though several did, was not on trial. I did not sleep well that night.

The order in which the prosecution called its witnesses puzzled many observers. Certainly, Christie might have performed with more assurance if he had been allowed to follow some of the secondary witnesses, rather than being called first.

The next day's testimony was either technical or routine: some RAF officers described the photographic and fingerprint apparatus; Mabel Ellis described the house and Sir Harry's usual schedule there; two constables described the room where Sir Harry had been murdered and mentioned that they had had to remove a chair that was near the bed and place it in the hall; Dr. Quackenbush told us that when he saw the body of Sir Harry Oakes, rigor mortis had set in.

The testimony of Hugh Quackenbush caused a visible stir in the jury. Sands and two other jurors put their heads together and whispered to each other, then Sands asked the Lord Chief Justice if the chair that had been removed from the room was the same one Rigor Mortis had sat in.

A ripple of laughter ran through the crowd. Sir Oscar rapped his gavel and, with great tact, explained to the jury that rigor mortis was not a person but a description of the rigidity of a dead body.

I looked at this jury of my peers and felt a twinge of uneasiness.

Sands did ask of the doctor one of the day's necessary

questions: "In your opinion, did Sir Harry move after receiving the blows?"

"In my opinion," said Quackenbush, "Sir Harry never moved after the blows were struck."

Dr. Lawrence Wylie Fitzmaurice followed his associate to the stand, and gave the best description yet of the four wounds: each less than an inch deep, forming a perfect square two by two inches, just above the victim's left ear. He admitted candidly that he did not know of an instrument that could, in four separate strikes to the head, cause such wounds.

Nor could he determine in what position, or by the use of what inflammable material, the pattern of burns on the body might have occurred. "Much would depend," said Fitzmaurice, "upon the size of the nozzle, and of the gun, and the number of squirts."

These responses were encouraging to Higgs and Callender, inasmuch as they meant the Crown had not yet found a satisfactory theory to explain the cause or nature of the fire. Nor was there any support here for the police theory that the killer had found in the room a half-filled spray can of insect repellent, and thus, acting on impulse, started the fire.

Hallinan called Dorothy Clark and Jean Ainsley, two of my dinner guests, as prosecution witnesses. Their account of how I drove them home would put me near Westbourne during the hours in which the crime took place. This would establish what the law calls "opportunity."

In fact, both witnesses gave evidence that was powerfully in my favor, and opened the way for Higgs to expose the shortcomings and disarray of the prosecution, whose attempts to use these witnesses backfired.

The two women were wives of Royal Air Force pilots whose husbands were stationed in Nassau. Dorothy was with Jean and Captain Clark, she testified, when Fred Ceretta introduced us in the bar of the Prince George Hotel. The captain encouraged them to accept my invitation to dinner at my home that night—a point that dismissed the insinuation of any marital misconduct.

Mrs. Clark confirmed that there were eleven people at the party, including myself and de Visdelou and his date, Betty Roberts. The party broke up around midnight, and she repeated the story of passing the pharmacy and checking our watches, establishing the time as a few minutes after one.

I would have driven past Westbourne, on my way home, at around one-thirty, well within the prosecution's essential time frame. There was no discrepancy here, but Higgs went briskly to his cross-examination. The testimony of Dorothy Clark was about to backfire on the prosecution.

She confirmed that I had lighted the candlesticks during dinner. She remembered petting an ash-gray Maltese cat. She identified the coat and slacks and two-tone shoes I wore. No one at the party was intoxicated; I was relaxed and in good humor on the drive home.

All of these comments went directly to charges that the prosecution made, or were helpful to my defense. But Godfrey was hoping for something more. He turned to the morning of Friday, the ninth of July, and the scene in the downstairs living room at Westbourne. She sat with de Visdelou, Betty Roberts, Mr. Hubbard, and Mrs. Henneage, all waiting to be interviewed by the American detectives, Melchen and Barker. Lieutenant Douglas, of the Bahamas police, looked on.

Q. Did you see the accused, Alfred de Marigny, taken upstairs that morning? A. **Yes,** I did.

Q. I **put** it to you. Was it between eleven and twelve o'clock? A. Yes, I am sure it was.

I felt a surge of excitement as I peered between my bars. We had spent countless hours debating the circumstances of the now-famous latent fingerprint that was the basis for much of the Crown's case. The Miami duo had sworn that at no time after the body was discovered was I allowed upstairs— not until the Chinese screen near the bed had been removed around three in the afternoon. Out of the blue, one of their own witnesses, not unfriendly to me but biased to neither side, had shot them down. I had been seen upstairs *before* the screen was removed—if, in fact, one accepted the claim that the print came from that source. Higgs, gambling, decided to follow up Dorothy Clark's answer.

Q. Where were you at the time you saw the accused taken upstairs by the American detective?

A. I was sitting in the western living room on a couch, on the south side of the room.

Q. When did you next see the accused?

A. I was in the dining room, and the accused was talking to Miss Betty Roberts. I heard her ask him, "Where have you been? You look as if you have been sleeping." Mr. de Marigny replied, "No, I have been upstairs with Captain Melchen."

Several of the jurors turned their heads to note the reaction of Hallinan and Adderley. I took this as a splendid sign.

Q. How long would you say that the accused was out of your sight from the time you saw him taken upstairs by the American detective until you saw him next in the dining room?

A. I would say at least three-quarters of an hour.

There would pass several days of volleying, in which one side would score and then the other, and to some of these moments I will return shortly. But the next dramatic breakthrough would come, predictably, when the bloodhounds from Miami took the stand.

In the magistrate's court, Melchen had testified that I had been taken upstairs after 3:30 P.M. Melchen even referred to a notebook he whipped out of his coat pocket with a flourish.

Melchen and two Nassau constables, Tynes and Knowles, confirmed the time. Now, in an embarrassment that could only be described as excruciating, they begged the pardon of the Lord Chief justice and paraded one by one to the witness stand to correct themselves.

The log kept by Lieutenant Douglas had been produced,

and my interrogation was listed as having occurred at eleven o'clock in the morning. It had been initialed by Erskine-Lindop, the absent witness now stationed in Trinidad. (Had anyone been tempted to tamper with the log, Douglas, it was later rumored, had warned the Miami cops that he would not cover for them.)

Melchen recanted, then Barker, then Tynes and Knowles, who said simply they had been in error.

In a remarkable gesture, Sir Oscar flipped a fountain pen straight up in the air. His voice dripping sarcasm, he asked how long they had been with the force, and if they had ever testified in court before. They were thirteen-year veterans, they replied, and had testified many times.

The Lord Chief Justice said he regretted very much such lax police work. It occurred to me that officers of the court find it difficult to say that someone lied.

It was Eric Hallinan who introduced the subject of the Chinese screen and the elusive fingerprint, also known as Exhibit J.

The Attorney General led Barker through his story: he had lifted between fifty and seventy prints, but only a few were legible. All were taken off with Scotch tape except the last three, which were raised with a strip of gummed rubber that was then covered with a transparent plastic sheet.

Unlike Melchen, who was squat and jowly and reminded one of a bartender, Barker made a strong impression. He was close to fifty, tall and athletic-looking, wavy-haired, a sharp dresser, bearing a resemblance to the movie actor Robert Ryan. He answered smoothly the powder-puff questions fed him by Hallinan.

Q. On the night of the ninth, when you examined those latent prints, did you find any one which you considered worth processing?

A. I did.

Q. Did you find on the screen an impression which bore any similarity to the fingerprint of the accused?

A. I did. I discovered this similarity after I had finished working on the screen in the hallway, which was around one-thirty P.M.

Q. ... What fingerprint, in your opinion, was that?

A. Finger number ten of the accused, that is, the little finger of the left hand.

Another fingerprint, he added, of digit number 5, was even clearer, but the pattern was reversed when lifted.

Godfrey Higgs was on his feet, took a step toward the bench, and bowed to the Chief Justice. "My lord," he said, "I reluctantly ask leave to interrupt my learned friend; but I must in all candor point out that this is the first time the defense has heard anything about *lifted* prints. When the evidence was submitted in the magistrate's court, I assumed that the fingerprints referred to were photographs of prints on the screen. I only learn today of something on rubber."

Visibly disturbed, Sir Oscar asked Hallinan when the photograph of the latent number 5 print was taken, and the answer given was July 9.

"My lord," Higgs implored, "that is exactly what I object to. This piece of rubber is not the best evidence, and I know of no case in which it has been produced in court before. The proper evidence would be to produce the print on the article on which it was found, and I submit that there is no print now on that screen.

"We have only the word of the witness to suggest that the print in question came from that screen. We for the defense are in a position to prove that a photograph of a lifted print *cannot* be produced as the original latent raised print of the accused, and that the best evidence is the screen itself, on which the print should be produced, and on which there is now no sign of a fingerprint."

SIR OSCAR: You would not object to a photograph of a raised print on that screen?

HIGGS: I would not, my lord. That is precisely my point. By

a "raised" print I mean a print that has been dusted with powder and is visible. It can then be photographed *in situ*. The original fingerprint can be preserved by covering it with Scotch tape. The original fingerprint in this way is not destroyed. It is there for all to see; and in addition, if need be and helpful, the photograph of the print *in situ* may be received.

SIR OSCAR: Your point is that they should have powdered the print, left it there, and taken a photograph?

HIGGS: That's it precisely, my lord.

SIR OSCAR: What you say is that since they did not powder the print and leave it on the screen, it might be a forgery.

HIGGS: That is exactly my fear and my contention. Whether this print came from that point on the screen which the witness describes now depends upon the uncorroborated evidence of the witness himself.

The Lord Chief Justice now addressed himself to Barker, who was looking much less confident and at case.

SIR OSCAR: So by your process of lifting this print on the rubber matting, you deliberately destroyed the best evidence, which was the print itself?

BARKER: This manner of lifting the print does destroy it, yes.

SIR OSCAR: And a photograph of this print *in situ*, taken with a (proper) camera would also have shown the background so that there would be no doubt where the print came from now?

BARKER: Well, the background doesn't always positively tell you exactly where the print came from.

Only the professionals in the courtroom clearly understood the dueling that was going on here. But no one could mistake the tone or demeanor of the Lord Chief Justice. "I have no hesitancy," he said, "in admitting that I am taken by surprise. It occurs to me that I may well admit this print, Exhibit J, into evidence and let the jury decide whether it is legitimate, and what weight to give it. If they have reason to doubt its genuineness, they can discard the print and, for that matter, the testimony of this witness altogether. We approach the hour of adjournment. The court needs time to reflect upon this critical matter. You will have my decision when we sit again on the morrow."

Sir Oscar Daly's words appeared in his own hand in the official transcript of the trial. There were no court reporters in the colonies, and no typed or printed record. Painstakingly, using a quill pen dipped in a well, Sir Oscar recorded the testimony. In some cases, reporters covering the trial kept their own, but adding to the color and suspense of the proceedings was the sight of the Lord Chief

Justice writing his summaries, at times requiring a pause to enable him to make up lost ground.

None of this concerned me, but only his indecision over the matter of the tenth digit. I could not believe, after the deceit so far uncovered, after attempts to falsify the evidence that could not be mistaken for errors of honest intent, that he could rule against me.

But the thought lingered and gnawed at me that yes, he could. If by his action, or inaction, the jury came to feel that he endorsed Barker and his evidence, the outcome of the trial was ordained. I would hang.

THE VERDICT

I overheard someone—it might have been an attorney, a jailer, or a reporter—say that our trial was a history-making one. For the first time, fingerprint evidence had been introduced in a Bahamas court of law.

I remembered a favorite story of an American lawyer named Abraham Lincoln, about a client who was tarred and feathered and ridden out of town on a rail. "If it wasn't for the honor," Lincoln quoted the man as saying, "I would just as soon have walked."

We did not have long to wait for the Chief Justice's ruling. Again, the courtroom was packed. No one in the room was unaware of what was at stake: without Exhibit J, the alleged print of the little finger of my left hand, the Crown's case would come apart. I had been arrested on the basis of Barker's claim that he had seen burnt hair on my arm; that I had quarreled with Sir Harry Oakes; and that her parents did not approve of my marriage to Nancy. All in all, pretty thin stew.

Sir Oscar Daly had decided to rule that Exhibit J was admissible. My whole body felt numb, even as I heard him say, "I am amazed that this question has not been settled either in England or in the American courts. I deem it not my duty to pass upon the ... propriety of what this police officer did or did not do. It may well be that his techniques and processes leave much to be desired ... I am faced only with this one fingerprint, Exhibit J ... and it is formally received. I must point out to the jury ... that the mere fact that the fingerprint is admitted does not mean that it must be accepted as legitimate and genuine by the jury. The weight to be given this particular item of evidence is a matter for them and them alone to decide."

I could find little comfort in how he qualified his ruling. But to my surprise, Higgs and Callender were not discouraged. They were eager to impeach Barker's testimony, and were confident the forgery would be apparent to the jurors. They also understood, as I had not, that had the judge ruled otherwise I would be haunted always by the claim that I had escaped the gallows by wriggling through a legal loophole.

And so the actors returned to their places on the stage, and Eric Hallinan completed his questioning of Captain James Otto Barker. His purpose now was to establish that a second expert had confirmed Barker's find.

Q. And what did you do with the pictures you made of the fingerprints?

A. I made duplicates of both the latent print and the known rolled print of the number five finger of the accused and forwarded them on July twenty-third to Detective Frank Conway, who is head of identification for the New York City Police Department.

Q. And why did you do that?

A. To get his additional opinion as to whether the raised latent print found on the screen was made by the accused's right little finger.

The "rolled" fingerprint, I knew, referred to the official prints taken when the police literally roll your fingertips across an inked pad and then onto paper. The reference to the number 5 finger puzzled me. Were they claiming now that I had somehow left impressions of both of my little fingers on the screen? Was it believable that a person, even by accident, could brush an object and leave no trace except the perfect imprint of both of his pinky fingers?

I realized that this was a serious matter, and the least detail could have a bearing on the outcome of the case. But to my ears, as they jabbered over the fifth finger and the tenth finger, latent prints and rolled prints, lifts and raises, it was like hearing people discuss their favorite noodle at a spaghetti dinner.

In a very few moments, much of the confusion would be swept away. Godfrey Higgs was about to begin his cross-examination of Captain Barker.

Q. You are not prepared to say that the fingerprint came off the area marked "5" in the second panel?

A. I am not.

Q. Do you know what portion of that top panel you took the print from?

A. I can only say with certainty that it came from the top portion.

Q. Captain Barker, will you please walk over to the screen and point out area number five, marked in pencil at the top of the panel?

Barker stepped down from the witness box and walked across the well of the court. Because ninety percent of a legal proceeding is verbal, sometimes more, any physical movement carries with it a certain drama, a sense of anticipation. The jurors and spectators all felt this was such a moment.

Barker stood in front of the screen, hesitating, reaching out with an arm, and then pulling it back. Finally he turned and looked up at Sir Oscar as if asking for help: "I wish to inform the court that this blue line which I now see on the screen was not made by me."

Higgs had to shout over the noise in the courtroom. "I beg your pardon?"

Barker pointed to the screen. "There has been an effort to trace over a black line with blue pencil. That is not my work. I made the black line in the presence of the Attorney General in the police station on August first."

No one spoke as Barker continued to stare at the screen. The room was electric. Had someone tried to sabotage the Crown's most precious evidence?

Suddenly, Barker took a step backward and his face turned pale. "I now withdraw what I said about the alteration of the blue line. I find my initials where the blue line is."

For the third time, a witness for the prosecution had been forced to reverse himself, to admit an error and deny his own testimony.

To my amazement and anger, the Lord Chief Justice attempted to ease his embarrassment. "My sympathies to you, sir. I have often been confused in such a way myself."

Sir Oscar was, of course, a compassionate man and, as his friends knew, a sometimes absentminded one. His expression was genuine. And I realized his kindness only emphasized the gaffe Barker had committed. Higgs would give him no relief.

Q. You have that area marked in two colors, in black pencil and blue?

A. Yes, the area was marked by me on two occasions, the first time in black and the second time in blue.

Q. And in what color did you mark the spot where your initials are now visible?

A. That was in black.

Q. You have the date "7/9/43" marked in black pencil?

A. Yes, the American way of writing July ninth. That is the date on which I found the print. I made the inscription on August first at the Nassau police headquarters. At the same time, I marked the figure "5" with a black pencil within the area marked on the black line.

Q. So until August first, there was nothing to indicate where that exhibit came from?

A. Nothing except my memory.

Q. You were certain, then, that that print came from this area?

A. I certainly was.

Q. And why are you not certain now?

A. Detective Conway of the U.S.A. and I last Saturday examined the area marked "5," but we could not find evidence of ridges which enabled us to say with certainty that that print came from within the marked area. Therefore, I had to confine myself to saying that it came from the top of the panel.

Q. Are you not saying positively that it did because you *know* it did not come from that area?

A. I doubt very seriously if it would be possible for the fingerprint to have come from area number five.

Q. Did you know that the defense had also photographed area number five for experimental purposes?

A. I did not know that.

Q. You made a trip to Nassau in September?

A. Yes, about this case. I came on a Saturday.

Q. I put it to you that this was two days after the defense conducted these experiments?

A. That is a coincidence.

Higgs nodded and replied, "I would say it was highly coincidental."

A murmur of appreciation spread through the gallery. Now Barker's motivation for changing his testimony was clear. And the work that had gone on behind the scenes had paid off. It was in September that Captain Miller had been visited by his son, who was employed by Scotland Yard. Together they had helped Higgs obtain an enlarged photograph of the screen, and had had a replica constructed by a local tradesman, reproducing each scroll and ridge and wavy line.

Then they had asked me to apply my left little finger to various spots, here, there, all over the screen. I pressed hard. I pressed lightly. They dusted the print and photographed it. But whatever the angle or the pressure, each lift, and each photograph, reflected the background of the screen. There was simply no way that Exhibit J had been taken from the Chinese screen. Not before or during or after the murder.

I had known this from the very beginning. But from the smiles and satisfactions on their faces, I accepted the fact that until this demonstration not even my closest defenders were entirely sure.

Higgs returned to Barker's retraction:

Q. Was it on that trip to Nassau that you realized that you could not get the print out of this area?

A. No.

Q. When did you first discover that Exhibit J could not have come from the area marked?

A. A week ago last Saturday.

Q. What made you reexamine the screen that day?

A. I knew that I would be called upon to produce the exact spot, therefore I examined the screen.

Q. Did Mr. Conway . . . tell you that it could not come from there?

A. He agreed with me.

Q. Realizing that you would be called upon to [locate] the exact spot where the print came from, you did not find out until two days before the trial began that you could not find the exact spot?

A. That is correct.

Q. When did you decide to change your evidence?

A. Immediately.

Higgs waited a few beats, giving the exchange more time to sink in on the jurors. When he addressed Barker again, there was just a hint of sarcasm in his voice:

Q. Where do you say *today* that Exhibit J came from? A. From the top portion of the end panel with the mark "5," but I cannot locate it any closer.

All this time Barker had been standing, as if naked, in front of the screen, unable to say how many lifts he had found, unable to pinpoint where he had found them, unable to conceal how inept his effort had been. Now Higgs suggested to the Lord Chief Justice that the witness could return to the box, and Barker actually gave Higgs a look of gratitude.

The tempo and nature of the questions changed. I could not guess what Godfrey had in mind, but he began to ask Barker about his law-enforcement experience, eliciting from him that he had joined the Miami police department in 1925, had been a motorcycle patrolman and a dispatcher, had been assigned as a clerk to the Criminal Investigation Department, and had been for eleven months the superintendent of this office, which employed two men. His rank was then reduced to patrolman on charges of insubordination.

Q. Is it customary in Miami to appoint superintendents with such meager qualifications as you have described to us?
A. No, I do not think that it is.

Skillfully, without venturing into unknown waters, Higgs had hinted that there were political favors in Barker's police career.

Q. Do you term yourself a fingerprint expert?
A. As the term applies, I think I am.

Q. Have you ever, in testifying, produced the object in court with the print on it?
A. Yes, when the objects were movable.

Q. Would it not be highly advantageous to have the print in this courtroom today still on the screen?
A. Yes, I suppose it would.

Q. Why did you not introduce the screen in this court? Is it not movable?
A. It can be moved. [At this point, Barker's eyes darted irresistibly to the screen, only ten feet from where he stood.]

Q. Did you not come prepared to look for fingerprint evidence?
A. Yes.

Q. But you left your fingerprint camera behind?
A. Yes. I thought the kit I brought sufficient to take care of a murder case. The fingerprint camera would have been desirable, but I did not know the conditions.

Godfrey did not press the point, but I wondered how many of the jurors remembered that Melchen and Barker had testified in the preliminary hearings that they thought they were coming to investigate a *suicide*.

Q. Could you not easily have got a camera flown over from Miami by Friday morning? A. I believe I could.

Q. And you never made that effort? A. No.

Higgs drew concessions from Barker that he could have borrowed equipment from a commercial photographer in Nassau, or from the Royal Air Force detachment. And while he had concentrated his efforts on the screen, he had not bothered to dust the headboard of Sir Harry's bed, or the thermos on the nightstand, or the railing of the staircase. Higgs was forcing him, in his own words, to admit that he was incompetent, or else to explain his actions with answers that were senseless.

Q. I suggest that there were numerous objects in that room that you did not process?

A. I suppose that is correct.

Q. If the accused left a fingerprint on the screen, don't you think it likely that he might have left other prints in the room?

A. Yes, under ordinary conditions, but the very nature of the crime in my opinion would most likely prevent the assailant, in his press of emotion and hurry, from handling a lot of objects in the room. In this case, there was no necessity for the assailant to handle many objects, in my opinion.

I have what I believe is a logical mind, and to my thinking, exactly the opposite was more likely. If the killer was an amateur, acting in emotion and haste, leaving a room spattered with blood and half burned, he would be knocking over objects blindly, moving whatever was in his way.

Q. Well, why did you process the downstairs powder room?

A. We could not exclude anything in an investigation of this type.

Q. But you did exclude a number of articles in Sir Harry's room?

A. In my opinion, yes.

Q. Had you excluded the possibility that the accused might have an accomplice?

A. I have not excluded the possibility of accomplices, nor have I advanced the theory that he had accomplices.

Q. In identifying a criminal, you require the rolled impressions of as many persons as possible who were at the crime scene?

A. Yes, for elimination purposes.

Q. And on Thursday you only got the rolled impressions of Major Pemberton, Dr. Quackenbush, and Harold Christie?

A. That is correct, and the right hand of Sir Harry Oakes.

Repetition is a favorite device of lawyers when a witness has been caught in a costly admission or contradiction. Higgs now turned up the heat.

Q. Did you roll the fingerprints of Mrs. Henneage? A. No, I did not. Q. Why?

A. I was not told that she had been in the room. Q. Did you roll the prints of Mrs. Kelly? A. No. Q. Why?

A. I was not told that she had been in the room. Q. But you now know that she had been in the room several times?

A. I know it now, but I did not know it then.

The litany was under way. Barker had not bothered to fingerprint the Attorney General, Erskine-Lindop, Corporal Muir, Constables Knowles, Tynes, and Nottage, Captain Melchen, Frank Christie, a Mrs. Gale, Mabel Ellis, or the coroner.

Nor had he fingerprinted one other person who had been in the room: the Duke of Windsor.

Q. Of the latent fingerprints you raised, how many did you identify?

A. The accused, Dr. Quackenbush, Major Pemberton, and myself.

Q. You did not find a single fingerprint of Harold Christie in that room?

A. No, I did not.

Q. You knew that Mr. Christie handled the drinking glass and the thermos?

A. I knew at the time.

Q. Is not a glass considered to be an excellent surface on which latent fingerprints can be found?

A. Yes, but I found no identifiable prints on the glass.

Q. Although Mr. Harold Christie and Sir Harry had been living there together for several days, you found no fingerprints of Mr. Christie?

A. No.

In one of the trial's more interesting vignettes, Barker chose that moment to ask for a glass of water. Higgs never moved, never took his eyes off him, as he drained it in one swallow, requested another, and drained that one also.

Until the court adjourned for the day, I felt mostly elation. I saw Barker as a creature to be pitied, not hated. But to my surprise and irritation, I learned that the members of the press were making bets on whether I would hang or go free, and there was more money against me than for me.

Erie Stanley Gardner, bringing Perry Mason's legend to his role as correspondent for the Hearst news syndicate, had been impressed, almost admiring, of both Christie and Barker in the witness box. Day by day, he seemed to feel my chances were slipping away.

I was amazed. It was like spectators at a boxing match, rooting for one fighter or another, arguing over the quality of the punches, no one appearing to see the same fight.

One could hardly wait to see what the next day would bring. And Godfrey Higgs had a wonderful piece of business up his sleeve, when Barker again took his place in the box.

Q. With regard to the handprints on the northern wall, did you measure these prints?

A. No.

Q. Why not?

A. It would not have furnished us with evidence.

Q. Why not?

A. There were no visible ridge marks or fingerprints for

identification.

Q. Did you not at least determine the size of the hand that might have made the prints?

A. It would have been difficult to determine the size of the hand. You could not necessarily get the length. It would all depend on how the hand was placed on the wall.

Q. Might not it be the palm print of a man in the room on the night of the murder?

A. It appeared to be an average hand, neither large nor small.

Q. Wasn't it a small hand?

A. I would say an average adult's hand, medium height in size, as I recall. If I had made a complete examination then, I could form an opinion as to whether the marks on the northern wall were those of a large hand or a small hand.

Higgs approached the bench. "My lord," he said to Sir Oscar, "I ask permission to have the accused hold up his hand."

The Chief Justice said, "Very well," and the two uniformed guards who were always at my side lifted the hinged lid of my cage and I stood to face the jury.

"Would you please hold up your hand, both of them?" asked Godfrey. As I did, he addressed Barker: "Would you say those were long hands?"

"Yes, I would say those are long hands."

Godfrey motioned me to be seated, and the guards lowered the lid and locked me in. To this day I am upset by the memory of my days in the dock, the freak-in-a-sideshow feeling, the sense of worthlessness. I was well dressed, well groomed, but I was still a man in a cage.

During the war in Vietnam, when I read about American prisoners of war kept on their knees in "tiger cages," I cried for them.

A rhythm developed between Higgs and Barker, Godfrey reciting the places and articles he had left unexamined, and the witness reduced to agreeing with him. Doors, windows, bloody towels, few of these had seemed important to him at the time.

Abruptly, Higgs invited Barker to demonstrate for the jury exactly how fingerprints are lifted. The chance to move around, to return to the ground where he was most comfortable, using his training, gave him new vigor. For thirty minutes he went on, working with his kit, explaining the tools, entertaining the jurors by lifting their prints from the railing in front of them. It was a nice show, a break in the monotony for all of us, but Captain Barker, poor fellow, never saw what Godfrey Higgs was doing to him.

Thinking back on that episode, many years later, I remember the great court-martial scene in the film *The Caine Mutiny*, when it suddenly, achingly dawned on Captain Quccg that the only sound in the room was the clicking of the steel ball bearings in his hand.

When Barker had finished, the court recessed for lunch. Later, in his closing arguments, Higgs would ask the jury to consider how an officer who, in court, was the ultimate professional, could so completely bungle his task when life and death were in the balance. How? Why? Could anyone make so many errors, unless the game was rigged?

The questioning moved on to the examination that had allegedly revealed to Barker the traces of burned hair on my arms. The witness said he knew that I was a sailor, out in the sun hours a day, and that I had told him of my having worked over the fires at the chicken farm.

Q. Then you could not say that the reddening on the skin of the accused was due to burns or not?

A. No.

Q. I suggest that you never examined [his] arms.

A. That is incorrect.

Q. Why didn't you show these hair burns to Major Pemberton, the head of the local CID?

A. Our highest authority in the United States is the chief

of police, and I therefore showed the hairs to Colonel Erskine-Lindop.

Q. So the only person who can corroborate the fact that you even examined the arms of the accused for burns is no longer available in the colony?

A. I don't know about that.

This oblique reference may have been the first indication some of the jurors had that Erskine-Lindop had been transferred to Trinidad.

Q. Did you not take specimens of hairs from the arms of the accused, from his beard, from his mustache, and from his hair?

A. Yes, I did.

Q. Was this so that these hairs could be examined under the microscope?

A. Yes, and to preserve them as evidence.

Q. And where are those hairs now? Do you propose to let us all see them here in open court?

A. The hairs were in Captain Mclchen's custody.

Q. He has already testified, and there was no mention of the hairs. Do you know what happened to them?

A. If Captain Melchen does not have them, I don't know where they are. It could be that they have been misplaced.

Q. Would these hairs from the body of the accused not be important evidence to you in this case?

A. No, not really. I saw them myself, so I know that he had varying degrees of burned hairs on his arms, face, and head.

Q. But we now have no other witness to corroborate what you tell us you saw?

A. I know what I saw, and I know that I saw burned hair from his body, and I know that I clipped off a substantial number of those hairs.

I was still displeased with the Lord Chief Justice for finding against us in the matter of Exhibit), but I will give him this: he did not preside, as many judges do, like a statue. He suddenly spun around in his chair so that his back was to Barker, a clear gesture of his contempt. He now spun back and demanded, "Who was in charge of this investigation?"

"Captain Melchen and I were working together, but neither of us was under the other."

"That *is* so!" snapped Sir Oscar. "That is so!" There was a tone of weary resignation in his voice.

Higgs went back to his task as if nothing out of the ordinary had happened.

Q. I put it to you that the accused told you he could not identify the shirt he was wearing that night?

A. That is untrue. I can remember his exact words. "It is very funny that I cannot find the shirt I wore."

Q. And isn't it very funny that you can remember those identical words, but cannot remember his description of the shirt?

A. It isn't very funny.

Q. The accused could very easily have picked up any one of those shirts and said, "This is the shirt I wore last night"?

A. Yes, as far as I was concerned.

Q. Would you have expected to find burned hairs on the legs of anyone who was in that room the night of the fire?

A. Not necessarily. It would be unlikely. The legs would be covered by his trousers, which would protect them.

Q. I take it, then, that is the reason you did not examine the accused's leg to see whether the hairs on his leg were burned?

A. That is correct.

Q. Is it safe to assume that you examined and found burned hairs on his arms because you considered his arms bare at the time the fire was started?

A. I did not consider it at that time. I just asked to see his arms.

Q. I put it to you that if you found singed or burned hairs on the arms of the accused, this would mean that he would have had to remove his jacket and shirt?

A. Unless the jacket and shirt were burned.

Of course, that would not be hard to determine. The Miami detectives had appropriated my coat and slacks as evidence, and I could see them, folded, on the clerk's table. Higgs walked over and, with the trousers draped across his arm, held out the coat in front of the jurors. Then he turned around and sort of flapped it, like a matador making a pass with his cape—a remarkably theatrical gesture for Godfrey—and handed the coat to Barker.

Q. I put it to you, show us some burns on the sleeves of this jacket or anyplace else on the jacket.

A. There are no burns on it.

Q. And would you be kind enough to point out the burned marks on these trousers?

A. I don't see any.

Q. But, sir, you did not take time to carefully examine either the trousers or the jacket. Are we to assume that you knew beforehand that there were no burns or soil marks on either one?

A. Yes, I had examined them before. There are no burn marks.

The point had been made. Higgs now had to return to his attack on the manner in which the investigation had produced Exhibit J.

Q. You told us yesterday, I believe, that you dusted some magazines and books. Did you think that the assailant was reading books and magazines in Sir Harry's room?

A. I thought he might have touched one.

It is possible, of course, to give an attorney too much credit. This may have been an innocent attempt to twit the witness. But some who analyzed the transcript thought that he had slipped in a passing slap at Christie, who had described how he read a copy of *Time* magazine before going to sleep.

Q. But you didn't think he might have touched the headboard of Sir Harry's bed, since you didn't dust there?

A. He might have touched it. I did not dust the headboard of Sir Harry's bed; the heat from the fire would have destroyed the latent friction ridges.

Q. Why would a latent fingerprint be preserved on the screen, which is blistered due to heat, and not on the headboard of Sir Harry's bed?

A. I could tell by looking for certain that there would be no fingerprints left on the bed.

Q. And you did not dust the foot of the bed either?

A. There is no foot of the bed there.

Higgs cocked an eyebrow. This was the kind of moment lawyers enjoy in their dreams. He walked over to the registrar's desk and selected one of the Crown's own photographs, showing Sir Harry's corpse still stretched out in his own bed. He all but sailed it into Barker's hands.

Q. What, pray tell, is *that*?

A. I see that the bed does have a footboard. I did not dust it.

The time had come to dispose of Barker.

Q. Please tell us again when you discovered the impression that is now Exhibit J.

A. On July ninth; but I did not mark the area.

Q. And you did not mark the area from which Exhibit J came until August first?

A. That is correct.

Q. And you left that panel to the last to work on?

A. I did.

Q. You said Captain Melchen folded the screen to protect area number five?

A. It was folded to protect all areas, not number five particularly.

Q. Can you indicate where any other legible prints came off that screen?

A. I don't think I could now.

Q. Is it a coincidence again that you can find no lifted area corresponding to Exhibit J?

A. I cannot find any such area.

Q. You said that you took three rubber lifts off the panel on July ninth. Have you got the other two?

A. No.

Q. You said that you did not identify the print described as Exhibit J before you left Nassau?

A. No.

Q. Will you please explain what you did with it?

A. I realized that it was a legible print. I took it with me to Miami, but I did not reexamine it until July nineteenth.

Q. Why did you wait until July nineteenth to reexamine it?

A. I left Nassau on July tenth and immediately resumed my unfinished work, which I had left in Miami to come over here the first time. I left for Bar Harbor at the request of Lady Oakes on the thirteenth and did not get back to Miami until the sixteenth. I returned to Nassau the next morning and remained here until Monday, July nineteenth. I found out at that time from the prosecution that there would be an early preliminary hearing. Consequently, I started to work on all the prints on July nineteenth and examined all the lifts. There were some latent prints which needed further examination. I was not entirely satisfied with my original examination made on the ninth. I came to Nassau again toward the end of September.

Q. Did you and Captain Melchen visit Lady Oakes in Bar Harbor the day of the funeral?

A. Yes, we did, at her request.

Q. This was after the funeral?

A. Yes.

Q. Mrs. de Marigny was there with her mother as well as other members of the family?

A. Yes.

Q. And did you tell Lady Oakes and Mrs. de Marigny that the assailant had entered the garage and picked up a stick from a pile of railings, crept upstairs, and struck Sir Harry on the head with it, and sprayed the bed with insecticide and set it afire?

A. I did not, nor did I hear Captain Melchen say that. I am positive of this. He might have said that some liquid had been used.

Q. And did you tell them that Sir Harry was revived by the flames and tried to fight off his attacker, that Sir Harry had been in great agony, and his assailant finally killed him?

A. No, I did not say that.

Q. That his assailant knocked over the screen and replaced it, and that you had examined the screen and found several prints of the accused on the screen?

A. I did not say that.

Q. I put it to you that you and Captain Melchen did say these things in order to arouse Lady Oakes's hatred of the accused?

A. I did not say this. We did not go up there on our own initiative.... They were asking for details.

Q. Did you not tell Lady Oakes and Mrs. de Marigny, and whoever else was present, about finding a fingerprint of the accused on the screen?

A. I believe I may have mentioned that we found such a fingerprint.

Q. And the funeral and your conversation were on July fifteenth?

A. Yes, that is correct.

Q. But you have told us not once, but several times, that you did not positively identify the accused's print, Exhibit J, until July nineteenth. How do you account for your statement to Lady Oakes and Mrs. dc Marigny on the fifteenth that you had found a fingerprint of the accused on the screen?

A. I knew of this legible print on the screen, and I thought it was that of the accused.

Q. Yet you told Lady Oakes and Mrs. de Marigny, positively, that you had found his fingerprint on the screen?

A. I believe I did.

Q. When did you first tell Captain Melchen that you had

positively identified Exhibit J as the fingerprint of the little finger of the accused?

A. I believe he heard it for the first time when I told Lady Oakes and Mrs. de Marigny.

In the spectator seats there was a gasp so strong that it was as if someone had sucked the air out of the room.

Q. I suggest that you chose the psychological moment to prejudice Lady Oakes's mind against the accused?

A. I would not do that.

Q. After you returned to Miami from Nassau on your first trip, did you see and consult with Captain Melchen?

A. Yes.

Q. And you rode together on the plane to Bar Harbor from Miami?

A. Yes.

Q. And you were with Captain Melchen in Bar Harbor some thirty-six hours from the time of your departure in Miami until you told him in the presence of Lady Oakes and Nancy de Marigny that you had positively identified the fingerprint of the accused on the screen?

A. Yes, if you say it was thirty-six hours, I will not object to that.

Q. Did you not think the discovery of the fingerprint of the accused on the screen was an important item of evidence in this case?

A. Yes, I did.

Q. Do you think it was quite the proper thing for you not to mention this to your co-worker . . . until this conference with Lady Oakes and Mrs. de Marigny?

Barker stood in the box, staring past Higgs, saying nothing. Sir Oscar joined in: "Isn't it strange that you did not tell Captain Melchen about the fingerprint of the accused that you found on the screen?"

Barker still did not speak, or move his head. "You did not answer the question, Captain Barker," the Chief Justice prodded him.

"Yes, it is strange," he said at last.

That seemed a fitting point to release the witness, and Higgs had started to walk away, when he had an afterthought.

"Did not His Royal Highness visit you at Westbourne and come to Sir Harry's room at the time you were processing for fingerprints?"

"Yes, he came up to see the crime scene."

I was holding on to my bars in expectation of where the questioning might lead, when I heard Higgs say, politely, "I do not think it would be proper for me to inquire as to why he came up, or what was said."

This was one of the areas I had pleaded with him to explore. But I knew it was futile. Godfrey had been conditioned by the old school rules, which dictated that one did not doubt or criticize the Royal Family.

The moment had passed.

Q. While you were working on the screen on Friday morning, did not Captain Melchen bring the accused upstairs?

A. I understand he did.

Q. And did Captain Melchen take the accused into the northwestern bedroom?

A. I understand he did.

Q. Did you not go to the door of that room and open it while they were together?

A. I did not.

Q. I put it to you that you did, and that you asked Captain Melchen if everything was okay?

A. I did not.

Q. I put it to you that Captain Melchen said yes.

A. I did not even know he was in that room until the next day, I believe.

Q. Wasn't the latent print of the accused, Exhibit J, obtained from some object in that northwestern bedroom?

A. Definitely not.

Q. But it was after he left that room that you claimed to have discovered his print, was it not?
A. Yes.
Now Godfrey's questions came in rapid succession.
Q. I suggest that you and Captain Melchen deliberately planned to get the accused alone in order to get his fingerprints.
A. We did not.
Q. I suggest that Exhibit J did not come from that screen.
A. It did come from that screen, from the number five panel.
Q. You can show none of that scrollwork from the screen on Exhibit J, can you?
A. I cannot.
Q. This is the most outstanding case in which your expert assistance has ever been requested, is it not?
A. It has developed into that.
Q. May I suggest that your desire for personal gain and notoriety has caused you to sweep aside truth. I put it to you, sir, you have fabricated evidence!

Higgs had turned and headed toward the defense table, his robes flying, as Barker called after him, "I emphatically deny that."

As Barker ended his testimony, a strange interlude took place. Melchen bolted out of the courtroom, and Raymond Schindler, the private eye, went looking for him. He found Melchen outside, leaning against the building, throwing up.

Years later, Marshall Houts, a law professor, former judge, and coroner, having researched the Oakes case, called Higgs's cross-examination of Barker "one of the most brilliant in common-law history."

The crown called Frank Conway, of the New York City Police Department, in an effort to restore what credibility he could to Exhibit J. Under cross-examination by Ernest Callender,

Conway's support turned out to be lukewarm indeed.

Callender had James Sands, the jury foreman, walk to the screen and put his thumbprint in the area marked number 5, then asked Conway to dust and lift the print.

The result was slightly blurred, but the lift clearly picked up the background of the screen.

CALLENDER: But Exhibit J has absolutely no background pattern of any nature in it whatsoever?

CONWAY: No, it does not.

CALLENDER: How many cases can you name where a lifted print not showing the background pattern has been successfully introduced in court?

CONWAY: I believe St. Louis had one around 1930. It was a murder case. I was not engaged in that case, I have just heard of it. I have never been engaged in a case where a lifted print without background material was used, and I have testified in hundreds of cases.

I suppose, in terms of legal fireworks, nothing in the trial would equal the work of Higgs and Callender in their attack on the fraudulent fingerprint. But there were dramatic highlights still to come.

Lady Oakes was called to the stand as a witness for the prosecution.

She had been preceded by Walter Foskett, Sir Harry's lawyer for many years, who described a letter he had intercepted from my former wife, Ruth Fahnestock, addressed to Lady Oakes. I had approached Foskett myself, asking his help in mending whatever differences existed between Nancy's parents and me. I called on him in the spirit of one gentleman to another, hoping this would be a step toward resolving a situation I knew to be causing Nancy pain. Foskett's response was to forward the vicious letter from my ex-wife to Lady Oakes.

Every eye in the courtroom followed her to the witness box, where she was allowed to be seated. She was dressed in a black silk dress, with a matching hat and gloves. I felt sympathy for her—I'm quite sure everyone did—but I still found it distasteful that she would testify against me.

She had sent me a birthday gift in March, a set of fine crystal glassware. I remembered a friendlier encounter, after I returned to Nassau after winning the Bacardi Cup in Havana. I attended a cocktail party at the Government House, one of the rare invitations I accepted from the Royal Governor.

Both the Duke and Duchess congratulated me on my victory. Lady Oakes arrived with Sir Harry, dressed in his familiar brown checkered suit with a matching shirt and a bright green tie. He quickly left his wife alone and went off to corner the Duke.

Observing this, I walked over to Lady Oakes, took her arm, and led her toward the large French windows overlooking the gardens. Two upholstered chairs seemed to be inviting us to sit down, and we chatted easily about Havana and Nancy and the other Oakes children. I noticed a reflection in a large mirror of a group of women moving toward us. The high backs of the chairs kept us from their view. Still, I could hear their conversation distinctly. One of the ladies, an American, asked the Duchess, "Darling, who is the quaint little man in the bookmaker's suit talking to David?"

The Duchess laughed and replied, "My dear, don't you know? That is Sir Harry Oakes. You must meet them. He and his wife are the Charlie Chaplins of our society."

I glanced at Lady Oakes, and her face was flushed. Neither of us made a sound, reluctant to reveal our presence. I breathed easier as the women moved away. Lady Oakes stood, and I offered her my arm and walked her to Sir Harry. She thanked me and, to my surprise, gave me a peck on the cheek. A few moments later, both left the party. She never did tell her husband about the offending incident. But within the week, Lady Oakes left Nassau, not to return until she testified at my trial and made clear her desire to see me hanged.

In my heart, I don't think she ever believed me guilty. But she blamed me for Nancy's health problems and pregnancy and, most of all, for what she considered her daughter's disrespect. For years she was willing to listen to anyone who claimed to have evidence of my guilt.

Her testimony did not harm me. She described receiving the news of our marriage, and how upset she and her husband were, though they were unwilling to risk a break with Nancy. At Bar Harbor, she said, I was "very nice" and took the children, who were fond of me, sailing.

Then came Nancy's bout with typhoid in August of 1942, and the surgery on her mouth, followed in January by the news that their daughter was pregnant. She made it clear that she regarded it as a failure of trust on my part: "I had told him to take the utmost care of Nancy, and there was no question as to what my meaning was."

In May, Nancy had rejoined me in Nassau after having returned a birthday gift, a check for two thousand dollars, from her parents. On the ninth of June, she wrote them a long letter, which I had not encouraged, but one that I felt was heartfelt and pleading.

Lady Oakes interpreted the letter as a demand that I be accepted by the family, or Nancy would cut off all contact with them. I do not believe the letter was in any way an ultimatum.

Godfrey Higgs was painfully aware of how risky it would be to subject Lady Oakes to any sort of piercing questions. But there was no need for it. She had been nowhere near the island when the crime occurred; she was in the courtroom, I suspected, only in an effort by Hallinan to toy with the jury. So Higgs needed little of her time, leading up to the two answers he wanted:

Q. Did you at any time ever hear the accused make any threats to do grave bodily injury to Sir Harry?

A. No, of course not.

Q. To your knowledge, was the only complaint of the accused that he was not accepted by you and Sir Harry into the family?

A. I assume that was all.

With that, the widow of Sir Harry, my mother-in-law, was excused.

November 4, 1943, was literally my day in court. I could leave that intolerable cage and stand in the witness box to defend my innocence.

Godfrey guided me through what amounted to the story of my life. I knew this ritual was necessary, but I also understood that he was attempting to give me time to adjust and relax before facing the onslaught of the prosecutors. But I felt no nervousness at all, a fact that frankly worried Higgs. He was afraid I would come off as arrogant. In truth, I often did.

To take the sting out of the questions he knew Hallinan would raise, Godfrey asked me about virtually every quarrel or dispute I had had with Sir Harry: our argument in front of my house; the time he yanked Sydney out of our guest room; his impatience with my unwillingness to mingle with the Windsors and the society crowd. I confirmed that I had last seen Sir Harry on the thirtieth of March. Nancy had left for the States in late May, to rest and attend school in Vermont; she was due back at the end of summer.

Godfrey brought up the issue of what shirt and tie I had worn the night of my dinner party. I said the shirt was identical to the one I was wearing now in court; it would be impossible to pick out the tie, I owned so many.

The Chief Justice was curious: "Five or six ties?"

"Dozens of them," I replied, and as if on cue, Raymond Schindler spread out across the defense table two or three dozen neckties in multiple colors. When he started to remove them, I instinctively called out, "Would you please wrap all of those ties in paper, Mr. Schindler, so that they do not get soiled?"

Laughter erupted in the courtroom. Even the guards smiled at my implication that I intended to wear them again. On my part it was unplanned.

Higgs led me through the day of the murder, my arrest,

the charade with Melchen over the water glass and the pack of cigarettes. Then he asked, "Did you, on the night of July seventh, or the morning of July eighth, go to Westbourne?"

"I **did not.**"

"Did you kill Sir Harry Oakes?"

"No, sir, I did not."

There was absolute quiet in the courtroom as Eric Hallinan advanced toward me. No one could miss the tension. My mouth was a little dry, my pulse a little fast, but I had been warned he would try to provoke my anger and I was determined to disappoint him.

His first questions were intended to cast doubt on my name, my birth, my title.

Q. When you first came to this colony you were called "Count"?

A. I never used it.

Q. Why were you then called "Count"?

A. In the family of my mother, the de Marigny family, there are lots of titles.

Q. Does it come from Fouquereaux?

A. It came from both sides.

Q. How is it that you became publicly known as Count de Marigny?

A. My former wife, Ruth, who was in New York at the time, called herself Countess de Marigny against my desires. I discussed the matter with the *Guardian* and the *Tribune* here, and I asked them not to use it. I have never used this title in Nassau or anyplace else.

He hoped, of course, to show that I was a counterfeit person, but we both knew that what his questions had to establish was my motive. The fact was, the prosecution had documents in their possession that already shattered their claim that I stood to benefit from Sir Harry's death. They had a copy of his will, which would not be probated until after the trial, showing that the Oakes children would receive no inheritance until their thirtieth birthdays. There was no fortune; Nancy would receive an allowance of a thousand dollars a month.

Even then, I had waived any rights I might have to whatever monies or property Nancy owned or stood to inherit. But one copy was in the possession of Sir Harry's lawyer, and the other in a file in New York, where I could not reach it.

In his charge to the jury, Adderley had said I had been motivated by greed and revenge, and Hallinan now picked up those themes:

Q. When Sir Harry turned you out of that room in the hospital in Palm Beach, and when he spoke in that rough way to you before the neighbors in the Victoria Avenue house, and when Sir Harry removed Sydney from your home, I take it you were humiliated?

A. No, not in the least. I knew Sir Harry was a man who was very moody and had a violent temper, and everyone knew it. He used to lose his temper for nothing.

Q. Did he call you a sex maniac?

A. Quite possibly.

That was too provocative a note for Sir Oscar to ignore. "Did this make you angry?" the Chief Justice broke in.

"I realized that he was very angry," I replied. "He was losing his temper more and more, and there was no sense in my getting angry. I thought he might not have meant what he said. If he had spoken coldly or in an insulting way, I might have been angry."

Either nothing else he could think of to ask was nearly so interesting, or else the Attorney General decided that the directness of my answers had done nothing to support his charges. The jurors could think what they wanted of my marriage, my interest in boats, my choice of friends, my sense of independence. But all they had to decide was: did I look like a man capable of murder?

So Hallinan ended his cross-examination more quickly than anyone expected. It was such a letdown that the foreman, Sands, proposed a courtroom demonstration to test my claim that I could have burned my arm while lighting the hurricane candles the night of the storm.

The three lamps that had been taken as evidence were even now on the registrar's table. While Sir Oscar was almost doubled over to get a good view, I picked up the first lamp, struck a match, and put my hand inside the shade. Instantly the flame caught, and curled upward over my hand. I jerked it back with a yelp of pain. Even Erie Stanley Gardner was impressed. He wrote that I had helped myself with my responses, which were bold, and that the demonstration with the lamp had provided a convincing alternative to the prosecution's claim.

The trial plowed on, through the second week. Freddie Ceretta testified that I asked him to accompany me while I drove Mrs. Clark and Mrs. Ainslie home.

Major Pemberton reported that Harold Christie's bed did not appear slept in, the morning after the murder. It was barely rumpled; from its appearance, someone had lain on top of the sheets.

Captain Edward Sears would not be shaken from his description of seeing Harold Christie at around midnight, when their cars passed on George Street.

The bankers, Gaffney and Anderson, went into boring detail about my personal finances, which fluctuated, sometimes wildly. There was a balance of five thousand dollars on the day of my arrest. I had been overdrawn by as much as twenty thousand dollars. I had made a loan to de Visdelou of ten thousand dollars.

But the Crown failed in its attempt to paint me as in debt and on the verge of bankruptcy. My chicken farm was profitable, he said; my credit was such that I could borrow twenty thousand pounds on my signature.

"And how much would you loan me?" asked the Lord Chief Justice.

"Possibly a thousand, my lord," said Gaffney. "No offense intended."

"None taken," said Sir Oscar, smiling.

There were two emotional hurdles ahead: the testimonies of Nancy and of my cousin, Georges de Visdelou.

There was no choice but to put Georges on the stand; he alone could verify what time I had returned home. But Higgs and Callender knew that the lights had burned all night in the Attorney General's offices. If their hopes of convicting me on the basis of Exhibit J were fading, they had an urgent need to disprove my alibi.

Georges was not a disciplined person, and he came across as more French than I did: a fashion plate, who dated Betty Roberts, the sexy young blonde who nursed his cold the night of the dinner party. To the stern Bahamian working class, this was sufficient to stamp him as a playboy and a Don Juan.

So it was with some reservations that Higgs called de Visdelou, my cousin and lifelong friend, to the witness box. Georges seemed nervous and unsure of himself, even in the hands of a friendly attorney. Still, his recital was routine: He had not been well that night; I had volunteered at one-thirty to drive Miss Roberts home; at three o'clock he had heard me call out to him to remove his cat, Grisou, from my room.

And then it was the turn of Alfred Adderley to cross-examine. There were more questions about the cat. Had de Visdelou entered my room to fetch Grisou? "I may have done so," he replied, "but I can't recall if I did."

Q. If you had done so, would you say so?
A. Yes.
Q. I will ask you, sir, if you did not give a statement to the police on July eleventh of this year?
A. I gave a statement at some time; but I do not remember exactly when.
Q. I hand you now this paper and ask you to examine it closely and tell us whether it bears your signature.
A. Yes, it is my signature.
Q. I will read from the statement: "... I retired to my room

from the party a little after eleven o'clock. At this time, I said good night to Mr. de Marigny and all of his guests. I did not see Alfred de Marigny from that time on until about ten o'clock the following morning. ..." I put it to you, is that what it says?

He looked at the page, and then nodded mechanically. "Yes," he said. In a state close to panic, the eyes of de Visdelou darted from me to Higgs to the ceiling to Adderley. I felt my stomach muscles tightening. What has he done? What could he have been thinking?

He blundered on: "I was terribly upset; my best friend, there, had been arrested. I didn't know exactly what I would say. It is not right, what I said in this statement. What I say now is right. I did talk to him about the cat, I got the cat out of his room after I took Miss Roberts home. I did! I did! I'm French. I get emotional. I forgot about the cat until Mr. de Marigny reminded me of it."

Georges had just taken a bad situation and turned it, for me, into a catastrophe. Not only had he contradicted himself, and appeared to have denied to the police my version of the events, but in near hysterics he had left the impression that I had coached him, had tampered with his testimony.

I looked at my cousin, a person I knew was incapable of hurting another. And yet with those few words de Visdelou had moved me close to the gallows. The lies of Melchen, Barker, and the local constabulary would count for nothing, now that the one person who could corroborate my account of the evening had, in effect, testified against me.

During the recess for lunch, Higgs and Callender reviewed the written statement of de Visdelou. The handwriting was all but illegible. In less than an hour they had to find a way to regroup, to find an explanation, a defense. Suddenly, Calender's eyes lit up. He had found the answer.

After the recess, Georges returned to the witness box and Callender began his redirect examination. He went through the same formality as Adderley, holding up the five-page document, asking if the signature was his. Then: "I shall read the statement to you. 'I and my girlfriend left and went upstairs. I was not feeling in a party mood. About one-thirty de Marigny came to my apartment door and asked if he should take my girlfriend home. I replied, "no." ' Is that what it says?"

"Yes."

The Lord Chief Justice asked for quiet in the courtroom as a babble of noise greeted this latest twist. Sir Oscar asked for the statement, read it, and asked Adderley to approach the bench.

"You led me and the jury to understand that Mr. de Visdelou's statement was a contradiction of his evidence. What we have here puts a completely different light on the matter."

Adderley replied weakly, "Begging your pardon, my lord, I was showing that the witness stated he did not *see* de Marigny from midnight on. The statement just read by my learned friend does not dispute that. It merely says that the witness *talked* to the accused." Sir Oscar did not try to temper his disgust: "I do not appreciate
the fineness of this distinction, Mr. Adderley, when a man's life is
at stake."

The chastened Adderley returned to his seat. I began to breathe
normally again, and de Visdelou looked as though he were the one
who had just escaped a death sentence.

Finally, the defense called Nancy Oakes de Marigny, and one could feel a different excitement inside the old courthouse. That she was there at all was a blow to my ill-wishers. Godfrey took her through the narrative of our first meeting, up to the difficulties with her mother and father.

Q. And to what do you attribute this estrangement between you, your husband, and your parents?

A. I attribute it solely to the attitude of my parents. My

husband and I tried hard to change that attitude, and we had still hoped to change it.

Q. Did you at any time ever hear your husband make any expression of hatred toward your father?

A. No, never. He never spoke ill of my father at all. When the differences and disagreeable episodes occurred, he was always sympathetic toward my father, attributing it to his age and health.

Q. At any time during your married life, did the accused ever try to obtain money from you?

A. No, never.

Q. What money did you and your husband use to live on after your marriage?

A. He had some money of his own, several thousand pounds. I had some savings. My mother gave us some money for our honeymoon trip. We were not destitute or dependent upon my parents or anyone else. We had planned to make our own way, and the chicken farm appeared to be a profitable enterprise.

Nancy kept looking in my direction. I was impressed with her poise, her self-control. Dressed in a dark suit with small white dots and a white collar, a white pancake hat and gloves, she looked like a model. She never wavered, even as Godfrey asked about the day of her father's funeral.

Q. Did Captain Melchen and Captain Barker tell you anything about who murdered your father?

A. Yes. Both on the telephone and at Bar Harbor, they gave me to understand it was my husband.

Q. Did they tell you why they thought it was your husband?

A. Yes. They said there could be no doubt about it. His fingerprints had been found on the screen next to my father's bed.

Q. Did they imply any doubt as to whether these prints had been positively identified as your husband's?

A. There was no doubt whatsoever; as a matter of fact,

they assured me that the prints positively were those of my husband.

In the give-and-take of courtroom sparring, the lawyers face the same problem of balance: how far to go, how hard to push, when to pull back and treat a witness with delicacy. Higgs had to walk the line with Lady Oakes. Now it was the Attorney General's turn in dealing with Nancy. Clearly, she had already won a certain respect from the jurors, to judge from the benign look on their faces. So Hallinan began with what seemed a fair and necessary question:

"Where were you when you first learned of your father's death?"

Nancy started to answer, "I was in Miami, and I received a telegram from my husband telling me to go to my mother, and I—" Then she broke down, lowered her head, and began sobbing, softly but unrelievedly. She had been holding her emotions in check for months, and now this one memory had torn down the walls.

In my prisoner's dock, my eyes were blinded with tears. They rolled down my face unchecked; I'm not sure I was even aware of them, as I saw Nancy vulnerable and wounded as I had never before seen her.

Sir Oscar offered kindly to call a recess, but Nancy insisted she wanted to continue. "I'm sorry," she said. "I'D be all right in a few moments."

After Nancy had composed herself, Hallinan read into the record the lengthy letter she had written to her mother on the May 26—nine days after her birthday, twelve days before her father's death.

Dearest Mother,

Several days ago I received a letter from the bank, advising me that you had instructed them to purchase two thousand pounds' worth of British War Loan Bonds in my name. These certificates have not arrived as yet from London; but as soon as they do I will request the bank to return them to you.

Nothing is more natural than for a family to give their children gifts on such occasions, but under the circumstances it is impossible for me to accept from either you or Father such gifts that have the smell of charity to a poor relative.

At the time that you and Father left Mexico, you both seemed to hold my husband in high esteem. In fact, you both took him into your confidence in many matters of a personal nature, indeed, much more so than you had ever done with your own child. As things were then, even you were very happy and looking forward to a normal family life of trust and good fellowship. However, since our return from Mexico the picture has changed erratically. You choose to believe the insinuations of third parties, in preference to inquiring frankly the truth and facts of certain matters of your own people, and, when an attempt was made by us to show you how you had been misled, you refused to cooperate with our lawyer.

In addition, when Father came to Nassau with Sydney, he was most insulting in his behavior toward us. At that time, he expressed in the most forceful terms his desire for us to sever further connections with the Oakes family. Painful as it was, I was forced to choose between my parents and my husband. Under the circumstances, there could be no question as to where my decision lay.

For this wholly unnecessary and unhappy situation, I place the responsibility on Walter Foskett, who has been, I believe, deliberately misguiding your judgment....

I want you to know that both of us can forgive this whole painful affair if you and Father can wash away your prejudices against my husband, and can regard him with the respect and trust to which he is entitled. Otherwise, I can never again feel any love or respect for you or Father or accept any of the natural advantages usually given to children by their parents. Sincerely, I am praying that you will not misunderstand the plain language of this letter, it may appear hard at first reading but no insulting or bitter feeling is intended. It is simply the bare truth as seen through my eyes. I pray God you will also see the truth and justice in these statements.

Your loving daughter, Nancy

To my ears, as the only other person who knew the emotions behind it, the letter was eloquent, a daughter asking not to be forced into choosing between her husband and her parents. But the Attorney General gave it a different interpretation, asking, "That was a pretty hard letter for a girl to write her mother, was it not?"

"You might think so," Nancy replied, "but you were not mixed up in all of this."

Now the Chief Justice intervened: "Did you wish to sever relations with your father and mother?"

"Not if I could help it. I had earnestly hoped that it would not come to that."

A final question came from James Sands, the jury foreman: "Did you ever discuss the question of your parents' wills with your husband?"

"No, never," Nancy said flatly. "That would not be a proper subject for us to talk about."

A trial could scarcely end on a more dramatic note than with the testimony of a beautiful young woman, her love and loyalties caught in the middle of a baffling murder case.

Godfrey Higgs rose, bowed to the Lord Chief Justice, and announced in a booming voice, "My lord, the defense rests."

The final arguments, and a summation by Sir Oscar Bedford Daly, would be heard the next morning. With luck, good or bad, we could expect a verdict by nightfall.

I observed my usual routine and was up early. To my surprise, a few minutes later Captain Miller came into my cell, followed by a prisoner carrying a bucket of whitewash and a brush.

"Fred, my boy," he said, "you have ruined government property by drawing on the walls, and I want you to clean up the mess." He walked out without another word.

I laughed. He was referring to my doodling, and marking

off the days. In his gruff way, Miller was being kind, trying to keep me occupied until I returned to court. Then, too, he knew I was superstitious and would want to leave a clean cell, with no sign that I ever expected to return.

Higgs drove me to court. Sir Oscar was punctual, and walked into a crowded but utterly silent room.

As the defense counsel, Godfrey went first and spoke for two hours and twenty minutes. He reminded the jury of the concept of "reasonable doubt," characterized Melchen and Barker in the bluntest possible language as liars, and called Exhibit J an obvious fake and forgery.

Eric Hallinan needed only sixty minutes for the Crown's closing argument. He virtually ignored the fingerprint evidence and concentrated on motive, which was, according to him, that I had been driven to kill Sir Harry because I hated him and was desperate to get control of his estate before he disowned Nancy and me.

Now came perhaps the most critical speech of all, the Lord Chief Justice's charge to the jury. In legal parlance, it turned out to be "a summation against the Crown." He dealt harshly, unsparingly, with the work and testimony of the American detectives. At the end of that lecture, he made an extraordinary announcement:

"I wish to state that never in my career as a lawyer, a prosecutor, or jurist, have I seen such a case. I am entering into the record a recommendation that a royal commission be appointed to investigate the conduct of the Nassau police force."

That aside, Sir Oscar said he could find no absolute proof that Exhibit J was fabricated; but he left to the jury that final determination.

The jurors, led by James Sands, the grocer, retired to their deliberations at 5:25 P.M., twilight time in Nassau. The winds were gusting in the dusk, and the courtroom began to empty. It seemed unlikely that we would receive a verdict this night.

By now I had joined my two attorneys at their table. Schindler was hovering nearby; Nancy had decided to wait at home until the jury returned. I felt a cheerfulness in sharp contrast to the unhappy and worried looks worn by Higgs and Callender. I asked Higgs a few questions about Sir Oscar's analysis of the evidence. He seemed unusually distracted and even somewhat annoyed by my good humor.

"Fred," he said, "this is a very serious moment for all of us, and for you in particular. Are you not fearful of the verdict?"

"Not one bit," I assured him, which was true. "You remind me of the priest who visited Maximilian, the Emperor of Mexico, in his cell just before his execution by a firing squad. The priest walked out of the cell with tears in his eyes and said to the people waiting outside, 'I came to comfort him; instead he comforted me.' "

"You are incorrigible," Callender said, smiling slightly.

By this time it was dark outside. The heat in the room had become stifling. I could hear the muffled talk of a gathering crowd impatiently awaiting a verdict.

At ten minutes past seven, one hour and fifteen minutes after the jury retired from the courtroom, the clerk announced that they were returning with a verdict. I returned to my cage, and the lawyers seated themselves in their regular spots.

Sir Oscar and the jury entered the silent room.

I watched Nancy in the front row as she made a sign to me to keep my chin up.

Sir Oscar's voice was loud and clear: "Gentlemen, have you considered a verdict?"

"We have, Your Honor," said James Sands in a clear, loud voice.

"What is your verdict?"

I closed my eyes and bit my lips.

"Not guilty."

The room erupted into noisy bedlam that echoed all the way down

Bay Street. My cage door opened and I walked out, a free man. I rushed into Nancy's arms and then was hugged by my friends and kissed by their wives. I shook hands with Higgs and Callender, and watched as Hallinan and Adderley made a quick exit. The judge remained on the bench, watching the proceedings with a benign eye.

I made my way through a wall of people, Nancy's arm around my waist. Outside, thousands of blacks and a handful of whites had gathered in Rawson Square; the police would call for fire hoses to disperse the crowd. (Ironically, I learned later that Hallinan had placed the police on alert, believing they would be needed to protect me from a hostile crowd.)

The crowd carried me on their shoulders to my car, where George Thompson waited, with the motor running.

Far into the night, the hotels and bars of Nassau were filled with people, many of them unknown to me, celebrating my victory. The champagne flowed, not for me alone, but for the underdog in each of us. Hundreds gathered on the lawn outside my home, singing, dancing, cheering.

Soon Nancy arrived and we drove over to the Trolles for a small reception in my honor. Most of my friends were there, including Basil McKinney and Oswald Moseley and, of course, Professor Keeler, Maurice O'Neil, and Raymond Schindler.

I yanked George Thompson out of the kitchen and into the front room, and pressed a glass of champagne into his hand. I quieted the crowd and gave a little speech.

"My friends, here is my best and dearest friend. George stood by me in spite of the efforts of our pal Hallinan." We all drank to George's health, I hugged him, and as soon as I turned my back, he slipped back to the kitchen.

That one glass may have been all I had to drink the entire night. I doubt that anyone noticed, but I needed nothing to enhance my high spirits. One by one the reporters left. After dinner, over brandy and coffee, Professor Keeler entertained the guests with his lie detector. In my euphoria, I volunteered to take the test. Higgs objected, as any lawyer would. I had nothing to fear. The jury had found me innocent. My curiosity demanded to know if this new machine would do the same.

Keeler attached the wires and asked his questions:

Q. When you took your guests home on July seventh, did you come straight home yourself?

A. Yes.

Q. Did you enter Westbourne?

A. No.

Q. Did you kill Sir Harry Oakes?

A. No.

Q. Were you in the room when someone else killed Sir Harry Oakes?

A. No.

Q. Do you know who killed Sir Harry Oakes?

A. No.

Q. Did you put your hand on the Chinese screen between the time of the murder and the discovery of the body?

A. No.

Every eye in the room was riveted to the white dial that sat atop the machine like a clock. The needle barely flickered. That night, and for the rest of his years, Keeler, a pioneer in scientific crime detection, swore that there was no doubt of my innocence.

It was after midnight before the party broke up and Nancy and I returned to Victoria Street. She went to bed, but I lingered in the living room, remembering my last night there, the police poking through drawers and closets. How naive I had been, not demanding a search warrant, not having a lawyer present, not sending them to the devil. I shook my head in wonder and went into the bedroom.

Nancy was already sound asleep. I stood there looking at her face for a few minutes, knowing that for me this would not be a restful night. My pent-up emotions were still churning. With no plan in mind, I went to my car and drove into town. I slowed down at the jail, and looked at the heavy iron doors that closed off the lives of those on the inside. In the distance I heard the music that had haunted me for so long. I turned in that direction and found myself in front of a nightclub that, I realized with a start, I knew well. I had driven by it several times a week when I visited property I owned in the neighborhood.

Some of the blacks at the entrance to the club recognized me, and soon a crowd had gathered. I walked inside, and a cheer greeted me. When I could finally regain my voice, I ordered drinks for everyone.

"Sorry, boss man," said the owner. "You buy no drinks for anyone. We buy *you* a drink."

I ordered a beer, sipping it slowly while listening to the sounds of life that had kept me company for so long. These people were not aware of the important part they had played in my life during the past months. I could not tear myself away from the laughter, the noises, the music.

The next morning, the fifteenth of November, brought a bitter surprise. Godfrey Higgs stopped by to deliver the bad news. The jury had attached a rider to the verdict, recommending that both de Visdelou and I be deported from the Bahamas as "undesirables."

In the uproar that had greeted my acquittal, the rest of the foreman's words were drowned out. The Chief Justice heard it, thought the action was improper, but said he would leave the ruling to other authorities.

The Governor in Council voted to accept the recommendation, and Georges and I were given two weeks to leave the islands. But the government had a dilemma. The only place to which they could deport me was Mauritius, six thousand miles away, and they had no way to get me there.

Records declassified decades later would show that Hallinan and Christie had provided daily reports on the trial to the Duke of Windsor while he and the Duchess traveled in the eastern United States. On November 19, the Duke cabled London in support of the deportation, although there was no legal basis for it, and asked that military transport be provided to carry out the order. London declined.

The outcome of the trial, so inconclusive, was a major embarrassment for the Duke. Even more troubling, the longer I remained, the more likely it was that questions would be raised, such as, why was no effort being made to find out who had actually killed Harry Oakes? And who had framed Alfred de Marigny?

The Royal Governor and his Attorney General had maneuvered themselves into a box: they had shot off a flurry of cables to London, to other British colonies, and to Washington, labeling de Visdelou and me as undesirables. The Foreign Office cabled back that (1) there were no legal grounds to deport someone for being "undesirable," and (2) the War Office could not issue a transit visa to anyone classified as "undesirable."

It was, in Joseph Heller's wonderful phrase, a Catch-22.

By the time the Windsors returned to Nassau, my status had become nearly an obsession with the Duke. In a long cable dated November 26, he included charges that one writer called "a list of libels which went far beyond the evidence at the trial." Among the accusations were these:

HIS MATRIMONIAL HISTORY SHOWS HIM TO BE AN UNSCRUPULOUS ADVENTURER [\VHOJ HAS EVIL REPUTATION FOR IMMORAL CONDUCT WITH YOUNG GIRLS. IS GAMBLER AND SPENDTHRIFT. SUSPECTED DRUG ADDICT [A REFERENCE TO MY INJECTIONS FOR HYPOGLYCEMIA]. ENGAGED IN TWO ENTERPRISES IN VIOLATION OF IMMIGRATION LAWS [HERE HE SEEMS TO HAVE IN MIND MY AID TO THE SURVIVORS FROM DEVIL'S ISLAND, AND MY RENTAL OF APARTMENTS TO JEWISH GUESTS FROM THE UNITED STATES].

Whatever the fears of the Duke of Windsor, I had decided for reasons of my own that it was not healthy to remain in Nassau. I said good-bye to de Visdelou, who was leaving for Haiti. Meanwhile, Nancy and I had friends in Havana, including Hemingway, and they were able to arrange Cuban visas.

On one of my last days in Nassau, I stopped by the bank to settle my accounts, then walked a few steps down the street to James Sands's grocery store. I wanted to thank Sands for the manner in which he had conducted himself as foreman of the jury.

The grocer seemed genuinely pleased to see me, and led the way to his office in the back of the store. He offered me a chair.

"You want to know about that rider, don't you?" he guessed.

"Frankly, yes."

"De Marigny, the vote was nine to three for acquittal," said Sands. "I had four Plymouth Brethren on the jury. To them you were more than a criminal, you were a person who broke the law of God. Not only did you sail on Sundays, but you enticed their sons and daughters to sail with you. Those four stuck together like glue. Without that rider, we would have had a hung jury and you would have spent many more months in jail. I wanted to avoid that at any cost, so we struck a deal. One of them would shift his vote, and in exchange I agreed to the rider."

"Good Christians," I snorted in disgust. "But I thank you, Sands. You did the right thing. I am leaving the Bahamas as soon as a boat can be readied to sail."

After nearly two months, passage had been arranged to Cuba. Roland Symonette, a power in the Assembly and a fellow sailor, had found a rickety old bucket available for charter the first week in December.

While I was sitting in his office, I noticed a roll of one-inch hemp rope, taut and smooth, coiled in a corner.

"That is a fine grade of rope," I said. "Where did you get it?"

He laughed in his usual good-humored way. "You can have it," he said. "It belongs to you anyway."

"What do you mean?"

"It was a special order from Hallinan. I imagine he had something in mind for it if you were found guilty."

Surely this was a classic example of what is called gallows humor. I laughed and said, "I don't think I want the whole coil. Just give me a small piece for good luck."

PART FIVE

THE ODYSSEY

Loue par ceci, blame par cela. Me moquant des sots, bravant les mechants. Je me presse de rire de tout de peur d'etre obliger d'en pleurer.

("Praised here, censured there. Disdaining the fools, defying the rogues, I am forced to laugh for fear of being obliged to weep.")

LA MOTTE HOUDART

CUBA LIBRE

IT was nine in the morning when our small craft sailed into Havana harbor under the looming presence of Morro Castle. A large crowd had been awaiting our arrival since before dawn. When we docked, the president of the Yacht Club, Emilio Pozo, gave me an *abrazo*.

The Cuban newsmen knew me from my yachting days. A few American reporters on the shore shouted questions about the trip and about our future destination, and whether Nancy was going to divorce me. On and on until, finally, we escaped in a private car to the Nacional Hotel.

Our corner room had a view of the ocean on one side, and from the terrace we could see the city all the way to the Prado Boulevard. Flowers had been delivered for Nancy, along with a bottle of champagne to celebrate our safe arrival, and a basket of fruit. The presents, together with an invitation to dinner that same evening, came from Aristmendie Trujillo, a guest at the same hotel.

Nancy clapped her hands. "Trujillo! You do remember him, don't you? He was Father's guest a few years ago in Nassau." Yes, I remembered Trujillo, the brother of the dictator of the Dominican Republic. I had acted as his translator. It was a small world. Smaller than I could have imagined. Nancy gave me a kiss. "My love, in no time we shall be the toast of Havana."

As if to lend credence to her words, the telephone began to ring. And ring. In the end, I had the operator hold our calls.

I had happy memories of Cuba, and respect for its people

and history. It was on these grounds that the officers of the army and navy took refuge during the revolution that toppled Machado. That revolution ended with the ascent of Fulgencio Batista, who had ruled the island since 1933, first through surrogates, then, since 1940, as the legally elected president.

Cuba still had the flavor of a banana republic, but Havana had flowered as a sin city, a haven for gangsters sitting out the last of the war. The casinos flourished, and the tourists couldn't resist the delicious bargains in rum and tobacco.

That evening, Trujillo and his beautiful young wife greeted us as old friends. He was exactly as I remembered from four years earlier: cocky, slight of build, haughty, with a faint smile always on his thin lips, giving him the expression of a snake about to strike. After dinner, we had coffee on the terrace and our host reminded me that during his visit to Nassau he had invited me to Trujillo City. He now extracted from me a promise to visit him soon. He could not have known—nor could I—that his invitation would be a safety net into which I would leap like a man from a burning building. I would find refuge there, after being released from jail in Haiti.

The next morning, Nancy ordered from the bellboy a copy of every U.S. and local newspaper in the city. After breakfast she sat on the floor, surrounded by dozens of publications; she read the headlines aloud and scrutinized the articles about us.

She showed me the front page of *Diario de la Marina*, the leading newspaper in Havana, which had devoted a full page to photographs and articles related to our arrival. A large photo of our little craft occupied the center of the page.

"Freddy, I must have that negative," she begged. "Please get it for me. I will have it enlarged and framed and hang it in our living room."

Her manner turned confessional: "I shall tell you the truth. When I saw the boat at the dock in Nassau, a boat the size of a peanut, I was scared out of my wits. Later, when we entered the Gulf Stream, those enormous waves frightened me to death. The trip was a nightmare."

I took her hands. "If I live a hundred years, I will never forget how you chanced that dangerous crossing to be with me—"

Nancy cut me off, laughing. I had missed the point of what she was saying. "Darling, stop being ridiculous. You are so dramatic. You act at times like a schoolboy. Did you think for one moment I would let you travel alone? And have all the headlines to yourself? Think of it. What an entrance, arriving in Havana on that little tub. The crowd, the pictures. I would not have been cheated out of it, no matter the danger or discomfort."

She touched her fingertips to her lips and blew me a kiss, then went back to her clippings, cutting and sorting them with care. I had the unpleasant sensation of having been slapped across the face. I got up and walked out of the room.

The sight of the shore and the smell of the sea cleared my head, and I felt better. I followed the seawall and sat on a large rock that was part of the breakwater. My thoughts turned to Nancy, and I asked myself what the future might hold in store for us. For the first time in our marriage, I was able to look at her objectively. I saw that a wide gulf separated us. I felt uneasy, and closed my eyes. The small waves broke against the stone wall in a soothing rhythm, and I remembered the evening of Nancy's debut, when we had sat on another wall and listened to nature's music.

I was irritated with Nancy for reasons I did not fully understand. Still, her reactions were so spontaneous that it was hard to take seriously what she had said. She had gone through an ordeal and emerged a heroine. She was oblivious of the unsavory portrait of her husband painted by the same stories. I had been branded "the man accused of the murder of Sir Harry Oakes." That label would follow me everywhere, all the years of my life.

I walked back slowly to the hotel, wondering what tomorrow would bring. Nancy had left a note: she had gone to lunch with a reporter who wished to interview her. From there she had an appointment at the beauty parlor. In a way, I was relieved to be alone. I tried to rest. The telephone awakened me. Hemingway! It was Ernest calling to invite us to spend a weekend at his *finca*. His voice, his profanity, cheered my soul.

For the next call I was unprepared. It was from Arthur Garfield Hayes, the eminent American lawyer, who had won lasting fame with his unfortunately unsuccessful defense of the anarchists Sacco and Vanzetti. Also a guest in the hotel, he invited me to breakfast.

The next morning I was mildly nervous as I rang the bell at the suite of Arthur Hayes. He was a short, graying man in his sixties who limped and walked with a cane, but his eyes were bright and gave his face a quality of strength. Breakfast was served on his terrace, from which we had a sweeping view of the city. Over coffee, he told me that he had come to Havana especially to talk to me.

He said he had followed my case from the beginning. "I was dumbfounded that it ever went to trial," he said. "They did not have a penny's worth of evidence against you. One could expect that sort of kangaroo justice in South America or Africa—even here. But in a British colony? It is beyond me."

When the waiter poured the thick black coffee from a large pot, he laughed and said, "You'd better get used to it if you're going to be in Havana long. Coffee and cigars are a must here."

He asked me if my lawyers had ever informed me that he had contacted them, offering his services free of charge to assist with my defense. I told him this was the first I had heard of it. But I had ceased to be surprised by any of the events of my trial.

He nodded. We sat for a moment in an uncomfortable silence. I asked what he thought of the case and especially of the deportation rider.

Hayes almost exploded. The deportation had been totally

illegal, he said, and had violated their own immigration laws. "I echo the words of the Chief Justice," he said. "In my career as a lawyer, a prosecutor, and a judge, I have never before seen such a case." We chatted easily about the various facets of the trial. He was like a general who had studied a strategic battle, hungered for more details, and now had a chance to question one of the survivors.

He was returning to the United States in the morning. He told me to remember that I had a friend and admirer in New York. I thanked him for his kindness and sat back. I pointed out to sea, to the place where I had raced two years earlier, and sailed across the finish line of the Bacardi Cup. "Those were happy days," I said, sighing.

"Forget those days," he said with great seriousness. "You enjoyed them. That is the past. Tomorrow matters, not yesterday. You have just been acquitted in a court of justice. Tomorrow you shall face the court of public opinion. It will be a long trial, and a painful one—ten times worse than the misery you have known so far. You shall need all your strength and fortitude. People will do their utmost to exploit you and your name, even your misery, to make a dollar through you. Never forget that you are a gentleman. Never allow anyone to cheapen you. Be leery of 'friends' who could easily bury you."

Arthur Garfield Hayes left Havana the next day. When I reached New York several years later, I visited with him. I accepted his gesture, his advice, as the courtesy it was, because it came at a time when I was unable to pay for such things.

Ernest Hemingway's *ftnea*, at San Francisco de Paula, was an hour's drive on the central highway going east out of Havana. An old, one-story home, with a touch of colonial Spanish, stood in a lovely garden surrounded by fruit trees, flower bushes, and well-manicured lawns. The small ranch occupied a hill overlooking the countryside, and from the terrace off the dining room one could detect the city in the distance. Down the hill was the swimming pool, with tables and benches in the shade of avocado and mango trees.

Ernie had canceled the shoot that Saturday to spend the day with Nancy and me. He had invited all his Basque friends to swim, eat, and drink at the *finca*. These were his *compadres* who had fought against Franco during the Spanish Civil War. The Basques formed a close-knit group, and many of them worked at the *fronton*, the jai alai arena. They included the immortal Guillermo and his rival, Ermua, who were part of the golden era of the sport.

As a race, the Basques were unique. Their attitude toward women was a complex one. Although it was a matriarchal society, the men gave the impression they ran the show. The men ate alone and were served by their women. Only after the men had finished did the women sit at the table. The men seldom spent time with their women, talked to them, or traveled together. They were respectful of their wives and daughters, but theirs was a world of men. Their sports were displays of brutal force.

It was a world that clearly appealed to Hemingway. Meanwhile, Martha Gellhorn was the perfect wife, who guided her husband's friends through the maze. She was more beautiful than ever. We chatted about the time we had met on the *Normandie* during my first trip to the States. She took Nancy under her protection and introduced her around.

Some of the guests swam, while others played dominoes, argued politics, or drank. Several of the women were drawn to Ermua, a young and extremely handsome bachelor. I joined Ernie at the bar and watched him toss down a large quantity of Pernod. This unfortunate habit, which I remembered from our previous encounter, had grown worse. I soon realized that he resented the attention focused on Ermua. He grew quieter, a dangerous sign, as he watched his wife among those laughing in the circle around the young star.

Suddenly, Ernie went off to the ranch house and returned with two sets of boxing gloves. He stepped in front of Ermua and, in broken Spanish, said, "You are young and a great athlete. Let us have an exhibition for our guests." And he handed him a pair of gloves. Confused, the Basque stood and protested that he had no idea how to box. Martha jumped to her feet and glared at her husband. "What are you trying to prove?" she demanded. "Don't be an ass. He told you he can't box."

I could see the alarm on Martha's face. Ernie was a fine boxer. He ignored her, and insisted that Ermua lace on the gloves. A dead silence floated over the party. Hemingway stepped around Erniua, who stood motionless, his arms dangling at his sides. "Put your hands up!" Ernie shouted.

In the next instant, Hemingway led with a left, and then threw a right hook to the jaw of Ermua. The *pelotari* made a semicircular loop into the swimming pool. He appeared to be unconscious when he was fished out by two of his friends. Martha was like an angry peacock as she scolded her husband, then followed Ermua and his companions to the house.

Ernie looked around and clumsily tried to explain that he had meant no harm, the right had slipped. No one seemed to care. A shadow had descended on the party. Martha left for New York the next day.

Ernie would not allow the departure of his wife to spoil his plans. The pigeon shoot would take place on Sunday. There would be two teams: the American group that would include Winston Guest, the famous polo player; Papa Montero, a millionaire from Long Island; our host, and me. On the other side were three Spanish aristocrats, among them one whose family owned the Merito cognac and sherry works, and two Cubans.

Ernie casually told me that the Spaniards were Fascists, and had fought on the side of Franco, against his friends, during the Civil War. I was puzzled and dismayed to discover this apparent hypocrisy in my friend.

The shoot was excellent, however, and everyone placed large bets to add zing to the sport. A great deal of liquor was downed, and to my chagrin, Ernie finished a full bottle of Pernod. I told him it was poison to the brain, and could make a man mad. "I am already mad," he retorted. "Madder than you may think."

Somehow the world moved smoothly at the *finca*. Ernie relaxed with his radical friends and Basque companions one day, and saved the weekend for the Fascists and wealthy Americans. The one exception was Father Andres, the priest who had fought alongside Ernie, who was welcome on all occasions.

Soon, Nancy had to return to Nassau, where she was needed to help settle her father's estates. She seemed genuinely sad about leaving, and I was touched, feeling that there was yet hope for our future together.

It would be three decades later that I realizxd what a twist our lives had taken in Cuba. While Ernest provided a diversion I needed, within a few years Nancy would enjoy the company of his son, Jack Hemingway, later a professional sportsman, and whose daughters Margaux and Mariel pursued careers in modeling and acting. Jack described the relationship, with what I thought was a certain enjoyment, in a book he wrote in the early 1980s.

Meanwhile, I had received a long letter from Basil McKinney, advising me to liquidate my few remaining assets on the island. He added that Gaffney, at the Bank of Canada, had promised to exchange all my pounds for dollars at the old rate of five to one. The second part of his letter had to do with the will of Harry Oakes. It had been probated, finally, some six months after his death.

Eric Hallinan, it developed, had advised the executors not to probate the will until after my trial, so as not to prejudice the jury against me. It was another of his dirty tricks. He had built his case on circumstantial evidence and hammered away at what he called my motive: to get my hands on the family fortune. The truth finally surfaced.

Harry Oakes, described as one of the richest men on earth, left an estate valued at slightly under twelve million dollars, most of it in land. Half was bequeathed to Lady Oakes. The five children divided the rest, each receiving the sum of twelve thousand dollars a year until the youngest, Harry Philip, then twelve, reached the age of thirty. (Thus Nancy would be eligible for her inheritance at thirty-seven.)

To fulfill the bequest of Oakes, the trustees would have to sell off properties over the next eighteen years to assure the monthly allowances of the children.

Nancy, the celebrated heiress, was to inherit one thousand dollars a month. At the time of her father's death, my income was twice the total annual inheritance of the five children.

So it was that Hallinan had tried to "protect" me by delaying the public disclosure of the will, which would have cast doubt on the most basic premise of his case: that I had married Nancy for her great fortune.

Soon after Nancy's departure, I rented an apartment in the Vedado, on the top floor of a quadruplex, surrounded on all sides by mango trees. My neighbor, two doors down, was Alvaro Caro, the Marquis de Villa Mayor. One block away lived Eduardo Chibas, the senior senator from La Habana Province, an orator and a patriot. In weekly speeches on the radio and in other public forums, he forcefully opposed the policies of Batista. The three of us became friends, talking politics far into the night.

During the week we would meet with Hemingway at the Floridita, where he had his private table, and his friends came to spend the day drinking daiquiris and eating seafood. One morning, Ernest asked me to keep him company at the *finca*. I accepted gladly. His was a complex nature, and I was curious to dissect it.

Life at the *finca* was well organized. Ernest rose early, swam, and took a run around the gardens. He ate a light breakfast, then sealed himself in his room to write. He typed standing up in front of an old-fashioned typewriter. After dinner, Ernie loved to relax and talk. He was a curious person, who wanted to know every tiny detail of my life. I found him to be a simple man, basically kind and even timid when sober. On occasion, he was capable of laughing at himself.

At such times, I had a glimpse of the Hemingway few people ever knew. He had a slight speech impediment, and used his hands to clarify words that were hard for him to pronounce. This disappeared when he drank Pernod, and especially when there were people around. The Pernod boosted his courage and he became excitable, testy, and unpredictable. He expressed his opinions *ex professo,* and in public he never missed an opportunity to look for a fight.

I had read every one of his books. They all depicted Ernie as a sentimentalist playing the role of the macho man. From *The Snows of Kilimanjaro* to *For Whom the Bell Tolls,* Ernie was always present, on every page.

Then came his failed novel, *Across the River and Into the Woods,* in which my friend apparently felt he had to bare the wounds inflicted on him by all the women with whom he had ever been involved. The years had taken their toll. It was his last love affair that led him to write *The Old Man and the Sea,* in a desperate effort to prove to himself that he still possessed the great machismo.

Nancy returned after two weeks in Nassau. I was amazed at how much money she had gotten for the articles in my house on Victoria Avenue. Everyone on the island wanted a souvenir, and Nancy made them pay dearly for the privilege of buying one. She had a large draft in dollars for me from the Royal Bank of Canada. The check was made out in my name. Gaffney had been as good as his word. "He didn't seem to trust me," she said peevishly. I said nothing, but I was very grateful to him.

The trip had left her exhausted and testy. The trustees had refused to advance any money for the dental work she felt she needed in New York. "Even in death," she pouted, "Father succeeds in controlling his family. He managed to keep a leash on all of us, from the grave."

She did not object to my choice of an apartment, but made it clear that she had no intention of languishing in Havana. I soon found out that she had made definite plans to leave Cuba. She hated the place, finding the women loud and common, the men coarse. I listened in silence, then said, "It's up to you. You have your own income. You are free to leave."

She looked at me in surprise. "I expected you to help me. How far do you think I can go with five hundred dollars a month? What about my surgical bills? You can't be serious."

I said, "Darling, I have to count my pennies."

She looked at me accusingly. "What about the draft for thirty thousand dollars I just delivered to you?"

"I repeat, I must count my pennies. I am not working. I must ration my capital, and not waste it on your whims. I might not like Havana any more than you do, but I am stuck here, and until I can get a visa to enter the States, I must be careful. I will pay your fare to New York. You can stay with friends and tell the surgeon to send me his bill. Your five hundred dollars a month should be enough to carry you."

She threw herself on the bed, buried her face in a pillow, and began to cry. After a while, I walked onto the terrace and watched the sun set in the distance.

In two days, Nancy left Havana, and I was not to see her again until I reached Montreal, a year later.

Now my life, which had been temporarily peaceful, took a strange turn. The Duke and Duchess of Windsor visited Havana and were honored with a luncheon. Among the guests were Hemingway and Father Andres. During the meal, my name was mentioned. The Duke flinched and said, "You know that man?"

Assured that they did, the Duke looked at my friends and said, "He is a very bad man, a dangerous man. Take my word for it." At that, Father Andres rose and said in halting English, "Don Alfredo is my friend, a gentleman. You must not speak evil of him in front of me again."

He pushed his chair aside and started toward the door.

Ernest flung his napkin on his plate. "That," he said loudly, "goes for me, too." Already half-drunk, Hemingway stumbled after the padre.

The presence of the Windsors had nothing to do with me or with the unsolved murder of Harry Oakes. But two other events surely did. I felt some pressure to rebuild my cash reserves as quickly as possible, and after the exchange of several telegrams and letters, I accepted a contract from Random House to write an autobiography, giving my account of the crime and the trial.

A news conference was held in New York, which I did not attend, to announce the agreement, with the publication date to be released later.

One stormy night that week, I came home from the jai alai matches and tossed my raincoat on the bed. My neighbors were having a birthday party, and I went next door to join them. It was late when I returned. The day was humid, and I slept in Nancy's room, the coolest in the apartment. I was awakened by the maid, wildly waving my raincoat. There were six bullet holes in it, and the shots had gone through the mattress.

I went to phone the police, and discovered that one of the glass panes in the window had been shattered and bits of broken glass had gone flying, landing on the bedroom floor and in the garden. Someone had climbed the mango tree outside the window and, seeing a shadow on the bed, had emptied a revolver.

Slowly it sank in that someone had tried to kill me. I called Hemingway and told him what had happened. Within the hour he was there, accompanied by one of his Basque friends, Paco Avcllanal, who was to stay with me for a while and act as my bodyguard.

Everything went along peacefully for a few days. Then, after a night out, Paco and I returned home at two in the morning. He dropped me at the front gate and drove the car one block to the garage. I opened the front door and went straight to the kitchen to make our nightly cup of hot chocolate. I was standing in front of the stove when I had the uneasy feeling that someone was close by, watching me. I immediately ducked, and as I did so, two shots rang out, just missing my head. I turned the light off, then heard footsteps running away. This time he had fired from behind me, through the open kitchen window. I reached the front terrace and saw Paco fumbling with the front door, but the gunman was already out of sight.

The neighbors gathered quickly, wondering what had happened. Eduardo Chibas was still in his pajamas when the police appeared. We discovered why Paco had been unable to open the door. The lock had been plugged with toothpicks between the time I walked in and the time the shots were fired.

Two attempts had been made on my life, with no clue as to why, or by whom. With the help of Chibas, from that day on I had a twenty-four-hour police watch around my home.

I had no threats, no written warnings, no real evidence, but there was no doubt in my mind that I had been sent a message. Twice. I marked off to coincidence the visit of the Duke of Windsor. But I had the very distinct impression that someone did not want me writing a book. My lawyer contacted the legal department at Random House, and they were very understanding. We canceled the agreement.

Forty years would pass, and nearly all of the principals in the case would be dead, before the urge to tell my story would return, and then so strongly I could not deny it.

Havana had suddenly become an empty, lonely, and shadowy place. Ernest left for Europe as a war correspondent for *The Saturday Evening Post*. He was elated, feeling at last that he was doing something important, as well as useful to his pocketbook. I had the feeling I was never to see him again. I sometimes wish the premonition had been true.

Seven years later, when I returned to Havana to live, the Hemingway I found was a very sick old man, one step from the grave. I saw him often, the last time just days before he left for Ketchum, Wyoming, where he ended his life. Whatever his weaknesses and faults, he lived and died by no one else's terms.

I still stopped by the Centro Basco (the Basque Club), at the corner of the Malecon and Prado Boulevard, on a street paved with mosaic all the way to the Presidential Palace. I ate there most days and played dominoes with the local boys, or in the afternoon played *pala,* a Basque equivalent of squash, played with a short, solid wooden bat and a ball like those used in baseball.

Pilar ate there also. We often shared a table, always ending the meal talking about Ernest. On her birthday, her friends held a small party for her and she seemed relaxed and gay. Still, a veil of sadness filled her eyes at times. That night she told me the last time she had celebrated her birthday had been many years ago, on the Spanish front, with Hemingway.

"He loved me like a madman in those days," she said. "Life was like being on a volcano. I was different from the other Basque women, who spend their lives in the kitchen, caring for their men. I was a fighter." Then she added, "Forgive me. I hate to be sentimental."

That night, over drinks, the conversation returned to Hemingway. "Such a romance could not survive between two domineering peopie," she said. "Ernie had to be the boss. I was wounded and went to the hospital. By the time I returned to the front, Martha Gellhorn had arrived in Spain. She was beautiful, blond, very different from me. She treated him as a woman treats a man. I treated him as an equal. I did not fight for his love. For me, for my country, it was life or death. For Ernest, it was the excitement of the moment. That changed nothing in my feelings for him. *"Asi es la vida,"* she concluded—"Such is life."

I offered a mild apology for my friend. "*Querida,* you must remember that Ernest is a great writer and, like most artists, a breed apart. He needs adulation. That is his food."

She drained her glass and tapped her fingers on the table, then said, "I worry that Ernie has no feelings for other people. After seeing death everywhere, people wounded, losing arms and legs, cities destroyed, he seems to consider war a game. He finds pleasure in selling himself for a dollar a word—the great writer telling us about misery and death."

Her expression was as cold and hard as flint. I tried to understand the two of them. She was right, yet he was not wrong. Ernie was a man in every sense of the word. He despised tears and sought no pity.

My curiosity got the better of me, and I asked her if Ernie was the lover he gave the impression he was.

She screeched with laughter. "Forget him as the great lover. That he was not. Never was."

My surprise must have shown. "Ernie had a complex," she said. "He drank a lot to forget his complex when he was with a woman. God was not generous to him in that way. He tried to make up for it by drinking and making love like a gorilla. He felt that acting tough and talking tough would make a great lover of him. He runs naked through the words he writes. The tough man proving his virility."

But that was not the impression of Hemingway she wanted to leave. "He is like a boy. His eyes become naughty and he smiles, a beautiful smile. He makes you melt, forget everything. That is the Ernie I shall love until I die."

That was my last evening with Pilar. Twenty-four hours later, I left Havana for good. I left behind me months of excitement. I left behind whatever love I had ever felt for Nancy, who was in the States, and had written only once.

Any pain I felt at the time of her departure had healed. Time was my medicine. I knew that everything was over. In spite of her support at the trial in Nassau, the entire year was a nightmare I wanted to forget. I decided to leave for Santo Domingo and begin a new life. I had to close my eyes on the past. I would soon find that destiny had decided otherwise.

As much as I liked Havana, there were disquieting things happening that made me queasy about remaining there. I had not forgotten that an assassin was on the loose, and might be tempted to try again.

I asked Eduardo Chibas if he could look into the government's files and find out what the Nassau authorities had told the Cubans about me. Two days later he informed me that he had discovered a letter from the Bahamas concerning me. It was a damnable document.

I asked if he could get me a copy, but before he could do so, the political process intervened.

Cuba was in the middle of an election to determine the successor to Batista. The president had promised to keep his hands off the election, but no one trusted him not to renege, least of all Eduardo, who was backing San Martin, the opposition candidate, against Batista's man. Eduardo, a volatile and unstable romantic, was stumping the countryside for San Martin. He made a strong anti-Batista speech on the radio, and then committed suicide at the microphone as a symbolic gesture of love for his country. The gesture must have had some effect, because San Martin won the election and Batista, true to his word, went off to Florida for eight years. He returned in 1952, after the corrupt and greedy civilian politicians botched the chance at democracy they had been given.

Needless to say, I never did get to see what the letter from the Bahamas said about me.

I asked for help from the British consul. To my surprise, he offered some. A Canadian merchant ship on its way to Halifax was in Havana. The third mate had died of a fever he picked up in Santo Domingo, and if I wanted his job, it was mine. Two days later I was cruising on board a tramp steamer heading for Canada.

A few miles from Cuba we hit a mine, which blew away part of the bow. We were able to stay afloat, however, and slowly steamed into Cape Cod, where we were to join a convoy to Halifax. The captain and I went ashore at the Cape for supplies, and on an impulse I telephoned Nancy. To reawaken the echoes of love, a man needs only to have a brush with death or disaster.

She told me she would be waiting for me in Montreal if I wanted to see her after I arrived in Canada.

The trip north was nerve-racking. We were in the most vulnerable part of the convoy, and during the night German submarines torpedoed a number of ships. The ocean around us was a mass of fire and debris. There was no time to be afraid. We took several hits from shells, but no lives were lost, and we limped into Halifax, escorted by planes and PT boats. We made our way through floating lumber, cargo, and crates of food into the harbor. The moment we dropped anchor, the reaction set in and I became sick to my stomach.

The ship would have to be repaired. I was given thirty days' leave and, promising to be back in time to sail, I headed for Montreal. This was not to be one of my wiser decisions.

CANADIAN SUNSET

LIKE interlocking rings, my fate was joined to that of Harry Oakes. In Canada, where Oakes had left his footprints long ago, where he found a fortune and his legend began, my marriage to Harry's daughter, and that phase of my life, would end. I had lost my freedom and risked my neck, or so it now seemed, as a result of the love I had felt for Nancy. Except for a casual letter, I had not heard from her for over a year.

I found my way to the hotel, to an empty room. A note had been left on Nancy's pillow, telling me to make myself at home; she had gone to the theater and would be back by eleven.

After a shower, I stepped back into the room to find, to my surprise, an attractive blonde in her twenties sitting comfortably in an armchair, smoking.

Greeting me with a smile, she said she was a reporter with the *Montreal Gazette*. She did not seem in the least embarrassed by my nakedness. I whipped a towel around my waist and asked her how she had managed to get inside the room and what the dickens she wanted. She laughed at my confusion and answered, coyly, that newspaper people had all kinds of friends. Since Nancy was at the theater with her boyfriend, she added, we might as well enjoy a drink in the bar in the lobby—as soon as I was more suitably dressed.

The bar was crowded with officers of the British and Canadian air forces, and she seemed to know them all. She was very much at home. It did not take long to learn that the

Gazette, the afternoon paper, had assigned her to interview me about my past, present, and future.

Out of that evening only bitter fruit would come. I would reestablish that I was only a pawn manipulated by the government of the Bahamas and the Oakes family. Their mutual objective was to have me deported to the island of Mauritius, where I would be isolated and forgotten, without a visa, unable to travel anywhere in the world.

Sally Dennison, as I shall call her, was eager to gain my confidence. She gladly informed me of my wife's activities. Nancy was having an affair with a pilot in the RAF Ferry Command, who delivered fighter planes from the U.S. to Montreal. Combat-tested English fliers took over for the final leg to air bases in Britain.

His name was Joerg "Hans" Edsberg, and my informant understood that he had a wife and five children in his native Denmark.

This romance had been going on for months. She confided, her voice a whisper, that she thought Edsberg was somehow involved with a racketeer named Count Navarro, who for reasons of his own was financing the conquest of my wife. After she obtained a divorce from me, Edsberg would then marry this heiress, whose great fortune would be available on her twenty-first birthday.

I could not repress a smile at the thought of the many eager fortune hunters that roamed the cocktail party circuit, in pursuit of the so-called heiress. They would be in for a sad surprise when Nancy disclosed her modest income of a thousand dollars a month, for the next sixteen years.

At eleven o'clock I left and returned to my room. Shortly, Nancy and her escort arrived. She threw out her arms and gave me a hug.

Behind her stood Hans Edsberg, who was short and pudgy. He left immediately.

I studied Nancy with genuine interest. I barely recognized

her. The youthful charm I remembered was gone. Her expression had hardened, her speech was measured, and her sentences were sprinkled with random profanity. She chattered nervously, injecting an occasional question about what I had been doing in Cuba after she had left. She asked about Hemingway and his friends, and about my duty with the Canadian Merchant Marine, her thoughts jumping, leaving me no time to answer.

I wondered how I could have been so much in love with her. The thought crossed my mind of how much this infatuation had cost me in emotional as well as financial terms.

"You seem to be miles away," she said. "Come, get back to earth."

"All right, then. Suppose we begin by discussing what you propose to do about your boyfriend?"

The remark caught her off guard and brought a flush to her face. I went on, in a dry tone, "Stop playing games. Let us talk like grown-ups. Tell me what you intend to do now that I am back."

She told me she hardly knew where to begin. They had met as passengers on a plane, and from that moment on she had lost her head and her heart. "If you really love me as you always told me you did," she said, "try to understand and let me go. I want to be free to marry him."

"What about his wife and five children?" I asked ironically.

She abruptly changed the subject, saying she had to leave for New York in a day or two to see her dentist. When she returned, she told me, we would have time to think and then talk about our plans.

The next day I drifted into the bar and, to my surprise, met several pilots I had known in Nassau. One of them was Lonnie Fredericks, who was recently divorced and living alone in a large apartment. He offered to share it with me.

After Nancy departed, I fell into the routine of having my lunch in the hotel bar. Sally Dennison was always there, and I began to find pleasure in her company. The interview seemed to have been forgotten, or at least postponed. One day she told me my wife was back and in the dining room on the roof garden, with Hans and a Mrs. Betsy Bloomingdale, from New York. As the elevator stopped on the top floor and the door opened, I came face-to-face with Hans Edsberg. Flustered, he turned and sprinted to the exit at the other end of the room.

Nancy greeted me coldly and suggested we meet the next afternoon in Mrs. Bloomingdale's suite, where she was staying. Her husband, Alfred, owned a large New York department store.

That evening, Sally asked me to walk her home. I felt warmly toward her. She had shown me kindness at a time when I needed it most. When I awoke the next morning, she had left for work.

I felt lighter of heart than I had in some time. But I was to learn another of life's painful lessons: you may regret the things you say when your head is on a pillow.

Unwisely, I felt no apprehension about seeing Nancy. But this meeting turned out to be a testing time. Nancy had not lost her capacity to take a bad situation and make it worse. She wanted everything her way. As we sipped tea in silence, I watched her. Her hands were trembling. Betsy Bloomingdale sat nearby, uncomfortably, plainly there because Nancy had feared facing me alone.

"I want to end our marriage," she said, her voice icy.

"You may have a divorce whenever you wish," I said.

She avoided looking me in the eye. "I do not want a divorce," she said, "I want an annulment."

I was taken aback. I had not even considered that possibility. "Why an annulment?" My mind spun; what was her game?

At that point, Mrs. Bloomingdale spoke up: "What difference does it make?"

"A great deal," I said. "To obtain an annulment, she would have to find some cockeyed reason to convince a judge that our marriage was fraudulent. That would close the door of U.S. immigration to me forever on the grounds of moral turpitude."

A nod indicated that her friend understood. But Nancy glared at me. "I shall get my annulment," she said. "My lawyers told me they could get me one easily."

"It will be a hell of a fight," I assured her, "and a costly one."

I could see the temper rising in her, and again the image of Sir Harry came through vividly, the disagreeable look that surfaced when things did not go the way he wanted. "I advise you," she said, "to return to your little island where you can marry some silly girl and have children and grow sugar cane. You were born for that plebeian life."

Betsy Bloomingdale could not conceal her dismay. She reminded Nancy of how she had stood by me at the trial. Why now this apparent hatred?

She believed in my innocence, Nancy said, adding that she also had no desire to be the widow of a man hanged for murder.

I have no idea what instinct prompted Mrs. Bloomingdale to try to mediate our differences. But she did try.

"Nancy," she said, "you're not a Catholic. You were married by a justice of the peace. Why in the name of heaven do you insist on an annulment? It would be damaging for him and costly for both of you."

Nancy moved to the edge of her chair and bit off each word: "I want an annulment because my lawyers assured me that the moral-turpitude statute would prevent him from ever setting foot in the United States."

"What have I done to merit this treatment from you?" I asked, appalled by her vindictiveness.

Nancy made it all sound very simple. She did not want me moving in her social orbit; did not want to read about my succeeding in business or marrying well. Somehow she would take that as a defeat for herself. "I want you out of my life, out of this part of the world," she said.

I made a futile attempt to reason with her. She refused to listen, and finally I exploded: "Nancy, left to your own whims, you will be no more than a social parasite and will end your life in the gutter."

I apologized to Mrs. Bloomingdale, and, ignoring Nancy, I walked out of the room, and literally out of her life.

I despised her at that moment, but I felt as much contempt for myself. The cool air outside refreshed me, and I continued to walk along the road to a hill overlooking the city. My mind continued to churn. Then, suddenly, I remembered having read in my youth an old Chinese proverb:

"Never avenge yourself, be patient. Sit on your doorstep and you shall see the corpse of your enemy pass by."

That thought calmed me, and I walked back to the hotel to rejoin my friends at the bar.

With my break from Nancy now complete, I moved into Lonnie Fredericks's apartment. It was convenient to town, and a peaceful change after the hectic days at the hotel. Lonnie spent half his time flying, which gave me the privacy I welcomed.

Sally Dennison grew more and more attentive. Through her friends, I met a lawyer named Marcel Gaboury, who had valuable political connections. He advised me to begin thinking seriously of my future, and of settling in Canada.

I had contacted Maurice Speiser in New York, and he agreed that I should consider Gaboury's advice. In the meantime, Speiser offered to retain a lawyer in the States to defend me in the event Nancy started annulment proceedings. Shortly thereafter, Bernard Shapiro arrived in Montreal to acquaint himself with my case.

His law practice was in Washington, and I found him a man of reassuring presence. We spent days discussing virtually every option, every action that might be taken. Shapiro recommended that we add to our legal team one Arnold Krakower, of New York. (Krakower later married Kathleen Winsor, who wrote the best-selling novel *Former Amber*, which caused a sensation with its heated sexual passages.)

I was suddenly up to my ears in lawyers, but they were bright men, and I had the uneasy feeling I might need them all.

Legally, I was still a merchant marine officer on a thirty-day leave. The war in Europe had just ended, and for an indefinite time a need would exist for transportation to bring Canadian and American soldiers home from foreign lands. My attorneys suggested that I solidify my status by transferring to the regular armed forces. I agreed. The idea seemed to delight Sally, and within days Gaboury had filed a petition to have me, a British subject by birth, become a Canadian resident.

I felt optimistic about my prospects, knowing that the government was even granting asylum to ex-Luftwaffe pilots and German officers who had been prisoners of war in Canada. It was with a light heart that I left for Quebec, where the 26th Regiment was stationed, an exclusively French-speaking unit. At the recruiting office, the doctor who examined me was none other than my old friend from Nassau, Ricky Obcrwarth. He asked me if I wanted in or out.

"In," I replied.

We made a date to get together the following Sunday. Ricky called for me at the barracks and we drove to his apartment in the center of Quebec. After my acquittal, he said, his medical practice began to drop off, and he felt fortunate to be accepted by the army. The conversation turned inevitably to the Oakes case. He had his own strong suspicion as to how Sir Harry had been murdered.

He told me he had not been allowed near the body shortly after it arrived at the morgue. Still, he had found an opportunity to examine the wounds on the head and probe **them**. Immediately afterward, he had been warned not to make any statement about the condition of the corpse, and the autopsy was assigned to a doctor appointed by the Attorney General's office.

There was no doubt in his mind that Oakes had been shot in **the** head with a small-caliber gun. The idea that a blunt instrument had caused the wounds struck him as ludicrous.

He urged me to make an effort to have the body of Oakes exhumed. He said he would stake his reputation that any objective medical examiner would agree with his point of view. I was grateful for his opinions, but we both knew how difficult such a process would be. I had no legal standing to make that request.

After we parted, however, I could not get the idea out of my mind. I called Speiser in New York, and he said he thought we could obtain the necessary court order, in time. There was no rush. Once I was established in either Canada or the United States, he promised his assistance in the matter.

And so the issue rested. Another forty years have since elapsed. Today the skeletal remains of Sir Harry Oakes might well hold the solution to the mystery that still shrouds this case.

Three weeks after my enlistment in the army, I was discharged *illicto presto*. I listened with growing puzzlement as my commanding officer, a major, described a call he had received the previous day from a general in the War Ministry.

The general was furious. "I have been told," he said, "that this son of a bitch de Marigny—you know, the man who killed Harry Oakes—is enrolled in your regiment."

The major said he reminded the general that I had been acquitted by a jury. "It seemed to have no effect on him. He wanted you out immediately. He added that you were to be given a dishonorable discharge. I asked him on what grounds. There was a pause, and he replied, 'I leave that to you. But I want him out within twenty-four hours.' "

Several Canadian officers went to bat for me. No one was quite clear exactly why the War Ministry had intervened. One officer, I was told, demanded that the general put in writing his reasons for insisting on a dishonorable discharge.

The next morning, the general consented to my receiving an honorable discharge. But he was adamant that I leave the barracks the same day. And so I did. Mine was a priority case, and I was mustered out ahead of soldiers who were returning from the battlefields of Europe, and who had been waiting weeks or months to be discharged. The date was July 26, 1945.

I returned to Montreal and headed straight to Gaboury's office. He could make no sense of the manner in which I had been dismissed. I called Sally, who told me to come to her place and not to mention to anyone what had happened. We spent the evening together and waited for Gaboury to call. He was crestfallen: the immigration office had rejected my application to become a resident of Canada.

That news hit me in the hollow of the stomach. I was still alone and homeless, a nomad wandering in the desert. Sally did her best to console me, then dropped me off at Fredericks's place while she went to her office to catch up on her work.

The next afternoon, the newspapers were on the street. A vendor was shouting, "Read about de Marigny... read about de Marigny being deported from Canada!"

I could not believe what I had heard. I bought the *Gazette*, and the front-page headline jumped out at me: CANADA REJECTS DE MARIGNY AS CITIZEN AND SOLDIER. The article covered most of page one, under the byline of my friend.

The next morning I learned that Sally had left for Toronto, where she was to marry her fiance, who worked there. She had played her cards with great craft and skill. Without a blush, she had given me her body to gain my confidence. She had entered my life through the front door and left it through the bedroom window. At that moment I vowed never again to place my faith in anyone connected with the press. If she was an example, they were a breed apart, who for a scoop would sell out their own mothers.

Marcel Gaboury stormed the *Gazette* offices at first light the next morning and informed the editor that unless they retracted the article, and gave my side equal space, he was prepared to sue them for slander. He pointed out that I had never applied to become a Canadian citizen. I had simply applied, as hundreds did every day, for permission to become a resident.

The *Gazette* printed a retraction in their next edition. But once again I was branded.

To my surprise, I was to find that my plight had aroused sympathy in unexpected places. One was the office of the ex-Prime Minister and leader of the Conservative Party, John Diefenbaker. He gave me an appointment to see him at his office.

Meanwhile, I was invited to a dinner party whose guest of honor was a jockey-sized character with a large head attached to tiny shoulders, and a body that seemed undernourished. He was introduced as Count Navarro.

During dinner, our hostess made a small speech to introduce the count to her other guests, and then asked him to tell some of the dramatic stories of his life with Al Capone.

Someone whispered that he had killed thirty people during his career. I watched him with interest and, in truth, admired his pluck. Everyone at the table seemed to be under his spell: a silly little crook surrounded by a bunch of impressionable fools. I spotted him instantly as a fourteen-karat phony.

After dinner, the "count" corralled me and we moved to the other end of the room. He asked me point-blank if I was the husband of Nancy Oakes.

I nodded. He then asked if she had turned twenty-one yet. He appeared startled when I told him that she had reached her twenty-first birthday in May, two months ago. He rubbed his chin and said sharply, "That little bastard she goes out with told me she was to come into many millions on her birthday. He wanted me to finance him. He was going to get a divorce and marry her, after she divorced you. I bankrolled the bastard for thousands of dollars. Are you certain she is already twenty-one?"

I assured him she was. I also added that she would not inherit millions of dollars, and that under the terms of her father's will, her allowance was limited to one thousand dollars a month for another ten years, at the end of which time she would receive whatever was left of the estate.

"God send his soul to hell," he swore. "He took me for a ride, and no one does that to Count Navarro and gets away with it. He will pay for it." Navarro had a suite at the Hotel

Rex, and invited me to meet him for lunch two days later.

Out of curiosity, I went. Navarro told me cheerfully that his "boys" had given Hans a preview of what was in store for him. He was in a local hospital with a smashed face and a couple of broken ribs.

Navarro was a shrewd man, a con artist whose victims included both His Eminence the Cardinal, and the Prime Minister of Quebec.

His eventual downfall came as the result of taking money from the president of a small airline that flew between Montreal and New York. This money was "clean," and when the man realized he had been duped, he started legal action. The count fled to Venezuela. There he was arrested and extradited to New York, where he was wanted for a long list of robberies.

Life magazine gave his story several pages. He had been born in Brooklyn, was known in the underworld as the Frog, and had some twenty-one aliases. He was flung into jail, where he barely escaped death at the hands of his fellow prisoners, when an investment scheme he conned them into failed.

Diefenbaker promised to do whatever he could to find out the truth behind my abrupt dismissal from the army. To my dismay, that turned out to be very little. I discovered that the immigration offices in the British colonies acted as a state within a state, and answered to no one. There was no appeal against their decisions.

From the visitors' gallery, I watched Diefenbaker put his questions to the minister, as he had promised. The minister replied that under the Immigration Act (Number 695), no British subject born outside England, Australia, New Zealand, or Northern Ireland could be accepted as a resident of Canada. It was not what I wanted to hear, but I had my answer. Having been born in Mauritius, I was excluded *de facto*.

(The purpose of the act, of course, was to make immigration difficult from those British territories that were still overwhelmingly black, such as the Bahamas, Bermuda, Jamaica, and Rhodesia.)

There was nothing more that Diefenbaker could do. Now I was informed by Gaboury that he had been ordered to deliver me to agents of the immigration department at eleven o'clock, in his office. Marcel assured me that he had prepared a writ of habeas corpus and I would be released immediately.

At eleven sharp, two customs agents walked in and I was handcuffed and my passport taken away. I was hustled into a waiting car and driven to the Immigration Building. There the judge announced that I would not be deported. However, the Office of Immigration was empowered to keep me in jail until the matter could be decided in court.

The jail was operated by the French, and they were kind to me. Most of my fellow prisoners were sailors absent without leave, or people who had entered Canada illegally. The guards placed me in a cell by myself. I could not help comparing this little guest room to the dungeon I had occupied in Nassau. The turnkey invited me to play cards with him, and on several occasions I was allowed to spend the evening with the sailors watching a movie. The turnkey knew that without our passports we would not go very far.

The day after my arrest, I received an interesting call from Gaboury. A man named Moses Miller would visit me that afternoon. When he appeared, I observed a man bearing an uncanny resemblance to Groucho Marx, down to the familiar cigar, the long black overcoat, and the dark-rimmed glasses.

Miller was a gregarious person who had made a fortune in the dry-goods business, selling mostly cotton shirts and caps, still hard to obtain at war's end. I had no idea what any of this had to do with my circumstances.

I was beginning to feel like Candide.

Miller leaned forward and told me somberly, "The government is against you. The Oakes family and their attorneys are against you, and the authorities in Nassau would prefer never to hear your name again. But you have nothing to fear.

I talked to Gaboury, and everything has been arranged. We will have you out of here. The entire Jewish community of Montreal is behind you, and we shall appeal this case all the way to the Supreme Court, if necessary."

I had only one question: Why? Why should the Jews of Montreal foot the bill for the personal battle of someone who was not even Jewish?

"It is not a personal fight," he said. "It is a fight against persecution. We Jews had to fight just to survive. Do not worry. Moe Miller is here to help you."

He left as abruptly as he arrived, telling me he would see me the next day.

That evening, Marcel Gaboury dropped by and confirmed what Miller had told me. "He has persuaded a friend of his, Philip Joseph, a distinguished lawyer from Israel, to take an interest in your case. Joseph has a brother named Dov Joseph who is a member of the Israeli government. A minister, or something of that importance."

Moe Miller visited me four times a week, and on every visit he brought with him shirts for the turnkey and guards. "Public relations," he said, with a smile.

At last, my case came to court the Wednesday before Holy Week. The legal maneuvering seemed endless, the sparring between the lawyers pointless and boring. During those days, a middle-aged man with red hair always sat one row behind me. He was accompanied by a dignified-looking woman whom I took to be his wife. Finally, late on Friday afternoon, the judge told the lawyers that he would review the testimony and that I was to remain in jail until a decision had been reached.

Gaboury approached the bench and asked the court to set bail so that I might be given my release, pending the outcome of the hearing. He pointed out that since my passport had been confiscated, there was no possibility I would try to leave the country.

It was four o'clock, the judge noted. He was prepared to set bond, but a steep one, at the government's insistence. The banks were closed, and Holy Week started the next morning. Even if I had access to cash or other negotiable instruments, there was no time to obtain them.

As Gaboury walked toward me, he was intercepted by the man and woman who had been sitting quietly behind me. She carried a briefcase. They stopped at the judge's desk. A dead silence filled the room. The judge looked with surprise at the little man with red hair.

"Your Honor, I shall post bail for Mr. de Marigny," he said. He nodded to the woman, who walked up and handed him the briefcase. He opened it. "Here is fifty thousand dollars in cash, and fifty thousand dollars in government bonds. If that is not enough, my secretary can get more from my office."

The judge cleared his throat. "Who are you?" he asked.

"My name is Harry Rajinsky. I am the owner of the Spring Mattress Company of Canada."

"What is your relationship to Mr. de Marigny?"

"None, Your Honor."

"May I ask why you wish to post bond for him?"

"Your Honor, I am a Jew, and Mr. de Marigny is a Catholic. I find it objectionable that a good Christian should spend Holy Week in jail, when only the lack of a sum of money denies his freedom."

The court buzzed with a loud murmur. The judge stared for a moment more, then said, "I know your name, Mr. Rajinsky. You are an important man in this community. Since you stand bond for the defendant, I shall set bail at one thousand dollars."

Rajinsky counted out the cash and placed it in front of the judge. His secretary scooped up the rest of the money and bonds and left discreetly. The spectators applauded, and surrounded us to offer good wishes. I grasped the hand of my benefactor and thanked him. Quickly, I followed him out of the building.

I had dinner that evening at the home of Harry Rajinsky and his wife, a concert pianist. Moses Miller and the Israeli lawyer, Philip Joseph, joined us. Later, in the library, Joseph asked if I ever heard from Edith Meyer. The question startled me. Yes, I had last seen Edith in Paris, after her escape from Germany, eight or nine years ago. I had received a letter from her while I was in the Nassau jail—postmarked Israel. I began to sense a connection.

"She is the reason we are helping you," he said. "You took a great risk once when Edith and her mother were in danger. Now we repay you in our own way. Edith asked us to say that she prayed for you every day while you were on trial for your life."

That night, alone in my room, I thought of those Jews I did not know, who had come as one to rally to my side. Tears welled up in my eyes. Destiny had not abandoned me, after all. Through a long series of quirks, it was watching over me.

Or so I hoped. Remarkably, even though I had entered Canada on a thirty-day visa, the case dragged on for two years. True to Moc Miller's pledge, the appeal of my deportation order went all the way to the Supreme Court.

My life seemed hopelessly snarled. In New York, Maurice Speiser was dying, and I had no way of tapping the money he had discreetly held for me. Nancy had acted on her threat to have our marriage annulled, filing suits both in New York and in Dade County, Florida. As limited as my resources were, I vowed to contest them.

Life—and death—went on. In April of 1946, Hans Edsberg died in the crash of an RAF transport plane over Denmark. Poor, pudgy Hans. I felt a moment of sadness for him, touched as he was by what I would come to believe was an Oakes family curse.

The New York gossip columns were soon reporting that Nancy was involved in a love affair with a handsome and very married British actor, Richard Greene. That liaison produced a daughter who, as Patricia Oakes, would one day become the wife of Franklin Delano Roosevelt Jr.

Nancy would move on to other romances, including one

with the exotic star Turhan Bey, and two more marriages.

In Canada, I worked for a few months as a lumberjack, and otherwise survived on the kindness of those strangers who were now friends. In November of 1947, my case reached the Supreme Court in Ottawa. The justices upheld the ruling of the Immigration Department, and I was to be deported to Mauritius "within a reasonable time."

Now a familiar problem appeared. There was no air travel to Mauritius, no military transport could be provided, and no passenger ships served the island. Nor could I wait for the first available cargo vessel out of London, where I was persona non grata, thanks to the efforts of the Duke of Windsor.

My stay in Canada was extended a few more weeks, while Moe Miller and Harry Rajinsky worked behind the scenes.

The right people were bribed, and finally the Haitian consulate granted me a visa. After brief stopovers in New York and Miami, I boarded a KLM airliner for Port-au-Prince, the capital of the island nation ruled by "Papa Doc" Duvalier, a place famed for its witchcraft and voodoo rituals. Perfect. How symbolic, I thought. I was bound for the Land of the Living Dead.

JOURNEY'S END

I hoped I would find tranquillity in Haiti; it was a quality I had learned to measure in days and weeks. I had been advised to stay in Petionville, a small resort in the mountains, a thousand feet above the capital. The population was under ten thousand, and the life was pastoral.

I rented a room in a charming inn called the Belle Creole, with my own kitchen and a fine view of the village below.

The morning after my arrival, I awakened to a dreadful racket of falling pots and pans. Walking into the kitchen, I discovered a cow in the middle of the room, waiting to be milked by my landlady, while two maids washed the cow's udders with soap and water. I was told that this was a daily routine, the only way to assure the guest that the milk had not been diluted with water from a gutter, and that the one doing the milking had clean hands. From my room, the entourage moved onto the next.

I was just getting adjusted to the pace of Haitian living when two immigration officers paid a visit and drove me into town. When I told their captain I could not pay the five-thousand-dollar bribe he demanded, I was arrested and thrown into jail, the only white man in a cell shared by sixteen of us.

The cell was so small that everyone had to stand. The stench was fierce. Since there was no toilet, everyone used a back corner of the cell to defecate and urinate. I was amazed at how calm and stoic my cellmates were. If three or four were taken out, they were instantly replaced by a new group. All were silent; no one complained or questioned why they were there.

After forty-eight hours of this indecency, falling asleep on my feet, if at all, I was taken before the same official who had interviewed me earlier. Nothing had changed except his price, which had now gone up to ten thousand dollars, and soon I was back in the cell.

The next morning I was released at the insistence of the British consul, whom the owners of the inn had notified of my arrest. Back at the Belle Creole, I had a bath and my first edible food in three days. The British consul regretted my treatment, but feared I would suffer more of the same if I remained in Haiti. He suggested I try Jamaica.

KLM, the Dutch airline, had a plane that made a daily circuit of the islands of Curacao, Haiti, and Jamaica. I bought a ticket for Jamaica, and arrived in Kingston later that same afternoon. From the air the city was green and picturesque, and by now I welcomed the chance to return to the consistency of British colonial rule.

I had reckoned without the ever-present manipulations of the Duke of Windsor. I had been effectively, if not legally, blackballed in every British possession in the Caribbean and Canada. It was all very neat; each rejection reinforced the last, and paved the way for the next. I had been found innocent of the charges against me. I was, in fact, the victim of a false arrest, a criminal attempt to frame me for the killing of Sir Harry Oakes.

Yet, wherever I tried to turn, I was made to seem a dangerous character, a fugitive from my past. The moment I stepped off the plane, I was escorted by two policemen to an immense barn of a building, separated by ropes into compartments for arriving anddeparting passengers, and one marked "Immigration."

Here I was received by a red-haired Irishman who told me bluntly that I was persona non grata in Jamaica. As I sat on a chair flanked by two policemen, I could hear passengers debating whether I was a gangster or a stowaway. Meanwhile, the customs officials were working to put me on the next plane out of Jamaica—a KLM flight to Miami. The captain refused to take me without a valid visa. He argued that I was a British subject, on British soil. He could not understand on what grounds the Jamaican authorities had refused to admit me.

How odd it seemed to hear a Dutch pilot defending my rights to British officials. The plane left without me. I spent the night in the immigration jail in Jamaica, and the next day I boarded a flight back to Haiti.

There I was refused permission to leave the plane. We went on to Curacao, and there again I spent the night in jail, until the same flight returned the next day.

The joyless merry-go-round continued: from Jamaica to Curacao to Haiti, where I was allowed only to leave the confinement of the plane for that of the jail.

By then I had grown rather friendly with the Dutch pilot who had ferried me from place to place. Grinning, he suggested that I get a job with KLM as a steward, and then I could stay on that run the rest of my life and get paid for it. At least I wouldn't have to worry about finding a land that would have me.

But then, sympathetically, he asked if I didn't know any important people anywhere who might use their influence for me. And, yes, suddenly I thought of one: the brother of the dictator of the Dominican Republic.

The captain radioed a wire in my name to Aristmendie Trujillo. Within hours, permission was granted to KLM to land at Santo Domingo and discharge its special passenger.

I felt no uneasiness at accepting the hospitality of a family viewed by many as tyrants. I gave little thought to their motives, if any. It was enough that I had been helpful to them once, in Nassau. But in truth, to be welcome in a small and outcast country, it is sometimes necessary only to be unwanted in larger and more powerful places.

I was to be the guest of the Trujillos at the Jaragua Hotel for as long as I needed. That would turn out to be for six months, a very long time, the way my life had been going.

I felt like a refugee, but from what? I was running from nothing, bound for nowhere. How weary I had grown of immigration cells. My skin had become touchy after the humiliations I had endured.

Santo Domingo intrigued me. The city had been rebuilt after the 1932 hurricane in which it was devastated. I was impressed by how clean it was; the streets and parks were immaculate, flowers everywhere. What a contrast with Haiti, where the people lived in hovels, amid filth and vermin.

Don Rafael Trujillo y Molina, president of the Dominican Republic, was, in his own land, as powerful as any man on earth. He owned the island and held the power of life or death over everyone who lived there. When I first met him, I was astounded at his lack of charisma. He was not a Pcron or even a Miguel Alcman. He was of medium height, pudgy, and wore gold-rimmed glasses. His hair was thin, and his appearance was that of a bank teller.

Don Rafael was a skilled organizer and administrator. There was no sign of his iron fist anywhere, and no police or soldiers in visible numbers. His home, next door to the Jaragua Hotel, was neither large nor pretentious.

The dictator used to walk every evening along the Malecon after dinner. When Don Rafael realized I spoke Spanish fluently, he invited me to join him on his strolls. He lived a rather spartan life, and his visitors were few.

He boasted quietly of how he had led the island out of the state of anarchy that existed when he took over. The national debt was in excess of twenty-five million U.S. dollars. The country had been occupied for four generations by Haitians, and then by the U.S. Marines for fifteen years. What had not been ruined or looted by man had been virtually destroyed by nature, in the form of the 1932 hurricane.

Still, the politicians fought one another, and had at one time produced three presidents in a single day.

Five years after Trujillo took office, the national debt was paid. He issued currency backed by gold, and no one in the government signed a check without his permission. There were no more middlemen.

His concern for the poor and uneducated seemed genuine. At tremendous cost, Trujillo had retained a New Jersey company to install a system to provide fresh water throughout the country. "We are the only country in Latin America," he said proudly, "that can boast such an achievement. No more typhoid, no more dysentery. Everyone on the island has been vaccinated."

I was brimming with enthusiasm for the new order in Santo Domingo when I met a Miss Atkins, from the American consulate. My goal, my hope, was still to be admitted to the United States.

Miss Atkins was intrigued by my case and, I suppose, the story that went with it. She invited me to lunch at a small restaurant owned by a French Jew, Joseph Levy. With his sister, a doctor, he had joined a group of European Jews who chartered a steamship and crossed the Atlantic to escape the Holocaust. No country, including the United States, would admit them. They roamed the Caribbean without success until Trujillo allowed them to settle in his country. My own odyssey was a smaller-scale version of theirs.

Miss Atkins took immediate pains to cool my exuberance. "Mr. de Marigny," she said, "your file has arrived. There are a great many questions to be answered. We know you are grateful to the Trujillos for what they have done for you. That's natural. Still, certain facets of their way of doings things are not agreeable to everyone. I ask you to be most careful. Be discreet. Sooner or later, investigators will be here to talk with you. They will want to know your point of view about things that concern our government. Remember, you have a tough record against you."

I was to learn that the American way of doing things was completely unlike that of any other country in the world.

Regardless of the letters, memoranda, or telegrams that the government of Nassau had fired off to the United States, warning their officials against me, the American tradition of examining the facts carefully, and then, on that basis, deciding whether one was innocent or guilty, still prevailed. In my case, the Immigration Department was at odds with the Department of Justice, with the latter taking my side at no expense to me. I found this remarkable. Nowhere else in the world had such a charitable and open attitude been shown toward the rights of the individual.

Letters began to arrive from abroad. Before his death, Maurice Speiser had arranged to have funds sent to me monthly. The balance he entrusted to one of his partners, Robert Lansdale.

Nancy was going ahead full speed in her effort to obtain an annulment of our marriage. So far she had lost the case in Miami, and had filed an appeal with the state supreme court in Tallahassee.

There was nothing else to do but enjoy the security of Santo Domingo and wait patiently for my visa.

Then, one day, Joseph Levy asked me to meet a friend of his. The man who later appeared was middle-aged, and spoke French and English without an accent. He was traveling on a Swiss passport and wanted to leave for the United States, where he could make arrangements to have his wife and children join him. I quickly gathered that the passport was phony.

Joseph hoped that I might enlist the help of Aristmendie Trujillo in obtaining for his friend a passport from Santo Domingo. The man was willing to pay dearly. Frankly, I was at a loss as to how to handle such a delicate matter. One false move, and I could easily find myself back on a plane to nowhere.

The next day I approached an officer known as El Negro, a childhood friend of the colonel, who also acted as a bodyguard. He never let the colonel out of his sight, and was at times his link to the outside world.

I posed the problem to El Negro, and his face remained blank as he listened to me. There was no indication that what I had proposed was anything unusual.

"This will cost your friend a pretty dollar," he said.

"How much?" I asked.

"Ten to twenty thousand dollars."

I reported my conversation to Joseph, and was told to go ahead. The next afternoon, during the siesta hour, I visited El Negro in his quarters, and told him my friend wished to proceed.

He looked at me sharply. "How much is there for you in this deal?"

"Not a penny," I said. "Bad money brings bad luck." I meant it, and the words came without hesitation.

I walked back to the Jaragua. I was wondering what to do. I wondered if I had the right to jeopardize my chance to enter the States. Should Aristmendie take the offer badly, he could easily order me out. To where was anyone's guess. It could still take a matter of weeks before I obtained my own visa.

Should I risk all this to help a man I did not know? Yet no matter how hard I tried, I could not forget the promise I had made to Moses Miller in Canada, when he helped me fight the immigration office and obtain a visa for Haiti. His words still echoed in my ear when I had asked how I could ever repay him: "If ever you see a Jew who needs help, do what you can. That will be my repayment."

The colonel was most receptive. He bowed his head several times during my short recital and then said, "Don Alfredo, I am an army man. My brother is the one who handles politics. Still, for our friendship's sake, I would be happy to talk to your friend. Bring him for breakfast next Thursday."

That gave us six days. I had to find a way to give to Aristmendie the ten thousand dollars without offending him. We finally settled on a plan:

Joseph's friend was to withdraw from his bank ten thousand dollars in high-denomination bills. We would then purchase a large, expensive book of Spanish poetry and place the money between the pages. The book was to be wrapped as a gift.

On the day of the interview, we brought the gift to the colonel. After breakfast, we followed him to his office. He sat behind his desk while we stood.

Aristmendie explained that this was a very complicated matter. Still, he was willing to make the effort and hoped that he would be successful. When he was through, my companion thanked him and offered him the gift as a token of gratitude.

The colonel undid the package and held the book in his left hand, flicking the pages with his right thumb. Without hurrying, he placed the volume in a drawer and locked it.

He then rose and, wordlessly, we all walked the length of the veranda toward our car. By the end of our walk, Aristmendie was all smiles. At the car door he held me back and whispered, "Tell your friend that I like his book very much. Tell him that I would like to have breakfast with him on Monday."

Then, casually, he added, "Ask him when he comes to bring me the second volume of that book of poetry."

We drove away in a hurry. So the price of a legal passport, an identity, was twenty thousand dollars. I had paid a price much dearer, I knew, for an identity others had imposed upon me. Would I ever have my own true identity back? Within the week, Joseph's friend was on his way. I watched the plane leave and felt a twinge of envy. When, I wondered, would my turn come?

Bribery, graft, and corruption were a way of life in so much of the world, the morality of the times. But money alone could not buy my way out of the Dominican Republic and into the United States.

In time, two customs agents arrived and I was introduced to them at the American consulate. They questioned and observed me, and I would up showing them around Santo Domingo.

Five months and a week had passed since I first became a guest of the Trujillos. I was offered a temporary visa and urged by the Consul General to decline it. I looked at him in disbelief. I was so eager, I would have gone if the United States had accepted me by the hour. Which was just about what the visa meant: no work, and no assurance that I could stay more than thirty days.

I would be putting myself once again in a no-man's-land. He asked me to be patient another week or more, to trust him, and he would resubmit my request with a recommendation for a resident visa.

It is hard to be patient when time has been your enemy. It is hard to risk your trust when you see lies and deceit working so well. But I heard the sense in what he said, and I agreed to wait.

The Consul General called for Miss Atkins and instructed her to begin this next process. Before I left, he offered to show me my dossier. It was incredible. Judging by the size of it, I was either a very notorious man, or a very maligned one.

The Consul was confident that this flawed episode of my life would have a happy ending. "I had to go over everything in those files," he said, "and prepare an answer. You will be secure in the United States. People are fair and honest and helpful. You can start life anew and will soon forget those bad times you endured."

One week later the new visa arrived from Washington. When my passport was decorated with the appropriate stamp, and handed back to me by Miss Atkins, my hands were trembling. I looked with awe at the small blue book that would open the doors to freedom.

I reached New York in September of 1947. My first move was to visit the lawyer who was coordinating my defense against Nancy's suit to annul our marriage. He told me we were facing two more years of litigation, but he was certain we would win.

What a Pyrrhic victory that would be, I thought. I no longer believed we could win, and didn't much care anymore, but the battle had cost me most of my remaining cash. So my next stop was to locate Robert Lansdale, who held in trust the money I had managed to take out of the Bahamas.

I was in for a series of shocks. Lansdale had died of a heart attack, not two weeks earlier. His partner knew me, but knew nothing about Robert holding any money or securities in safekeeping for me. There was a mound of private papers to go through, and something might turn up about my assets. He was sorry, he said, but it might take months.

Suddenly I was broke. All I could lay my hands on were a few hundred dollars. I moved to a room in a cheap walkup hotel, and tried to figure out what to do to survive.

In the worst of times, the people you can count on are few, and sometimes they are the ones you would least expect. Igor Cassini had on several occasions upset me with his silly or misinformed items in the gossip column he wrote for the Hearst papers. After I wrote him a snotty letter, we became friends.

It was Cassini who tried to help, who introduced me to the manager of the St. Regis Hotel, a Belgian named Boltnick. When he heard I was nearly destitute, he told me to come by; he might have something for me to do.

Assuming I would be given a minor position at the hotel, I was waiting outside his office at three the next afternoon. The job turned out to be dog-walking for three old ladies who lived at the St. Regis. The pay was twenty dollars a day and meals with the kitchen help. I jumped at the opportunity and felt no shame in it. Anything was better than starving, and starving was better than begging.

In December the little old ladies headed for Florida, dogs in tow. I was facing disaster once more.

When you are desperate, you will do almost anything, and I soon found myself working as a scab laborer in a shoe store hit by a union strike. I was issued green overalls and sent to the basement, where rows and rows of shoes were stacked from floor to ceiling. As the shoes would be taken upstairs to be sold, my job was to keep moving the boxes to fill all the empty slots. It was back-bending work, and not without physical risk. To get to the basement I had to make my way each morning through an irate mob of strikers.

However, the pay was seventy-five dollars a week, which wasn't bad for those times. When Christmas came, the strikers caved in. They needed money to buy toys for their kids, and they put away their picket signs. I was out of a job again.

It is not a moment I look back on with pride, but I did not try to hide my circumstances. When friends asked what I did during that low point in New York, I admitted that I walked dogs, sold pints of blood to a hospital, and worked as a scab in a shoe store.

And, to my amazement, I discovered I still had a short way to go before I struck bottom. I moved into a Salvation Army shelter and shared soup with the rest of the homeless men. I looked for a job anywhere, but had no luck at all. After one rejection, I went outside and walked up Madison Avenue, on a cold and bitter night. At Fifty-third Street I stopped for a light and watched the traffic go by.

The thought crossed my mind: maybe if I stepped in front of a cab I would break a leg, and be taken to the hospital. At least I would have a bed and a hot meal. I almost did it, then felt ashamed of the impulse and kept walking west on Fifty-third.

Out of nowhere I heard a voice call out, "Fred!" A taxi had pulled up to the curb. Inside was Cassini, whose friends called him Ghigi. "Where the hell have you been?" he asked. He had been trying to find me, he said, but I had left no forwarding address. When I told him I had been staying at the Salvation Army shelter, he knew why.

He invited me to his apartment and warmed me up with a cup of hot chocolate. He had good news: an opening for me in a travel agency on Forty-second Street, at a salary of fifty dollars a week, plus commissions, and he would steer all his friends to me.

I tried to thank him, but the words would not come. That day marked another turning point in my life. I had sunk as low as possible and had, I hoped, accepted the blows as a man,

with whatever dignity I had. Now I would begin to live again.
My luck suddenly changed. It wasn't long before Robert Lansdale's partner called. He had found the records Robert had kept, confirming the money he was holding in my trust. All I had to do was come to his office and pick up the check.

The murder and the trial were never very far from my thoughts. I talked often of "putting it behind me," but when I tried, others brought it up; a character in the case would surface again, or a news story would appear based on the latest odd development.

Nancy was busy pursuing the life she imagined she wanted. She won, of course. Our marriage was annulled in October 1949, and she married a German prince, Baron von Hoynengen Huene, the son of the man once involved in the Nazi plot, hatched in Spain and Portugal, to detain the Duke of Windsor.

In September 1950, information reached the FBI that for the first time mentioned the name of Harold Christie as the likely culprit in the killing of Sir Harry Oakes. The information came from a seaman named Edward Majava, who, while on leave in California, had been arrested for being drunk and disorderly in a bar in Oakland. In jail he boasted that he knew who was behind the murder, on the face of it the rantings of a not-very-reliable source. But something in what Majava revealed to the authorities was significant enough to bring Augustus Robinson, the new police chief of Nassau, by plane to California.

The FBI office in San Francisco tcletyped to Washington a description of Majava, who was born in Michigan, of Finnish descent, and a copy of a letter in which he said he had received threats on his life because he possessed "intimate knowledge" of the murder. In his interview with Robinson, Majava revealed that his information came from a society artist in Fort Lauderdale, Mrs. Hildegarde Hamilton. Her connection to the case was never made clear, nor who her informants might have been.

Robinson returned to Nassau satisfied that the essential

elements of Majava's story, pointing to the guilt of Harold Christie, were true, according to the FBI. And there the matter sat. The Bureau took no action; this was not its case. For whatever reason, Robinson brought no charges.

Fifteen years after the murder, in 1957—motivated, as far as I can tell, by nothing but the empty passage of time—Cyril St. John Stevenson stood on the floor of the House of Assembly and called for the government of the Bahamas to reopen the investigation. In a moment of high drama, he declared, "The man responsible for the murder of Harry Oakes sits among us, and must be brought to justice."

No leap of imagination is required to picture heads turning toward Harold Christie, who remained motionless in his seat. When the house voted on Stevenson's resolution calling for an inquiry by Scotland Yard, Christie, for transparent reasons, voted in favor. Within days, Scotland Yard issued a terse announcement: the Yard considered the case closed.

The reluctance of law-enforcement agencies in the Bahamas, London, and Washington to reexamine the crime has been nothing if not consistent. But the public has kept it alive. "Like the sinking of the *Titanic,*" noted the writer Geoffrey Bocca, "it is one of those stories which will always intrigue people."

Slowly, painfully, fitfully, I slipped into the obscurity I had craved for so long. In 1952 my luck took a sweeping turn for the better: I met a lovely, charming, and intelligent young woman who became my wife and the mother of my three sons. The years ahead were to be the most fulfilling of my life. I hope the reader will not resent my selfishness, if I choose to disturb as little as possible the privacy of my wife and sons.

We settled in Florida, where I took the first steps to becoming a U.S. citizen. The times were comfortable, but did not last. We were too much in the shadow of the Oakes case. A burglary in our home one night—nothing more than a thief making off with jewelry and silverware—alerted the local newspapers that one of the key figures in the mystery now lived among them. The result was a series of stories in which I was nearly always referred to as "the man who was accused of killing Harry Oakes."

When the news became public that I had applied for citizenship, another round of stories followed, with more probing into my life, past and present. Letters to the editor appeared in print, complaining about the government giving asylum to criminals. I quietly withdrew my application.

We moved again to Cuba, where I had found refuge once before, and where memories of old friends were still strong. I opened a lithograph shop, reproducing prints, and for the first time in years I could renew my love of the sea. I acquired a sixty-five-foot sailboat.

We might have stayed in Havana indefinitely, if Fidel Castro had not ventured out of the mountains to launch a revolution. For a time I used my sailboat to help smuggle refugees out of the country. When it became too dangerous to continue, I packed up our possessions and moved my family to Mexico.

From there we returned to the United States, and Texas, where we lived, contented and undisturbed, for most of the subsequent thirty years, until the present. There would be an occasional call from a newspaper reporter, or a magazine writer, or someone researching a book on the Oakes case. And every year, on March 29, Nancy would call from wherever she was to wish me a happy birthday. I preferred that my wife take the calls and relay to me whatever news or gossip Nancy wanted to pass on. I never tried to analyze this gesture, or make of it more than it was. They were just phone calls, an acknowledgment, I suppose, that we were once part of each other's lives in what became an extraordinary time.

Several years after we settled in Texas, another couple invited us to take a cruise on their yacht, which was moored in Florida. We made a stop in Grand Bahama, which had been developed as a tax-free island with casino gambling. I have never found the frantic action of a casino especially tempting, and so I left the hotel and went for a walk. I sat down on a bench near the dock, overlooking the boats, feeling a little melancholy on a soft, starry night, knowing where I was.

A voice roused me from my reverie. He called me "boss man," a phrase I had not heard in twenty years or more. I looked up and encountered a middle-aged black man whose face was partially hidden by a large hat.

"You don't remember me?" he said.

"Should I?"

"Boss, I worked for you once in Eleuthera. Then I moved to Nassau and worked for Mr. Oakes."

I peered more closely at him, but still **didn't** recognize the features.

"What is your name?" I asked.

"Rawlins. You remember me, boss. I was one of the night watchmen at Westbourne."

Memories came flooding back. Rawlins! He was one of the men who had disappeared after the murder of Sir Harry. I asked about the man who had worked with him, his brother-in-law, I thought.

He nodded. "That was Cordner. He died two years ago."

I asked what he was doing in Grand Bahama, what had brought him to the dock at that moment, and, more puzzling, how he had recognized me.

"I work in the casinos," he said, "cleaning and taking care of things. I saw your yacht come in, and got to talking with one of the men on board. He told me that his boss was from Texas, a big oilman there. Then I saw you, and something was familiar. I asked who you was. He told me your name. Your beard and your hair got white, but you got the same look, the same walk. You ain't changed that much, Mr. Fred. I always thought I would see you again someday."

He had to leave, but we agreed to meet the next morning at eleven, in a little park north of the town. That night I rejoined my wife and our friends in the casino, but I told no one about my meeting with Rawlins. I wasn't in a mood to rehash the whole story, and I had no idea what he would be able to tell me. I only knew that the case had blown through my life like a Gulf storm, and here it was again.

The next morning, Rawlins led me to the small hut where he lived, which contained a bed, three stools, and a table. This was my first chance to really study him. His hair was partly white and he had lost most of his teeth. Although he was younger than I, he looked ancient. I asked him, point-blank, if he knew what had happened on the night Harry Oakes died.

"The devil himself came to earth that night," he said. When he started rambling about evil and the spirits, I prodded him to get on with the story. I did not want a long satanic buildup.

"There was thunder and lightning all over. We stayed in the shed where they keep the tools. We was going to leave soon as the rain stopped. We was cold and soaked.

"Then we saw Mr. Harold acting strange. He walked down the outside stairs and run to his car next door at the golf club. He drove towards town. Cordncr and I wondered what he was doing out in that weather. Cordncr said he might have gone out to meet some girls.

"We waited. The weather was still no good. We lived on the other side of the hill, in the pine barrens, and we had to get there on our bicycles. Then, about half an hour after Mr. Harold left, a car pulled into the drive on the west side of the house. It was a black car that belonged to Mr. Harold, the office car, the big one he used for taking people around.

"We watched the car stop at the front door. One man came out and went upstairs. The other man went up the side stairs to Mr. Harold's room. There was a lot of lightning and I could see the man behind the wheel. It was Mr. Frank Christie. Cordner got a good look at him, too.

"We heard a noise like the tearing of a thick cloth. Heard it three, four times. Then we could see the light of a fire burning in the bedroom of Mr. Oakes. I was cold in my blood. Cordner said, "What the shit is going on?' He was shaking just like me. If Mr. Frank wasn't in the car, ten feet away, we would have run for it, rain or no rain."

I asked how long the two men were in the house.

"Not long," he said. "Fifteen minutes, twenty, maybe a little longer. Then they both came down the same way they had gone up. They hurried into the car and it drove west."

"Toward Lyford Cay?"

"Yes, boss."

"What happened next?"

"The wind was strong and it came with the rain in squalls. About an hour later it stopped, and we got out of there."

"What about the fire you saw upstairs?"

He shrugged. "It just died down."

"What happened to the two of you after that?" I asked. "At the inquest, the police said you had just disappeared."

"We was both scared to start with. Then we heard about the two men at Lyford Cay turning up dead, one of them drowned. They was sponge fishermen—how could he drown? I was going to hide out, but after dark the next day, Mr. Frank drove by the house and caught me in the yard. I wasn't expecting nobody at that hour. He told me to take him to where Cordner was, and I did. You remember, boss, Cordner stuttered when he got excited. He couldn't talk at all—just made a noise in his throat.

"Mr. Frank asked us both where we was the night before, and I told him the weather got bad so we left early, real early. He asked me what time and I say around ten-thirty, maybe eleven, just before the big rain.

"I prayed he'd believe me. Then he said, 'You're both liars. I bet you never went to work that night.' And he took two rolls of bills, handed us each one. Said, There's one hundred pounds each. You bastards pack your clothes and be out of Nassau by the time the sun rises tomorrow. If you open your mouths about any of this I'll cut your damned throats myself.'

"We both had people in Grand Bahama, and we sailed here. I changed my name, they call me Bethel here. I prayed to God you would go free, Mr. Fred."

I gave him a couple of pounds and walked back to the yacht. I believed the story Rawlins told, and his account of Frank Christie's actions, but knew that nothing could come of it. I was eager to get as far as I could from the Bahamas, and the memories I could never bury.

Back in Texas, there was only one thing missing in my life, and that void was filled on March 7, 1975. I was notified to appear at the Federal Building in Houston, to be sworn in as a United States citizen.

Before the ceremony, I was invited to meet with Leonard Chapman, then the director of the Houston office of the Immigration and Naturalization Service. Chapman was aware of my history, and that I had spent four of the past six years collecting documents from the various places I had lived since Nassau. He made a special effort, I thought, to put me at ease. And he had an unusual request.

"My daughter collects passports," he said. "You have one of the really rare ones. In a few more minutes you'll be a citizen of the United States. My daughter insisted I ask if she can have your passport from Mauritius."

"Gladly," I said, with a laugh.

I don't believe I had ever felt more nervous than I did that day—not even when I testified at my own murder trial, or waited for the jury to come in. I was one of about two hundred people who were assembled in an auditorium to receive their citizenship papers. To my surprise; I heard my name called out. I felt a moment's panic, then the presiding judge explained that anyone who held a hereditary title, or any rank of nobility in a foreign state, had to renounce those claims.

Standing alone in the room, I raised my right hand and repeated the oath of renunciation.

I sat down momentarily, my heart pounding, and then I

was asked to rise again with the rest of the applicants. Tears streaming down my face—and I was not alone—I repeated the words, swearing to uphold the Constitution of the United States, and pledging my allegiance and fidelity to my adopted country.

I looked straight ahead, neither to the left nor the right, but I could feel the eyes of my wife and sons shining on me. Then the judge smiled and offered his congratulations, and a cheer went up in the room.

It was a wonderful, remarkable time for each of us who became an American citizen that day. But for me it represented even more, the greatest test that I could pass. The United States of America had reviewed my life and my trial, and had given me the verdict no mere jury had the power to extend; I had been accepted as a citizen.

There was no clearer or more meaningful way to confirm the verdict that I knew in my heart I deserved: *Not guilty.*

EPILOGUE

IN my mind there is no doubt whatsoever that Harold Christie should have been tried and hanged for the murder of Sir Harry Oakes. While hired hands acted for him, it was Christie who ordered the fatal act committed that turbulent night in Nassau, in the summer of 1943.

In the matter of how and why Oakes died, I do not subscribe to the more complicated theories.

First, the fire was not a diversion, but indeed a failed attempt to leave the body so burned, in the ruins of the house, as to conceal the nature of Oakes's death. In their haste, the killers, two professionals, botched the job. They failed to ensure that the fire would catch and spread. Gasoline was the liquid they splashed on the body and floor; it flares and burns off quickly. Kerosene, less volatile, would have burned more evenly. The spray gun partly filled with pesticide, which fascinated some witnesses and reporters, can be dismissed as a touch of local color. It was not a factor.

The high winds and moisture that blew through Sir Harry's open windows were enough to extinguish the worst of the flames and limit the damage. But the intent of those who set the fire is crucial to the understanding of Harold Christie's claims.

Christie actually did spend part of the night with his mistress, Mrs. Henneage. He returned to Westbourne around five-thirty in the morning, expecting to find the house at least partly destroyed, and the body of Oakes so scorched that no one would doubt he had died in the fire. Upon discovering the tragic "accident," Christie would have been only mildly reluctant to explain his whereabouts. Nor was there reason to think Mrs. Henneage would hesitate to support his story. Their relationship was no secret. It was hinted throughout the trial, in gossip and in print, that he was protecting a married woman.

The problem developed only when it became apparent that the death was not accidental, and Christie's absence had allowed the killers a clear field. That implication could only have distressed Mrs. Henneage. Called as a witness, she would have been required to testify about Harold's state of mind, his mannerisms, when he had arrived, and how long he had stayed. It is significant that she was never asked to testify.

Suddenly it became a matter of personal urgency to Christie that he deny ever having left Westbourne, though he had been seen in town by Captain Sears, who had known him since boyhood.

I contend that when Christie, in a near panic, first disclosed to Etienne Dupuch that Oakes had been shot, he knew this to have been so. The later guesses by the officers and medical examiners, that a blunt or pronged instrument was the death weapon, served his purpose. He was relieved of the burden of explaining that he had not heard the gunshots, among the several intrusive sounds he did not hear that night.

It is likely that Sir Harry was drugged—the thick, dark fluid in his stomach that the doctors did not bother to test—and killed as he slept. No one but Christie, the only overnight houseguest, was in a position to spike Sir Harry's bedtime drink. I do not believe that Christie participated in the killing, or was present when it occurred. Yet the web Barker and Melchen wove for me raised more questions for him. In their scenario, Sir Harry had fought off his attacker, struggling with him in the hallway before being forced back into the bedroom. How could Harold fail to hear those exertions? Moreover, how could he not have gone to the aid of his closest friend?

I have never found acceptable the theories of Mafia involvement in the crime. The suggestion that Oakes had blocked or even opposed attempts to bring casino gambling to the islands is faulty on the following grounds: (1) Sir Harry had made up his mind to move his family and his interests to Mexico, because the future of the Bahamas no longer engaged him; (2) the laws had been changed in 1939, four years earlier, to legalize gambling; only the war and the lack of tourists delayed the arrival of the casinos, not Sir Harry; and (3) even if he had objected, Oakes lacked the political power to decide such matters; Christie was the one to deal with, and he wanted the casinos, or, to be more exact, what the casinos would attract.

In his biography of the Duchess of Windsor, Charles Higham identified Christie as the man responsible for the death of Harry Oakes. He speculated that the killer Christie hired was from a tribe or sect that practiced black magic, and attributed the peculiar circumstances of the death scene—the spotty fire, how the body was burned, the scattering of feathers—to a ritual murder in which Christie himself took part. The murder weapon was described as a fishing spear used at very close range.

In another meticulous book about the Windsors, *The King Over the Water*, the author, Michael Pye, stops just short of naming Christie as the killer. But he touched on the motive: "Christie had a crisis on his hands. For months, even years, the trend of Oakes's thinking was clear ... if he actually decided to go, then Christie was in deep trouble."

For nearly fifty years the focus has been, understandably, on who killed Harry Oakes. The injustice done to me was a secondary issue. But Pye addressed it: "One point remained ... Alfred de Marigny had been framed. It had taken perjury by two Miami policemen and also by members of the local force ... de Marigny as killer was always implausible."

Harold Christie may have been a frightened soul trying to save his own neck. Eric Hallinan may have been a loyal civil servant trying to carry out his duties. But logic, as well as the rules of common practice, tells us that no one is going to perjure himself in a Crown case without the encouragement of a higher authority—if not the Attorney General, then the Royal Governor.

The murder of Oakes posed a terrible dilemma for the Duke of Windsor. He resisted every effort to reopen the Oakes case; any serious investigator would have done what those in the original quest did not. They would have followed the money trail left behind by Sir Harry, a trail that led to Axel Wenner-Gren, to the Banco Continental in Mexico. It was a trail that would have coughed up the under-the-table dealings of the Duke himself.

For many years, this aspect of the case held little interest for me, a question of business that did not concern me. But as the war receded into the fog of time, as cables once classified slowly began to surface, those events took on a clear shape. It dawned on me that what I had regarded as a personal vendetta was more likely the Duke's attempt to conceal his secrets.

Windsor was unfortunate in having attracted the dislike of two important Americans, who would monitor his activities with a special intensity: J. Edgar Hoover, director of the FBI, and Adolf A. Berle, the assistant secretary of state. While many have justified the Duke's political opinions and actions— he was pro-peace, never pro-Germany; he felt that fascism was less a threat than communism, and so forth—Berle did not tailor his view to fit the polite fashions of the day. In more than one report, he characterized the Windsors as "Nazi collaborators."

It ought to be acknowledged that the Duke and Duchess were often the object of vicious and unfounded gossip and crackpot stories. But they had a strange capacity for picking friends whose loyalties were clouded.

Robert Young, the American railroad tycoon, and James D. Mooncy, who had been targeted by Hoover as a double agent, entertained them. In his memoirs, John Balfour recalled an evening after the war when both the Duke and Young spoke wistfully of Hitler, "as though the outcome of the war had been bad for business."

Two months before Pearl Harbor, the results of a tap on the German legation's phone in Havana were relayed to both J. Edgar Hoover and Adolf Berle: "Duke of Windsor is seen as no enemy of Germany. Considered to be the only Englishman with whom Hitler will negotiate any peace terms, the logical director of England's destiny after the war."

None of which, of course, has on the face of it any earthly connection to the murder of Harry Oakes or the trial of Alfred de Marigny—with one exception. All roads lead back to Wenner-Gren. One week after the Japanese bombed Pearl Harbor, the elusive Swede was placed on the Allied blacklist. Ironically, since Wenner-Gren was then a resident of the Bahamas, the Duke, as governor, had to sign the document identifying his friend as a suspected enemy agent.

As early as 1933, British Intelligence had received information that Wenner-Gren would be an "important international asset" if the Nazis were to embroil Europe in war. As late as March 1941, Winston Churchill wrote to Windsor, pleading with him to discontinue any business dealings he might have with the man whose best-selling products were vacuum cleaners and guns.

It was too late. The Windsors had personally arranged for Wenner-Gren to meet with the pro-Nazi Mexican general Maximino Camacho. The purpose was to set up a bank through which the Germans could launder the currencies of foreign treasuries.

The first indication of this arrangement came from the famous British spy, H. Montgomery Hyde, who served on the staff of Sir William Stephenson, the inspiration for the book and movie *A Man Called Intrepid*. It is no longer clear, if it ever was, who was first used by whom. But Camacho and Wenner-Gren were introduced by Windsor, and next the name of Harold Christie appeared in the files, followed by that of Harry Oakes.

In January 1941, a confidential memorandum had been sent to the U.S. State Department by Sumner Welles: "The most recent information I have regarding Mr. Wenner-Gren indicates that he is in constant and close touch with the Duke of Windsor. . . . Reports have reached me that Mr. Wenner-Gren is anxious to participate in an American consortium planning the investment of a considerable amount of capital in Mexico."

All that year, U.S. agents were slipping in and out of Cuba, Florida, Bermuda, and Haiti, attempting to untangle what the Windsors were doing, and with whom. If that seems an overreaction to the life-style of a couple misplaced by society, or history, one must remember what a potential weapon Windsor represented to the Nazis. This was the former King of England, a man whose image still enchanted the masses.

One of the FBI warnings singled out Mooney, who ran the European interests for General Motors and was therefore heavily invested in Germany. One source wrote: "I consider him a dangerous individual. He is one of those Irishmen who is so against England that he would be prepared to see the whole world go down in order to satisfy his feelings with respect to England. In my opinion, he is as mad as any Nazi . . . and an even more dangerous person than Wenner-Gren for the Duke and Duchess of Windsor to be associated with."

That the Duke invested in the Banco Continental was confirmed to me by Oakes, Christie, and the man who, on at least one occasion, delivered funds for him to Mexico, John H. Anderson, whose boss was Wenner-Gren. It was from Anderson, the Nassau banker, that I heard the first garbled account of the murder of Harry Oakes.

On any of several levels, the Duke of Windsor could have been charged under the Trading with the Enemy Act. My own instinct is that greed motivated him more than politics. The accumulation of wealth was always a worry to him. He had no way of knowing what the value of his holdings in England and France would be by war's end. And so he had a pressing need to salt away as much money as he could, and to take part in schemes that would enable his funds to grow.

There is some doubt about the accuracy of Wenner-Gren's records, but his accounts indicate that the Duke deposited nearly two million dollars in the Banco Continental. How much of that might have been borrowed from Harry Oakes is unclear. What astonished J. Edgar Hoover was the paltriness of Wenner-Gren's own investment. Into the future he sank, according to the FBI, a total of twenty-five thousand dollars of his own funds.

So, before the trial, and into the 1950s and beyond, Windsor was no supporter of the calls to follow loose ends in the Oakes case. Surely not to Mexico, where Wenner-Gren laundered the currency taken by the Germans from occupied lands, and where it was mingled with money held in the Duke's name.

In whatever way one reads the law, in spite of whatever immunity his position might have entitled him, the former King of England was a willing conspirator in a plot to send an innocent man to his death. I further believe that by the end of the trial, certainly by the time of his return to the Bahamas, he was aware of Christie's guilt. He could not by then put the genie back in the bottle.

These conclusions, as they relate to the murder, are based on my own reading of the evidence, on my intimate knowledge of the characters involved, and on the statements made to me by Dr. Ricky Oberwarth and, years later, by the caretaker Rawlins.

As the figures in the Oakes case, large and small, died off, it became ever more important to me that the truth, as I remember it, not be left to the custody of strangers. The human odyssey begun in 1943 is nearly done.

Harold Christie was knighted by the Queen, in 1964, for "services to the Crown," married late in life, and died of a heart attack in 1973. His fortune was assured when the Assembly, at the urging of the Duke of Windsor, in virtually his last act as

Royal Governor, approved a funding of seventy-seven thousand pounds to develop the Out Islands.

The Duke of Windsor died of cancer in a Paris hospital on May 29, 1972, thirty-six years after the Abdication. What part his embarrassment in the Bahamas played is unknown, but the British government never found for him the substantial position he had always sought, and felt was his due.

Wallis Simpson, the Duchess of Windsor, outlived her husband by fourteen years. Upon his death, she realized one of her lifelong objectives, being received at Buckingham Palace. Her final years were lonely and, near the end, almost vegetative. She was ninety when her remarkable life ended on April 24, 1986. Queen Elizabeth kept a promise made to her uncle, and the Duchess was buried in a plot next to her husband.

Captain James Otto Barker was shot to death by his son, on Christmas morning, 1952. The elder Barker was described as high on drugs at the time. His son, twenty-four, tried to take his gun from him during a scuffle. The death was ruled a justifiable homicide. Barker's drug addiction, and his ties to organized crime, were known to the FBI at least two and a half years before my trial. In a memorandum dated March 6, 1941, J. Edgar Hoover wrote, quoting his sources, that "Barker is dishonest and is receiving payoffs in Miami from various types of crooks. ... In view of his activities, the Bureau should have a minimum amount of dealings with him." It strikes me as ludicrous that Barker was neither fired nor charged, and was allowed to become a point man for the Duke of Windsor.

Captain Melchen slipped from public view, his career ruined, and died of natural causes.

A year after the trial, Hallinan was posted to Trinidad. He ended his legal career as the Chief Justice of the Windward and Leeward Islands, retired to Spain with a knighthood, and died in 1988, one of the last survivors of this extraordinary case.

In his candid letter to Marshall Houts, in 1971, Hallinan

made what I considered a stunning admission: "Barker took photographs of the Oakes corpse and of the bedroom where he was murdered. I remember seeing the imprint of a hand on the wall as if someone had groped his way around the room. . . .

"[Later] I enquired what had happened about the hand prints . . . but was told they were 'negative.' I regard the way in which the investigation of these handprints was covered as one of the most sinister and mysterious features of the case."

Alfred Adderley continued his lucrative career as an attorney. He founded a new black political caucus in 1944, but was excluded from the black governments that would eventually rule the Bahamas.

Of the four attorneys who dueled in the courtroom, only Ernest Callender is still alive as these words are written. He never left Nassau, and retired there in comfort and respect.

Time left George Thompson virtually unmarked, if the photographs he has sent me can be trusted. Now nearly seventy, he is active and in demand as a captain of the fishing fleet that sails out of Nassau harbor.

Until his death, Raymond Schindler insisted he could solve the Oakes riddle. A heart attack silenced him in 1959, only weeks after the House of Assembly had called on Scotland Yard to reopen the case.

Axel Wenner-Gren, a magician in the ways of making money, remained on the Allied blacklist through the rest of the war, and never fully succeeded in clearing his name. With the end of hostilities, he returned to Nassau and sold his properties to Huntington Hartford, the American millionaire. Hog Island became Paradise Island, and new hotels and casinos attracted a fresh generation of tourists to the Bahamas.

Typifying the dual life he led, Wenner-Gren renewed his business ties to the Krupp family, builders of the Nazi war machine, and donated millions to charity. He was eighty when he died of cancer in 1961.

Although the boom in land values increased the estate left

by Harry Oakes, more grief and misfortune followed the baronet's children.

Sir Sydney Oakes, the eldest son, abandoned his first wife and children to marry a girl he met in a Palm Beach nightclub. He was killed in a car accident.

William Pitt, the second son, suffered from years of mental illness, during which he would run through the house naked, barking like a dog and raising his leg to relieve himself on the furniture.

The brightest member of the family was Nancy's sister, Shirley, who earned a law degree and, with her husband, started a small bank in Nassau. They were among the victims of Robert Vesco, the fugitive international swindler, and lost nearly everything they owned. Shirley and her husband divorced, and she was crippled in a car wreck, paralyzed from the neck down.

Harry Philip, the youngest son, lives quietly in Nassau, well established in business. Alone among his siblings, he has enjoyed the trappings of a normal life.

And what would I want said of Alfred de Marigny? That the shadow of the Oakes case followed me all of my years, but it did not break, embitter, or humble me (so my friends assure me). For the official record, the case will never be solved; no one else will ever be tried. I find no satisfaction in my memories of it. I have always known that, for me, the case would never be closed.

SELECTED BIBLIOGRAPHY

Bocca, Geoffrey. *The Life and Death of Sir Harry Oakes.* New York: Doubleday, 1959.

Donaldson, Frances. *Edward VIII.* Philadelphia and New York: J. B. Lippincott, 1974.

Higham, Charles. *The Duchess of Windsor.* New York: McGraw-Hill Book Company, 1988.

Houts, Marshall. *King's X.* New York: William Morrow, 1972.

Leasor, James. *Who Killed Sir Harry Oakes?* Boston: Houghton Mifflin, 1983.

"The Murder of Sir Harry Oakes," *The Nassau Daily Tribune,* 1959.

Pye, Michael. *The King Ch'er the Water.* New York: Holt, Rinehart and Winston, 1981.